International economic integration

International economic integration

Miroslav N. Jovanović

Foreword by Richard G. Lipsey

London and New York

First published 1992
by Routledge
11 New Fetter Lane, London EC4P 4EE

Simultaneously published in the USA and Canada
by Routledge
a division of Routledge, Chapman and Hall, Inc.
29 West 35th Street, New York, NY 10001

© 1992 Miroslav N. Jovanović

Typeset in [Linotron Times] by
Columns Design and Production Services Ltd
Printed in Great Britain

British Library Cataloguing in Publication Data
Jovanović, Miroslav N. *1957–*
    International economic integration.
    1. International economic integration
    I. Title
    337.1

ISBN 0–415–03819–7

Library of Congress Cataloging-in-Publication Data
Jovanović, Miroslav N., 1957–
    International economic integration/Miroslav N. Jovanović.
    Includes bibliographical references and index.
    ISBN 0–415–03819–7
    1. International economic integration. I. Title.
    HF1418.5.J68   1992
    337.1—dc20   91–10671
                              72663   CIP

To Jovan

Contents

Figures

Tables

Foreword by Richard G. Lipsey

Mirsolav Jovanović has written a comprehensive work on the economics of integration, passing from customs unions to common markets to full economic integration. The most distinctive aspect of his treatment is his own creative union of theory and applied material. For him, theory is no abstract game played for the amusement of the players, but a tool for enlightening our understanding of what we see in the world around us. For him, the major interest resides always in the problems created by working out various forms of union in real situations.

Thus, theoretical and applied considerations are blended from the outset. After a brief, stage-setting, introductory chapter, Chapter 2 deals with customs unions (with some reference to free trade areas where appropriate). It begins with the static, partial-equilibrium analysis of tariffs and customs unions. Even here, however, we find discussions of the EC's Common Agricultural Policy (CAP), employment policies, national security objectives, infant industries, bilateral and unilateral tariff reductions.

The analysis of tariffs and customs unions is followed by a brief consideration of subsidies. The theory is presented first, followed by a discussion which covers, among other things, the GATT (General Agreement on Tariffs and Trade) position on subsidies and countervailing duties, political issues in the choice between subsidies and tariffs, procurement policies, output and export subsidies, and the American DISC (Domestic International Sales Corporation) policy.

In the section entitled 'Dynamic Models', we find nothing about nonlinear dynamics, chaos theory, self-organizing systems, or evolutionary biology. Instead, we read about technology, competition, intra-industry trade, the EC's competition policy, the case for state intervention in non-competitive markets, scale economies in various industries, predatory pricing, and pre-emptive investment.

In short, Chapter 2 sets the tone for the whole volume. It selects topic areas one after another; it reviews the relevant theory of each, on the assumption that the reader already has some acquaintance with it; it then goes on to consider a host of important, applied issues in the area under consideration. The reader wanting to know the relevant theory, and the main applied issues that have arisen around any topic relating to customs unions will find that this chapter provides excellent source material, as well as a valuable consideration of most of the issues.

Chapter 3 takes a similar approach, this time with respect to issues surrounding a common market. It starts with the theory of factor price equalization and then goes on to consider labour mobility from the points of view of both the sending and the receiving countries in general. This is followed by a short discussion of the experience of the EC. The coverage then passes to capital mobility in general, which leads naturally to a consideration of foreign direct investment (FDI) and transnational corporations (TNCs). The experience of Canada, the US, and the EC illustrate the issues that are involved in the important question of the appropriate policy stance for national governments to adopt towards FDI of various types and in various situations. There is unlikely to be anything as simple as 'the' correct stance for all countries in all situations in anything as complex in its costs and its benefits as FDI. This is why Dr. Jovanović's pragmatic approach of looking at specific cases on their merits, rather than looking for universal theoretical presumptions, is so useful.

Chapter 4 on economic unions is by far the longest chapter, slightly over half the book. This is as is should be, since economic union is the final goal of many of the looser associations. Sometimes this is their stated goal, and sometimes forces unleased by looser forms of integration push their members in that direction. Dr. Jovanović's treatment of these issues verges on the exhaustive.

Coordinated monetary policy is a central part of economic union. Often, as EC experience shows, it is the next step after a common market. The issues around monetary policy are studied in detail, both in terms of the traditional model and a cost–benefit analysis. This raises the well-known issues of optimal currency areas, as well as the less well-known, but probably more important, issues involved in delimitating an optimal policy area.

Fiscal policy is an important aspect of any economic union. A complete unification of all spending and taxing measures in the various units of the union is not necessary – as the US economic union illustrates with its substantial variations in tax and spending patterns among individual state governments. A desirable characteristic, however, is that differences in tax policies do not exert major influences on the decisions of firms choosing locations within the union. In contrast, it does seem possible to accommodate significant differences in spending that reflect different philosophical positions on the place of the state in providing such measures as income security, welfare, environmental protection, and public goods. These spending differences call for using taxes that do not affect business costs to raise different sums of money in different jurisdictions, while keeping rates of taxes that do affect business costs relatively similar. These, and many other issues, arise on the fiscal side of economic integration.

Miroslav Jovanović devotes considerable space to the important topic of industrial policy, which is occupying much government attention in the 1990s, sometimes under different names. Governments are concerned about footloose, knowledge-intensive industries, both when they have them (lest they lose them), and when they do not have them (in hope of attracting them). Rightly or wrongly, new industrial policies are key issues in many countries today, and harmonizing them poses major problems for jurisdictions that belong to economic unions. In view of the vast complexity of the subject, Dr. Jovanović's treatment must be sketchy in places. He does, however, cover virtually all of the important issues that might need further, in-depth study by those seeking a detailed appreciation.

Inevitably in so broad a treatment of industrial policy, there will be things that each reader – including this reader – will not agree with. Given the available space of one monograph, however, it is hard to quarrel with the extensive coverage given. One of my caveats is that, by concentrating strictly on the level of Federal governments, Dr Jovanović makes US industrial policy seem less interventionist than it in fact is. Much US industrial policy is carried out at the state and local levels where US authorities vie with each other, and with foreign governments, to attract industries and to keep them. Competition is often so fierce that one suspects local tax payers are paying to firms, by way of subsidies and tax expenditures, most of the benefits the community would otherwise get from attracting a new firm. For example, Canadian studies consistently show the Canadian federal government engaging in a larger volume of subsidization of industry than the US federal government, but with this margin being reversed at the State and local levels, so that, overall, US inducements more or less equal Canadian inducements.

Regional policy poses even more vexing problems than does industrial policy. Over the years, and in most countries, regional policies have had much more uniformly disappointing results than industrial policies – perhaps because regional policies have so often concentrated on supporting sunset industries, and on locating isolated new enterprises with no consideration for Michael Porter's point about the need for clusters of related firms if a genuine competitive advantage is to be created. Dr. Jovanović deals with key issues of regional policy in general and then illustrates them with the experience of the EC.

Social policies pose another difficult set of issues for jurisdictions that are integrated economically, particularly when the regions have widely different levels of income. In many ways social policies pose the most intractable of issues, since there seem to be no easy solutions even in principle, let alone in the practice of modern democratic governments, subject to the usual political pressures. These issues are briefly explored.

Chapter 4 concludes with brief overviews of two other attempts at economic cooperation, if not full integration. These are the ambitious, but largely unsuccessful, CMEA (The Council for Mutual Economic Assistance), covering the countries of the former Eastern Bloc, and the ASEAN (Association of Southeastern Asian Nations), covering a number of countries of Southeast Asia which, with the exception of the Philippines, are now growing rapidly. Although this latter association has been loose, and has had limited objectives, it has been a success in many ways – perhaps for just those reasons.

Readers who set out on these pages have a rich and varied experience awaiting them. The coverage is remarkably comprehensive, considering that it is all condensed into less than 300 pages. For every reader there will be things to agree with, and things to argue with – as is to be expected in so rich a survey. In the end, however, many readers will agree with the author when he writes in the course of his summing up (pp. 280–1):

It is hard to forecast with a high degree of accuracy when and how the effects of integration will happen. In the short-term 'just after the lifting of barriers to trade', production, GNP and trade may increase while some prices fall. . . . In the medium- and long-term, structural adjustment takes place and economies of scale occur. . . . It is in this context where the dynamic effects of integration are materialized. International economic integration is not an economic policy choice which [should] frighten small and medium-sized countries. The only thing which these countries would lose while integrating is the illusion that international economic integration is a bad policy choice.

R. G. Lipsey
Vancouver, B.C., Canada

Preface

The traditional theory of international economic integration is an elegant and a quite convincing academic exercise. The conclusions are straightforward and offer useful insights into international economic integration. With that in mind, the first aim of this book is to introduce students to international economic integration. The other aim, equally important, is to update the theory of integration by introducing the arguments of the new theory of trade and strategic industrial policy. For the most part the exposition is descriptive and makes use of diagrams where appropriate. Thus, it is hoped that this book will be readily accessible to readers.

It is not yet possible to present a general theory of international economic integration. This is due primarily to the absence of a generally applicable theory of international trade. The traditional trade theory has looked at comparative advantage. The existing theory of international economic integration has largely been presented in this framework. Recent trade theory has, however, identified other, often more important, determinants of countries' trade patterns. In a world of imperfect competition and economies of scale, there are many reasons for trade, foreign investment and integration, even if countries are identical in their factor endowments, size, technologies and tastes. In such a situation, there are a number of second-best choices about economic actions. This book considers those choices. Also, this book argues – in particular in the chapter on economic union – that various market imperfections can be corrected by economic policy.

The new theory of international trade and strategic industrial policy, acknowledges the importance of the traditional, neo-classical theory of trade (countries trade because they are different in the endowment of resources, technology and/or tastes). The traditional model of trade is, however, more appropriate to trade in goods like wheat, while the new theory is more suitable as a theoretical tool for the analysis of trade in goods like aircraft.

The new theory adds to the traditional model a new quality. It is the consideration of market imperfections, in particular economies of scale. Being inconsistent with perfect competition, increasing returns to scale were left out of the picture in the traditional model. The new theory questions the traditional argument that free trade is an optimal economic strategy. The real world is full of market imperfections. In these circumstances, economic policy may simply add an adjustment mechanism to the already highly imperfect and sub-optimal situation. Once one does not have a simple situation, many outcomes become feasible. Therefore, the new theory is an eclectic mix of various approaches to trade and investment.

The new theory does not give *carte blanche* to protectionism, because retaliation and counter-retaliation makes everybody worse off. Also, the governments do not always have the necessary information for proper intervention (but neither do free markets always bring desirable solutions). What the new theory argues is that with a bit of smart intervention, under certain conditions, economic policy may improve a country's international economic position.

The treatment of the theory of international economic integration is basically Eurocentric, only because of its longer history. There are no theoretical differences between integration among industrialized and among less developed countries (LDCs). The arguments in favour of integration are the same. What may differ are the intentions and ambitions of countries. This is, however, a matter of choice. The LDCs may still wish to employ international economic integration as their development strategy.

The book is organized as follows. After the Introduction (Chapter 1), the subject matter of Chapter 2 is customs unions, which is the most rigorously developed part of the theory of international economic integration. The analysis is carried out in both static and dynamic models in both partial- and general-equilibrium frameworks. All considerations are from the standpoint of the general theory of the second best. Increased competition, specialization and returns to scale receive special treatment since they are the most important dynamic effects. A discussion of adjustment costs suggests that they do not represent a serious barrier to integration.

Chapter 3 is devoted to common markets. Factor mobility is here the central concern. Equalization of factor prices and the prospects for increased investment by transnational corporations (TNCs) are evaluated.

Chapter 4 examines economic unions. Monetary, fiscal, industrial, regional and social policies are tackled in turn. The point is that all these policies in an economic union can be defended by the same arguments which are used to defend these policies in a single country which consists of several regions. Monetary policy is the area where the effects of integration are felt first. Fiscal policy refers to taxation problems among countries. The creation of comparative advantage is considered in the discussion of industrial policy which is aimed at creation of wealth. The distribution of wealth is stressed in both regional and social policies which are used as a buffer against the potentially negative consequences of other economic policies.

Chapter 5 deals with the measurement of the effects of international economic integration. There are serious limits to quantification. Most importantly, it is not possible to create a reliable counterfactual situation which would simulate what would occur with or without integration. It is stated that the end result of the estimations is an amalgam of various effects, some of which have nothing to do with integration.

Chapter 6 concludes the book. The Bibliography may serve as a reading list for further research.

I hope that the book will be of interest to economists specializing in international economics, international trade and integration, European studies and European integration. If it is also of interest to those that have an interest in economic development, international business and policy makers, I do not regret such an outcome.

Acknowledgements

My involvement in international economic integration began when I was studying European integration at the Europa Institute of the University of Amsterdam during the 1980–81 academic year. The Dutch government generously gave full financial support for these studies. However, another event was responsible for the writing of this book: my study and research programme at Queen's University, Kingston, Ontario, during the 1986–87 academic year. All funds were generously provided by the Department of Economics of Queen's University and the World University Service of Canada. I continued working on it at the University of Belgrade and finalized it at the United Nations Centre on Transnational Corporations in New York. My gratitude to all of these institutions is very great indeed.

I have benefited from discussions with many economists. There are, however, several to whom I owe special gratitude. Michael Spencer helped me the most. Mića Panić, George Yannopoulos and Oskar Kovač have read the whole manuscript and gave numerous useful comments. Richard G. Lipsey, Lorne Carmichael, Yngvi Hardarson and Ed Saperstein kindly commented on certain problems. Christopher Matthews and Brian Sloan kindly provided many Eurostat data which Randi Moi processed. Joanna Wheeler swiftly provided data on the tax structure in the EC countries. Vilborg Hjartardottir typed one version of the manuscript, while Slobodan Gatarić was solving many PC-related problems. Finally, Alan Jarvis of Routledge favoured this project from the outset.

Thanks are due also to the Editor of *Economic Analysis* for kind permission to rely heavily on the article 'Industrial Policy and International Trade (Shaping Comparative Advantage)' which was originally published in no. 1, 1989.

The writing of this book would not have been possible without the understanding of my wife, Lilian. It was her ability to organize the family that allowed me the time necessary to complete this book. Our son Jovan hated it when I was away (even in mind) doing economics, but enjoyed to the full making a mess on my desk. At one time this book has 'divided us', but now it integrates us still further.

I am grateful to all of them. The usual disclaimer, however, applies here: it is I who am responsible for all shortcomings and mistakes.

Miroslav N. Jovanović

Abbreviations

ASEAN	Association of Southeast Asian Nations
CFA	Communauté Financière Africaine
CMEA	Council for Mutual Economic Assistance
DISC	Domestic International Sales Corporation
ECU	European Currency Unit
EC	European Community[1]
EFTA	European Free Trade Association
EMS	European Monetary System
ERDF	European Regional Development Fund
FIRA	Foreign Investment Review Agency
GATT	General Agreement on Tariffs and Trade
GNP	gross national product
IBEC	International Bank for Economic Cooperation
IIB	International Investment Bank
IMF	International Monetary Fund
LDC	less developed country
MITI	Ministry of International Trade and Industry
OECD	Organisation for Economic Cooperation and Development
R&D	research and development
SITC	Standard International Trade Classification
TNC	transnational corporation
USSR	Union of Soviet Socialist Republics
VAT	value added tax
WAMU	West African Monetary Union

---

[1] The European Community or Communities consist of the European Coal and Steel Community, the Euroatom and the European Economic Community (EEC). The three communities have had common institutions since 1967. Most of the activities of the EC relate to the EEC. The Treaty of Rome refers often to the treaty which established the EEC, although the Euroatom was created at the same time and the same place as the EEC.

1 Introduction

The interdependence of economic life among countries creates a situation in which national economic problems increasingly become a matter of international concern. The predominant form of solution for these international problems is still found at the national level where the most decisive influence is wielded by a small number of large and highly developed countries and a few oil-exporting countries. While free market competition can create a situation in which large firms can absorb their small competitors, such an analogy is not possible when one deals with countries. Large and developed countries cannot always behave like firms. If large countries attempt to appropriate some of the functions of small ones or even to absorb them, then small countries will adopt protective policies. The result is international economic disintegration (Panić, 1988, p. 284). Countries are not firms. They cannot be driven out of all business. But countries can, perhaps, be driven out of some business. Such a temporary shock can have permanent effects on trade (Krugman, 1990, p. 107).

Coordination of economic policies and international economic integration may solve the largest part of international economic problems. Economic nationalism, as opposed to coordination and integration, is still quite a strong economic strategy. This is because the mechanisms for the protection from unfavourable effects of integration, which are of a short-term nature, are not developed. This book argues that international economic integration is a desirable strategy, at least for small and medium-sized countries; that the benefits of integration come in the long run; and that the benefits are much greater than the possible short-run costs.

Economic efficiency can be fostered by free trade, which

stimulates competition. It rationalizes production of goods and services, and provides for a higher standard of living and greater welfare in the future. The adjustment to free trade, at least within the integrated group, should not be traumatic. There is substantial evidence in the relatively frictionless adjustment to the successive General Agreement on Tariffs and Trade (GATT) reductions in tariffs, as well as smooth adjustment in both the European Community (EC) and the European Free Trade Association (EFTA).

Large and developed countries depend to a lesser degree on external relations than small countries do. These countries may have a diversified economic structure which gives the possibility for an autarkic economic policy, while such a policy for small countries in a situation with economies of scale does not have an economic rationale. A relatively small domestic market in small countries often prevents the employment of the most efficient technology with the consequence of short production runs, higher prices and lower standard of living. The efficient operation of many modern technologies requires secure access to the widest market which does not exist in small, and sometimes, medium-sized countries. Elimination of tariffs, non-tariff barriers, restrictions on factor movements, as well as international coordination of economic policies and international economic integration can be solutions to this problem of country size. The aim is to increase, improve and secure access to markets of the participating countries.

A liberal trade and flexible adjustment policy for a small country may be a superior alternative to the policy of long-term protection. The competitive position of small countries can be jeopardized if protection increases the prices of inputs. Moreover, protection can provoke retaliatory measures from trading partners. It can also inhibit the adjustment incentives of the protected industry with an overall, negative, long-term impact on the whole economy. While having a limited influence on the events in the world economy, small countries can have leverage over their own competitive future by means of a liberal economic policy and/or international economic integration.

Global negotiations over tariff reductions were organized by the GATT with moderate success. These achievements, however, do not undermine the case in favour of international economic integration. Consequent rounds of negotiations have significantly reduced tariffs on selected manufactured goods. Little has been done, however, to liberalize trade in agriculture, services, textiles and clothing, or to lower non-tariff barriers which have mush-roomed as tariffs were dismantled. Due to different economic, political, climatic, cultural and other characteristics, it is unlikely that countries around the world would offer universal concessions in trade. One can imagine that these can be exchanged within a smaller group of countries with significantly less effort than on a universal scale.

Free trade and the unimpeded movement of factors is the first-best policy in a world which does not have any distortions. This is only a hypothetical situation. The rationale for international economic integration may be found in the case where there are distortions. When one distortion (a universal tariff of a country) is replaced by another (a common external tariff of a customs union) the net welfare effect may be unchanged, positive or negative. The theory of international economic integration is the analysis of a second-best situation, and it is not surprising that general principles may not be found. What matters, however, is not solely the prediction of theory, but rather what happens in real life. This book shows that despite the second-best character of international economic integration in theory, in practice integration may, under certain conditions, be a workable and acceptable economic strategy. A policy recommendation for small and medium-sized countries is that in a world of continuous technological and market changes, integration may expand and secure markets for the greatest variety of a country's goods and services in the future and, hence, mitigate the possible costs of adjustment.

DEFINITIONS

The aim of all economic activity is an increase in welfare. The approach towards this goal is at the core of the issue which deals with the organization of the human community because agents have various and often conflicting interests. The organization should make agents able to maximize their utility in the pursuit of their own aims and expectations subject to the limitations presented by the environment.

International economic integration is one of the means by which to increase welfare. By this arrangement, countries may increase the welfare either of the integrated group, or of some countries within the group, or of the world as a whole. Machlup (1979, p. 3) states that the term *integration* in economics was used first in industrial organization to refer to combinations of firms. Horizontal integration refers to linkages of competitors, while vertical integration refers to the unification of suppliers and buyers. As a term, the integration of economies of separate states is not found anywhere in the old, chiefly historical literature on the economic interrelationship between states, nor in the literature about customs unions (including the German Zollverein 1834–71), nor in the literature on international trade prior to the 1940s. Viner (1950) was the first to introduce the foundation for the theory of customs unions which represent the core of the theory of international economic integration.

One of the first definitions of integration was introduced by Tinbergen (1954, p. 122). He defines, on the one hand, negative integration as the removal of discriminatory and restrictive institutions and the introduction of freedom for economic transactions. On the other hand, the adjustment of existing, and the establishment of new, policies and institutions endowed with coercive powers is identified as positive integration. This introduces some confusion, since freedom is described as negative while coercion is positive. Experience teaches us that it is easier to advance in the direction of negative integration (removal of tariffs and quotas), than towards positive integration (introduction of common economic policies) because the positive approach deals with sensitive issues of national sovereignty.

Pinder (1969, pp. 143–5) cites the *Oxford Dictionary* which describes integration as the combination of parts into a whole. Union is the outcome of the combination of parts or members. He concludes that integration is a process towards union, and defines economic integration as the removal of discrimination between the economic agents of the member countries, as well as the creation and implementation of common policies.

Balassa (1973, p. 1) defines economic integration both as a process and as a state of affairs. As a process (dynamic concept), integration means the removal of discrimination between different states, while as a state of affairs (static concept) it means the absence of different forms of discrimination. The Achilles' heel of this definition is its restriction in concentrating only on the process or state of affairs among the countries that integrate. One can distinguish among intranational (interprovincial), international and world (universal, global) integration. Agreements among states about adjustment or coordination of some economic sectors could be called integration, so one could deal with sectoral and general integration. Balassa's definition does not say if economic integration is the objective or a point on the way towards some target. This ambiguity can be avoided by making a distinction between complete and partial integration.

Maksimova (1976, p. 33) argues that economic integration is the process of development of deep and stable relationships of the division of labour between national economies. This is a process of the formation of international economic entities, within the framework of groups of countries with the same type of socio-economic system, which are consciously regulated in the interests of the ruling classes of these countries. It is true that international economic integration is a highly politicized process, but this definition excludes the possibility of integration even by means of preferential and/or cooperative agreements between countries that have different socio-economic or political systems. This is important in practice, for there is a whole spectrum of integration agreements between the EC and developing countries which have the widest range of political systems.

Holzman (1976, p. 59) states that economic integration is a situation in which the prices of all similar goods and similar factors in two regions are equalized. This makes the two regions in essence one region or market. This definition implies that economic integration is the realization of factor-price equalization between two regions. This definition implicitly assumes that there are no barriers to the movements of goods, services and factors between the two regions and that there are institutions that facilitate those movements. This interesting issue of factor-price equalization is presented in the chapter on common markets (Chapter 3).

Mennis and Sauvant (1976, p. 75) look at integration as a process whereby boundaries between nation-states become less discontinuous, thereby leading to the formation of more comprehensive systems. They think that economic integration consists of the linking up and merging (not the abolition) of the industrial apparatus, administration and economic policies of the participating countries.

Pelkmans (1984, p. 3) defines economic integration as the elimination of economic frontiers between two or more economies. An economic frontier is a demarcation across which the mobility of goods, services and factors is relatively low. Potential mobility of factors is the criterion for economic integration according to this passive definition of integration. There is no indication that policy is actively promoting mobility and cooperation. The mere removal of 'economic frontiers' does not necessarily offer either a carrot or a stick to factors, in particular, to move. There are many non-economic obstacles to mobility which include: language, custom, the propensity to stick to the place of birth and the like for labour, while political and other risks inhibit capital movements.

El-Agraa (1985a, p. 1) refers to international economic integration as the discriminatory removal of all trade impediments between participating nations and the establishment of certain elements of coordination between them. This definition implies the removal of barriers to trade in goods and services, as well as freedom of movement for factors of production. Hence, this definition only partly covers free-trade areas and customs unions as types of international economic integration. El-Agraa (1988, p. xiii) accepts that international economic integration means an act of agreement between two or more nations to pursue common aims and policies. This is an active definition of integration.

Robson (1987, p. 1) notes that economic integration is concerned with efficiency in resource use with particular reference to the spatial aspect. He defines full integration as freedom of movement for goods and factors of production and an absence of discrimination. Freedom of movement for factors is not allowed for in some of the types of international economic integration, so this definition can not be applied to all such arrangements.

Marer and Montias (1988, p. 156) point out that economic integration has traditionally been equated with the division of labour in a geographical region, although it is usually not made clear what minimum level of trade would justify speaking of integration. Recently, economic integration is assumed to consist of the internationalization of markets for capital, labour, technology and entrepreneurship in addition to markets for goods and services. They argue (p. 161) that the necessary and sufficient condition for complete integration is the equality of prices of any pair of goods in every member country (adjusted for transportation costs). The same criticism as to Holzman's definition applies here too.

Panić (1988, pp. 3–5) distinguishes among openness, integration and interdependence. An economy is open if it has few barriers to international trade and factor movements. The fact that an economy is open does not necessarily mean that it is integrated in the international economic system. International integration has its full meaning only when it describes an active participation in the international division of labour. Two or more economies are said to be interdependent when they are linked to such a degree that economic developments in each of them are significantly influenced by economic situation and policies in the partner country.

All these definitions of international economic integration reveal that integration is a complex notion which is to be defined with care. Definitions of international economic integration are often vague and do not offer adequate tools for the easing of the process of integration among countries. International economic integration means different things in different countries and at different times. In the developed market economies, integration means a way to introduce the most profitable technologies and allocate them in the most efficient way; in the centrally planned economies it means the planning of the development of certain activities; and in the developing countries it has the meaning of a tool for economic development. At the time of the German Zollverein (1834–71) the grouping of countries meant the development of economic inter-dependence and self-reliance. Today, international economic integration refers to the increase in the levels of welfare.

Machlup (1979, p. 24) states that one of the most obvious signs of international economic integration is the non-existence of customs posts between integrated countries. Total economic integration among countries with market economies is not achieved until these countries know the level of their mutual trade. There does not exist a statistic which can show the volume of trade between Pennsylvania and Ohio. This measure does not apply to international economic integration among countries with central planning. In these countries the central plan always directs flows and decides volumes of foreign trade.

There is an unresolved question about what is to be integrated. Is it to be citizens, markets, production, consumption, commodities, services, regions, factors, money, resources, something else, all of these together or just some of these components? What are the measures for the advance, stagnation or decline of international economic integration? What is the essence of international economic integration and what are the criteria for the appraisal of this process? Machlup (1979, p. 43) offered the greatest part of the answer to the last question. He says that trade is the quintessence of economic integration and the division of labour its underlying principle. If one neglects transportation costs, then the basic principle for the appraisal of international economic integration is equality of prices for comparable goods and services in all integrated countries. Machlup's test is much easier for standardized goods and services than for differentiated ones. A meaningful comparison of the price gap of a good in different markets should take into account not only the transport costs but also, and more importantly, the consumption patterns in different countries. This is an extremely difficult exercise. Income, tastes, traditions and climate may be homogeneous in relatively small areas, sometimes even within a single country. The more homogeneous are the countries, the easier the test.

Finally, we can conclude that international economic integration is a process and a means by which a group of countries strives to increase its level of welfare in relation to the present level or some past one (it is possible that the past level of welfare was higher than the current one). It involves the recognition that a weak or strong partnership between countries can achieve this goal in a more efficient way, than by unilateral and independent pursuance of policy in each country. International economic integration requires the division of labour and freedom of movements for goods and services (at least) and factors of production within the integrated area, as well as restriction of these movements between the integrated area and countries outside of it. The essential point is that those countries together adopt a kind of inward-looking approach and concern for what happens in all member countries more than what happens outside of them. At least some consultation, if not coordination, of monetary and fiscal policies is also a necessary condition for the success and durability of integration, as is the case in the United States. The process of integration may be practically unlimited, just as is the continuous integration of various regions within a single country. From a technical point of view, international economic integration can be a limited process – i.e. the elimination of tariffs and quantitative restrictions, as well as the introduction of a common external tariff in a customs union. Ultimately, competition, new technologies and the like, require continuous adjustments for countries in a customs union, which makes integration more of an unlimited than a limited process. International economic integration is a process by which the economies of separate states merge in large entities. This definition of international economic integration, incorporating the ideas in this paragraph, will be maintained throughout this book.

TYPES OF INTERNATIONAL ECONOMIC INTEGRATION

Consumption in an integrated area is potentially higher than the sum of the consumptions of individual countries which are potential partners for integration in the situation in which trade is impeded by customs duties, quotas and barriers to factor mobility. International economic integration removes, at least partly, these and other distortions to trade and, possibly, investment. In this sense, international economic integration between at least two countries can have the following seven theoretical types.

- A *preferential tariff agreement* among countries assumes that the customs duties on trade among the signatory countries are lower in relation to customs duties charged on trade with third countries.
- A *partial customs union* is formed when the participating countries retain their initial tariffs on their mutual trade and introduce a common external tariff on trade with third countries.
- A *free trade area* is an agreement among countries about the elimination of all tariff and quantitative restrictions on mutual trade. Every country in this area retains its own tariff and other regulation of trade with third countries. The bases of this agreement are the rules of origin. These rules prevent trade deflection, which is the import of goods from third countries into the area by country A (which has a relatively lower external tariff than country B) in order to re-export the goods to country B.
- In a *customs union*, participating countries not only remove tariff and quantitative restrictions on their internal trade, but also introduce a common external tariff on trade with third countries. The participating countries take part in international negotiations about trade and tariffs as a single unity.
- In a *common market*, apart from a customs union, there exists free mobility of factors of production. Common regulations (restrictions) on the movement of factors with third countries are introduced.
- An *economic union* among countries assumes not only a common market, but also the harmonization of fiscal, monetary, industrial, regional, transport and other economic policies.
- A *total economic union* among countries assumes a union with a single economic policy and a supranational government of this confederation with great economic authority.

Table 1.1 shows selected types of international economic integration. The process of international economic integration does not have to be gradual from one type to another. The establishment

Table 1.1   Types of international economic integration

	Type 1 Free trade area	Type 2 Customs union	Type 3 Common market	Type 4 Economic union	Type 5 Total economic union
Removal of tariffs and quotas on trade among the countries	Yes	Yes	Yes	Yes	Yes
Common external tariff	No	Yes	Yes	Yes	Yes
Freedom of movement of factors	No	No	Yes	Yes	Yes
Harmonization of economic policies	No	No	No	Yes	Yes
Total unification of economic policies	No	No	No	No	Yes

of any of these types depends on the agreement among the participating countries. Spontaneous or market integration is created by actions of TNCs, banks and other financial institutions – often without the involvement of their governments – while formal or institutional integration asks for a formal agreement among governments to eliminate selected or all restrictions on trade and factor movements on their economic relations (Panić, 1988, p. 6–7). There is substantial historical evidence to support the argument that the formal (*de jure*) approach to integration asks for a spontaneous (*de facto*) way, and vice versa. The decision about entering into a customs union or any other type of integration is in fact political. A decision to abandon a part of national sovereignty with respect to the taxation of trade (all in a customs union, part in a free trade area) should be made by politicians.

SOVEREIGNTY

International economic integration is popularly criticized on the grounds that it reduces a country's national sovereignty (undisputed political power). When two or more sovereign countries sign a treaty, they agree to do and/or not to do specified things. Therefore, it is not a valid criticism of any international treaty to say that it entails a loss of national sovereignty. All treaties do so in one way or another. The real issue is: do the countries' concessions constitute a mutually beneficial deal. Is the surrender of sovereignty justified by the results? Consider, for example, the Canadian debate leading up to the Canada-United States Free Trade Agreement in Lipsey and York (1988).

Canada is a small (in economic terms) and open economy. The competitive future of this country has been seriously jeopardized by the uncertain future of the relatively liberal international trading system. Canada therefore negotiated, and subsequently signed in 1988, a Free Trade Agreement with the United States. The negotiations and the pre-election period at that time were subject to one of the greatest debates in Canadian history. The opponents of this Agreement tried, with initial success, to persuade a majority of Canadians that the Agreement would significantly reduce Canadian sovereignty and distinctiveness. The ado made by the opponents is probably the greatest one in the history of international economic integration. Giving their vote to the Conservatives, the Canadians, however, supported the Agreement.

There was a fear that Canada should have to harmonize a range of economic policies with the United States. If experience is a reliable guide, then this fear is not relevant. The Netherlands has a developed and costly social policy while Belgium spends little in this area. Yet, these two countries have been in a free trade area for more than a half a century without harmonizing their social policies. As for other economic policies, pressures for harmonization do exist. If tax rates differ among countries and if factors are allowed to move, then, other things being equal, factors will move to countries where the tax burden is lower. It should be noted, however, that these harmonizing pressures exist even in the situation without integration. Within, for example, a common market, apart from the agreed matters, countries will have to give each other national treatment. This means that countries can have any policy they wish, even those which are completely different from policies in the partner countries – with just one important condition. The country should not use these policies to discriminate between partners on the basis of their nationality. International economic integration is not the enemy of diversity in many economic policies. In others, like fiscal policy of the EC, integration does reduce the diversity of the main policy instruments. It is this that raises all sorts of problems when economies at different levels of development, facing different problems, become integrated. They ought to harmonize such policies.

If a small country accepts a long-term policy of protection, as opposed to liberalization or international economic integration, it chooses a long-term deterioration in its competitive position. It is coupled with a reduction in living standard in relation to countries which do not practise protectionism and/or to the level of welfare which could have been achieved by an alternative economic strategy. Can a country preserve its sovereignty and the welfare of its citizens with a long-term trend of deterioration in the standard of living?

The expectation of a net economic gain compared to the situation without integration is the most fundamental incentive for international economic integration. Anticipated gains include an increase in the efficiency of the use of factors due to increased competition, specialization, returns to scale, increases in investment, improvements in terms of trade, reduced risk and equalization of factor prices. Integration will be beneficial when cooperation and coordination of policies takes place instead of the disintegrated exercise of power through often contradictory policies. Sovereignty is pooled, rather than given up. Small, open countries need to realize that it is much less a choice between national sovereignty and international economic integration and much more a choice between one form of interdependence and another. If one's aim is to increase the competitiveness of a small country and secure widest markets for its goods and services in the future, then international economic integration is a serious alternative to the national freedom to implement and continue with bad economic policies.

2 Customs union

INTRODUCTION

All types of international economic integration provoke interest because they, to different degrees, both promote and restrict trade. Trade is liberalized, at least partly, among the participating countries, while it is also distorted because there are various barriers between the integrated grouping and other countries. On these grounds the analysis of international economic integration is complex. A customs union is the type of international economic integration which has received the most attention in research and is the most rigorously developed branch of the neo-classical theory. Here, the effects of the removal of tariffs and quotas and the introduction of the common external tariff on the trade, specialization and consumption of the integrated countries are analysed.

The tariff system may discriminate between commodities and/or countries. Commodity discrimination takes place when different rates of import duty are charged on different commodities. Country discrimination is found when the same commodity is subject to different rates of duty on the basis of country of origin. Lipsey (1960, p. 496) defines the theory of customs unions as a branch of tariff theory which deals with the effect of geographically discriminatory changes in trade barriers. This is true in the static perspective. In a dynamic perspective, however, a customs union may be, among other things, a means for economic development.

The efficiency criterion used most often in economics is that of Pareto optimality. An allocation is said to be Pareto-optimal if there does not exist another feasible allocation in which some agents would be better off (in a welfare sense) and no agents worse off. By a judicious definition of welfare, the Pareto-optimal allocation is that allocation which best satisfies social objectives. Pareto optimality (the first-best solution) is achieved exclusively in the state of free trade and factor mobility, so that other states, in which there are distortions (duties, subsidies, taxes, monopolies, minimum wages, local content requirements, to mention just a few), are suboptimal. It may happen that the Pareto-optimal allocation can not be achieved because of one or several distortions. Can a second-best position be attained by satisfying the remaining Pareto conditions? The theory of the second best answers in the negative (Lipsey and Lancaster, 1956–57). In the presence of distortions, if all the conditions for Pareto optimality cannot be satisfied, then the removal of some of the distortions does not necessarily increase welfare, nor does the addition of other distortions necessarily decrease welfare. It may remain unaffected, increased or decreased. This implies that there can be no reliable expectation about the welfare effect of a change in the current situation. The theory of the second best has a disastrous effect on welfare economics. However, Lipsey (1960) was not discouraged enough to prevent him from writing a seminal article on the theory of customs unions.

The intuition behind the classical theory of customs unions is the proposition that the potential consumption of goods and services in a customs union is higher than the sum of individual consumptions of the potential member countries in the situation in which trade among these countries is distorted by tariffs and quotas. In this situation one should, at least partly, remove these impediments. The following chapters spell out static and dynamic models of the theory of customs unions.

STATIC MODEL

A static model of the theory of customs unions considers the impact of the formation of a customs union on trade flows and consumption in the united countries. After outlining the assumptions to be maintained, partial and general equilibrium models, respectively, are analysed. Also, attention is devoted to conditions for a welfare-improving customs union.

Assumptions

The classical (orthodox or static) theory of customs unions relies on a number of explicit and implicit assumptions. This approach makes theoretical consideration easier, but it also simplifies reality so much that the policy recommendations of this theory are to be considered with great care.

Assume that there are three countries. Country A, a relatively small country in relation to the other two countries, forms a customs union with country B. Country C, which may represent all other countries, is discriminated against by the customs union by means of a common external tariff. Duties are levied on an *ad valorem* basis in all countries. Rates of duties are the same both for final commodities and inputs, so that the rate of nominal protection equals the rate of effective protection. The assumption of equal rates of tariffs removes the possible dispute about the level of the common external tariff. Tariffs are the only instrument of trade policy and there are no non-tariff barriers to trade. The price of imported goods for home consumers (P_{mt}) is composed of the price of an imported good (P_m) and tariff (t):

$$P_{mt} = (1 + t) P_m \qquad (2.1)$$

where $t \geq 0$. State intervention exists only at the border, and trade is balanced. Free or perfect competition exists both in markets for goods and services as well as in markets for factors. Perfect competition (or complete equality of opportunity) exists in all economies, but for the existence of tariffs.

Production costs per unit of output are constant over all levels of output. To put it more formally, production functions are homogeneous of degree one, i.e. to produce one more unit of good X, inputs must be increased by a constant proportion. Costs of production determine the retail prices of goods. Producers in an industry operate at the minimum efficient scale at the production frontier. Countries embark upon the production of certain commodities on the basis of the prices (relative abundance or scarcity) of home factors.

The theory of customs unions refers to the manufacturing sector: a fixed quantity of factors of production is fully employed. There are no sector-specific factors such as specific human and physical capital, entrepreneurship and the like. In a dynamic model these specific factors can be transformed in the long run, but this would require adjustment costs which are ruled out in the static model. Factors that can not be transformed include natural resources. Mobility of factors is perfect within their home country, while commodities are perfectly mobile between the united countries. TNCs are ignored.

There are no transport, insurance or banking costs. Prices are given irrespective of quantities produced or traded.

All countries have access to the same technology and differ only in their endowments of factors. Economies are static, with static expectations. This is to say that rates of growth; technologies; tastes; propensities to consume, save, import and invest, are given and unchangeable. There is no depreciation of the capital stock. All goods and services are homogeneous, i.e. consumers do not have a preference for the consumption of goods and services from any particular supplier. They decide upon their purchases exclusively on the basis of price differences. All goods and services have unit income elasticities of demand, i.e. every increase or decrease in income has a proportional change in demand for all goods and services in the same direction. This means that demand is 'well-behaved'. Non-tradeable commodities do not exist. There is no intra-industry trade or 'cross-hauling', i.e. a country cannot both export and import any good. There are no inventories. All markets clear simultaneously. Such equilibrium must be both sustainable and feasible, i.e. firms can neither profitably undercut market price nor make losses.

In this model there is no uncertainty. Firms and resource owners are perfectly informed about all markets while consumers are fully familiar with goods and services. Fiscal (taxes and subsidies) and monetary (rates of exchange, interest, inflation, and balance of payments) operations are ruled out. Finally, a country which is not included in a customs union is assumed not to retaliate against members of a customs union.

The above assumptions are clearly highly restrictive, but greatly simplify the analysis so that the essential properties of the model can be highlighted.

Partial equilibrium model

The partial equilibrium model deals with the market for a single good. International trade can be a response to differences in the availability of resources (factor proportions), differences in technology and efficiency in production (production functions), economies of scale, differences in tastes, differences in market structures and/or differences in output or factor taxes. This section deals with the case where the three countries produce the same commodity,

Table 2.1 Unit cost of production of a commodity

Country	A	B	C
Unit cost of production	60	50	35

but with varying levels of efficiency: their production functions differ. This model is described in Table 2.1.

Country C has the lowest unit cost of production, hence this country will become the world supplier of this commodity. Suppose now that country A wants to protect her inefficient domestic producers from foreign competition for whatever reason. This intention of country A can be criticized from the outset. Tariffs are an available means of protection which have distortionary effects. The most important effect is that they move the country away from free trade towards autarky. Gains from specialization are sacrificed because resources are diverted away from the pattern of comparative advantage. In addition to reducing potential consumption, tariffs redistribute income in favour of factors which are used in production in the protected industry and decrease the income of other factors used elsewhere in the economy. Regardless, if country A wants to protect her home production of this good, an import duty must be levied. This tariff of, for example, 100 per cent not only increases the price of the imported commodity to country A's consumers, but more importantly it shifts consumption away from imports towards country A's domestic production. In these circumstances, country A could increase domestic consumption of this good if it enters into a customs union with either of the countries in this model. Table 2.2 presents prices of the imported commodity with the tariff on country A's market.

Table 2.2 Price of an imported commodity with the tariff on country A's market

Import duty (%)	Price of a commodity from country B	Price of a commodity from country C
100	100	70
50	75	52.5

If country A forms a customs union with country B, then consumers in country A could import the good from country B at a cost of 50 dollars per unit, rather than to buy it from domestic suppliers at the cost of 60 dollars as before. Hence, they are better off than in the case of non-discriminatory tariff. If country A embarks upon a customs union with country C, then country A's consumers are in an even better position compared to a customs union with country B. Now, they purchase the good at a unit price of 35 dollars. In both cases, consumers in country A are better off than in the situation in which they were buying the domestically produced good. The final effect in both cases is trade creation.

The formation of a customs union encourages *trade creation* as the result of a change from a dearer to a cheaper source of supply. Other things being equal, this is a move towards free trade because a less efficient, protected, domestic supplier is replaced by a more efficient, foreign one. Country A gives up a product in which she has a comparative disadvantage in order to acquire it more cheaply by importing it from a partner country, so trade is created. This welfare-improving effect depends crucially on our assumption that the freed domestic resources can find alternative employment elsewhere in the economy.

Suppose now that prior to the formation of the customs union, the duty on imports was 50 per cent in country A. Table 2.2 shows that in this case the supplier of country A would be country C. Country A's domestic industry offers this good at a unit price of 60 dollars, country B at a price of 75 dollars, while country C is the cheapest source of supply at 52.5 dollars. If instead, country A enters into a customs union with country B and if the common external tariff for the commodity in question is 50 per cent, then country A will purchase this good from country B. In this case country A pays 50 dollars per unit to country B, while at the same time, a unit of the good from country C costs 52.5 dollars. The outcome in this case is *trade diversion*. Trade creation and trade diversion are often called Vinerian effects due to Viner (1950) who first introduced the terms.

Trade diversion works in the opposite way from trade creation. The cheapest foreign supplier is changed in favour of a relatively dearer customs-union supplier. Due to the common external tariff, business is taken away from the most efficient world producer and trade in this commodity is reduced. This creates a global welfare loss. Trade within a customs union takes place at a protected level of prices. A higher union level of prices relative to the international one benefits internal exporters. Importers lose, for they pay the partner country suppliers a higher price per unit of import and their country forgoes tariff revenue which is not levied on intra-union imports.

The net impact on world efficiency of a move to a customs union depends on which of the two Vinerian effects dominates. It may be positive, negative or neutral. Therefore, the favourable attitude of the GATT towards customs unions and free trade areas as trade-liberalizing moves can not be accepted without reservation.

The Common Agricultural Policy and the Common Commercial Policy (customs union) in the EC are the policies which are oriented towards producers. The interests of the consumers are largely neglected in the EC. This is obvious from the relatively low influence of the European Parliament which can represent most directly the interests of consumers. Continuous reforms are gradually increasing the influence of this Parliament. Nevertheless, producers in the EC have a dominant say. Hence, a trade diverting bias of the EC should not come as a surprise (Pomfret, 1986, p. 112).

Trade diversion may be more beneficial than trade creation for the consumption of the country that, like country A, gives preferential treatment to certain suppliers. It is because this country does not sacrifice home production (Johnson, 1973, p. 89). The source of benefits is *anticipated* trade creation, since, by assumption, bilateral trade flows must balance. The comparison here is between trade creation and the autarkic volume of domestic production. An integrating country will not benefit from trade creation unless it increases its exports to the partners (as compared to the pre-union level) which from the partner's point of view can represent trade diversion (Robson, 1987, p. 52).

Flows of trade among countries A, B and C may have the following patterns. Suppose that country A and country B form a customs union. If only country A produces a particular good, but inefficiently, then the choice between domestic production and imports from country C depends on the height of the common external tariff. If both countries in the customs union produce the good, but inefficiently, then the least inefficient country will supply the customs-union market subject to the protection of the common external tariff. If neither country in the customs union produces the good, then there is no trade diversion. The customs union is supplied by the cheapest foreign source. If only one country in the customs union produces the good in question, but in the most efficient way, then this country will supply the market even without a common external tariff. By offering a common level of protection, the common external tariff may promote a more efficient allocation of resources within the customs union. Figure 2.1 shows flows of

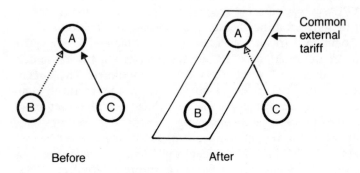

Figure 2.1 Flows of imports of a commodity to country A before and after the creation of a customs union with country B

imports of a commodity to country A prior to and after the creation of a customs union with country B.

Figure 2.2 illustrates the effects of a tariff and a customs union on economic efficiency for a single good in country A's market. Supply curves for a single good may equally be assumed to represent quantities of different goods which offer equal satisfaction to consumers as the consumption of a single good (Johnson, 1962, p. 55). SS represents country A's domestic supply curve, similarly, DD shows the domestic demand curve. Country B's supply curve is BB, while country C's supply curve for the same good is CC. Both foreign countries can supply unconditionally any quantity of the demanded good at fixed prices. Both foreign supply curves are flat (perfectly elastic). It is a consequence of the smallness of the country in our example. This country cannot exert influence on its terms of trade, but in a customs union with other countries this is likely to change. Prior to the imposition of a tariff, at price 0C home demand for the good is $0Q_6$. Domestic producers supply $0Q_1$ while country C supplies Q_1Q_6.

Suppose that country A introduces a tariff on imports such that the price for domestic consumers is 0T. Now, country A can expand domestic production from $0Q_1$ to $0Q_3$ and curtail home consumption of the good from $0Q_6$ to $0Q_4$. Of course, the government collects tariff revenue equal to CT $\times$ Q_3Q_4. This choice by country A may be questioned. There are at least two good reasons to object to trade restrictions in the medium and long-term. First, new barriers to trade can provoke retaliation in the foreign countries in

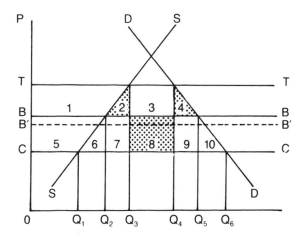

Figure 2.2 Effect of a tariff and a customs union on production and consumption in country A

which exporters intend to penetrate. Second, and more subtle, if intermediate goods exist, all trade barriers raise the price of imported inputs. Therefore they act as a tax on exports. This is a part of the reason for the poor export performance of highly protected countries (like East European ones were until recently). With the tariff, country A employs more resources in an industry in which it does not have a comparative advantage. Keeping in mind the assumption that the amount of resources is fixed, and stepping out shortly from the partial equilibrium approach, resources are diverted from the activities in which this country may have a comparative advantage. If a home industry is not competitive, a tariff may save jobs in this sector in the short term. This may, however, lead to reduced activity in other home industries. If the uncompetitively-produced home good is an input for other industries, their export performance may be compromised and investment reduced with the overall consequence of increased unemployment in the longer term.

  Policy makers can easily identify jobs that are saved by various forms of protection, but do not easily recognize adverse conse-quences of this protection, hence the need for a general-equilibrium model. Through protection in the long term, resources are wasted on inefficient production. Everybody loses except the government (because of increased revenues) and the protected industry. In the short run, the problem is that the general-equilibrium consequences of a given policy are not easily quantified. This policy of import substitution as opposed to a policy of export promotion may be substantiated only on the grounds that foreign markets for country A's exports are closed.

The national-security argument for tariffs can be questioned. Trade-impacted sectors lobby for protection. This plea does not take into account the fact that industrial decline rarely, if ever, implies the actual demise of an industry. Possible nuclear warfare and 'smart bombs' remove the classical national-security argument for protection. Risk-averse governments may consider stockpiling and/or guaranteeing supplies of goods and services from allies before imposing a tariff (Tyson and Zysman, 1987a, p. 41). Apart from security of supply, there are other reasons why a country may wish to preserve at least a part of (declining) domestic industry which is exposed to international competition. Possibilities for domestic production increase bargaining power in negotiations about long-term supply contracts with foreigners. Also, if the cost situation changes in the future, some domestic research and development (R&D), as well as production capacity may be a good starting point for regaining competitiveness.

With regard to protection, the infant-industry argument and similar arguments of learning-by-doing state that entrants to an industry suffer losses while they acquire know-how, suppliers, customers, trained labour and the like in the period of infancy, so they need protection. It takes time for a firm to become profitable. Everybody knows it. If bankers, investors and entrepreneurs are not prepared to accept short-term losses as their investment toward long-term gains without government intervention, that is a clear indication that the market does not consider the enterprise to be viable, and so does not deserve tariff protection.

A free trader would argue that every firm profitable by market criteria does not need to be protected. If the infant-industry argument is to make sense, then there must be some evidence of market failure, either in capital markets (entrepreneurs can not obtain adequate loans), or labour markets (such as inadequate training or fluctuations in the labour force) or some evidence that the production structure warrants protection. For example, there may be increasing returns to scale or positive externalities that require a certain level of protection. These market failures may be corrected by economic policy (intervention). Still, there are many old infants. What starts as an infant-industry-protection argument turns into an employment-protection argument. Finally, old infants are often nationalized at continuous cost to the country (Brander 1987, p. 19). If a government bails out a declining sector and/or firm and creates a precedent, this produces expectations that the cost of poor management of business will be socialized. This may be one of the main sources of the adjustment difficulties in the 'problem' sectors in industrialized countries.

Returning to Figure 2.2, assume that country A which imposed a non-discriminatory *ad valorem* tariff on imports, enters into a customs union with country B. The price of imports from country C with a common external tariff CT is 0T. Country B will supply country A's market. Country A's inefficient production contracts from $0Q_3$ to $0Q_2$, while consumption increases from $0Q_4$ to $0Q_5$. *Trade expansion* due to the customs union equals the sum of the reduction in home production Q_2Q_3 and the increase in home consumption Q_4Q_5. Country A's government does not earn any proceeds from imports of the good from the customs-union partner, country B. Trade expansion inevitably effects rationalization in production. This takes place through an improved employment of existing factors, increased size of production units (reallocation of resources within sectors) and a reallocation of factors among integrated countries. The consequences of these rationalizations are decreased unit costs of goods and services, as well as increased standards of living on the average.

Trade-expansion effects, however, should not be overemphasized. The downward adjustment of the domestic tariffs to the common external tariff need not result in an increased trade-expansion effect in a customs union. This alignment will first lead to a reduction to normal levels of the profit margins of the protected domestic producers. If there is excess capacity in the protected industries, a possible increase in the domestic demand – which comes as a consequence of the fall in price – will be met firstly by the country's own production (if it exists), rather than through imports. Thus the trade-expansion effects due to the creation of a customs union will not be as large as would be suggested by the difference in tariffs before the creation of a customs union (Yannopoulos, 1988, pp. 41–2). Therefore, the scope for trade diversion is, indeed, smaller than it may first appear. It is just the potential for trade and competition that does this good work for consumers (and producers in the long term).

Consumers' surplus is defined as the difference between the consumers' total valuation of the goods consumed and the total cost of obtaining them. It is represented by the area under the demand curve above the price that consumers face. Any decrease in price, other things being equal, increases consumers' surplus. Country A's consumers benefit when their country enters into a customs union with country B in relation to the situation with an initial non-discriminatory tariff. Their gain is given by the area $1 + 2 + 3 + 4$. These consumers are, however, worse off in comparison to the free-trade situation in which country C is the supplier. This loss is given by the area $5 + 6 + 7 + 8 + 9 + 10$. Domestic producers lose part of their surplus in a customs union compared to the situation with a non-discriminatory *ad valorem* tariff (area above SS up to the price 0B which they receive). This is represented by area 1. From the national stand-point, area 1 nets out as part of both the consumers' gain and the producers' loss. Country A loses tariff revenue (area 3) which it collects in the initial situation. Hence, the net gain for country A is area $2 + 4$.

The formation of a customs union has increased trade and consumption in country A in comparison to the initial situation with a non-discriminatory tariff. In the situation prior to the formation of a customs union, country A imports the good from country C, pays for it an amount equal to $Q_3Q_4 \times 0C$ and collects revenue equal to the area $3 + 8$. After the formation of a customs union, area 3 is returned to consumers in the form of lower prices for the good, while area 8 represents a higher price charged by the customs-union partner country. The return of the area 3 to the consumers may be regarded as Hicksian compensation. When tariffs change, compensation is seldom paid. Hence, demand curve DD may be regarded just as an approximation to the compensated Hicksian demand curve. It is important to note that country A pays, for the same amount of imports Q_3Q_4, a higher price to the customs-union partner ($Q_3Q_4 \times 0B$) than was paid to the country C suppliers prior to the customs union formation. It has a greater outflow of foreign exchange and does not collect revenue, which it had done when it had imposed a non-discriminatory tariff on imports from country C. The outflow of foreign exchange from country A was equal to $Q_3Q_4 \times 0C$ while area $3 + 4$ illustrates the transfer from consumers to producers within the home country.

The net welfare effect of the creation of a customs union in country A depends on the relative size of the Vinerian effects; trade creation (area 2 + 4) minus trade diversion (area 8). Instead of a revenue-generating obstacle to trade (tariff), a government may introduce cost-increasing barriers (customs, health and testing documentation) whose effect may be a reduction in trade. (Let the effect of the non-tariff barriers be BT in trade with country B.) If the set of non-tariff barriers is removed, the effect on domestic consumers and producers would be the same as in the situation when the tariff was removed. The government which has never earned revenue from the set of non-tariff regulations, would lose nothing. The social gain from reducing these barriers is area 2 + 3 + 4.

If one introduces dynamics into this model, in the form of increasing returns to scale, then country B, as the customs-union supplier of the good, faces an increased demand. Production would become more efficient and the price might fall from OB to, say OB'. This enhances trade creation and decreases the size of the trade-diversion effect.

Figure 2.2 belongs to the family of standard microeconomic partial-equilibrium figures. Unfortunately, they all deal just with a part of the business cycle – that is, only with the first third of the cycle when demand rises. Other cases, like stagnation or reduction in demand, are seldom considered.

If the initial situation included tariffs on trade among countries, then after the creation of a customs union, consumers face lower goods prices. Hence, their real income is increased. Viner implicitly assumed fixed proportions in the consumption of various goods (Michaely, 1976, pp. 86–7). If one abandons this possibility and if one allows for a change in relative prices, then the structure of consumption will change.

After the creation of a customs union, patterns of consumption will change. Inter-country substitution occurs when one country replaces the other as the source of supply for some good. Inter-commodity substitution happens when one commodity is substituted, at least at the margin, for another commodity as a result of a shift in relative prices (Lipsey, 1960, p. 504). The latter occurs, for example, when country A imports from the customs-union partner country B, relatively cheaper veal which replaces at least some of the pork produced in country A and at least some of the chicken which is imported from country C, and when consumers in a customs union replace a part of demand for theatre and opera by relatively cheaper stereo and video equipment.

There are many aspects to efficiency. One can ask if there are superior alternative policies. Unilateral, non-discriminatory reductions in import tariffs may seem to be a superior policy to the formation of a customs union. It seems better to obtain trade creation exclusively as a result of unilateral tariff reductions than to create a customs union which uses both trade creation and trade diversion (Cooper and Massel, 1965a, pp. 745–6). This argument cannot be accepted without serious reservations. A customs union offers something which is not offered by a unilateral reduction in tariffs – that is, an elimination of tariffs in customs-union partner countries. A unilateral reduction in tariffs exaggerates the price reduction effects on consumption, while it eliminates the possibility of penetration into customs-union partner countries' markets.

In spite of the trade-diversion costs of a customs union, the terms of trade of member countries may turn in their favour, so that, on balance, each member country may be better off than in the unilateral tariff-reduction case. The classical approach to the theory of tariffs is mistaken. This approach, on the one hand, finds gains in the replacement of domestic goods for cheaper foreign goods, while on the other hand, expansion of domestic exports does not bring gains in this model to the exporting country (except possible improvement of the terms of trade), but rather to the foreigners (Johnson 1973, p. 80).

Suppose that transfer payments between countries are allowed for. Then any customs union is potentially favourable for all countries considering participation, since they can be compensated for losses when they join. This means that customs union among n countries can be extended to $n + 1$ countries. By expansion, this implies that there is an incentive to extend the customs union until the whole world is included, until free trade prevails throughout the world (Kemp and Wan, 1976). This may lead to the classical proposition that a customs union is a step towards free trade. This conclusion depends on the existence of inter-country transfers within the customs union. This is a severe restriction and the greatest weakness of this approach. The more countries there are in a customs union, the greater will be the potential need for compensation. If compensation schemes are adopted in reality, they are often the products of political bargaining and not purely of economic impact. These schemes are too complicated and they never compensate in full since compensation schemes are never perfect, which limits the actual size of customs union. This leads to the conclusion that non-economic reasons may also play a prominent role in economic integration. The experience of the EC illustrates that the political considerations play a prominent part in integration.

Subsidies

Consideration of the impact of tariffs on imports would be incomplete without comparing them to production subsidies. The effect of a tariff on imports of a commodity is equivalent to a combination of a tax on domestic consumption and a subsidy on home production of the same good. Tariffs and subsidies are close substitutes. A reduction in one of them may be compensated for by an increase in the other.

A domestic tariff increases prices both of imported goods and home-made protected goods (at least in the short run). This distortion has as its cost the losses both of gains from exchange and gains from specialization. A cost of subsidies is a loss of gains from specialization due to the distortions of prices of home-made goods. Thus, at least in the long run, a restriction of imports is equal to a reduction in potential exports when a fixed amount of resources is fully employed prior to the introduction of distortions. Resources are being shifted out of exports into import-substituting industries. But in the short run (before elections), authorities might be more concerned about the level of (un)employment than about income transfers which both tariffs and production subsidies imply.

If country A is subject to subsidized supplies of good X from country B, country A should consider the consequences of such circumstances. Subsidies are based on potential earning of economic rents from foreign consumers and producers (beggar-thy-neighbour). These rents refer to the proceeds of the exporters which are in excess of what is necessary to cover costs of production and to yield an average return on investment. Such subsidies will improve the social welfare of the exporting country only if profits of the exporting industry on exports exceed the cost of the subsidy to the taxpayers. If country A obtains the good X at a lower price from country B than from its domestic producers, then domestic consumers are better off, although its home producers of good X are worse off. All this is at the expense of country B's taxpayers. If country B is willing to supply country A with the subsidized good X indefinitely, then a smart policy for country A is to accept these supplies and shift domestic resources to activities where the return is higher in relation to the return to home production of the good X. However, if country B subsidizes its exports of good X in order to discharge cyclical surpluses, or in order to prevent the entry of country A's firms into the market of good X, or to drive them out of it in the long run, and intends later to charge monopoly prices, then country A need not accept this offer as the only source of supply.

Although tariffs and subsidies have similar effects on trade and production, the GATT does not prohibit tariffs, while its Code on Subsidies and Countervailing Duties (1979) prohibits export subsidies (with the exception of certain primary products) if such subsidies cause material injury to the importing country's firms. The injury must be proven prior to the introduction of a countervailing duty which aims to offset the effect of foreign subsidies on domestic business. Of course, the maximum countervailing duty permitted by the GATT is limited by the amount of subsidy embodied in imports of the country that introduces the duty. The effects of such a policy are limited only to the competitive situation in the home market of the country that introduces countervailing duty. Similarly, in the situation of a balance-of-payments deficit, the International Monetary Fund (IMF) recommends a tariff, but does not advise the use of export subsidies.

Foreign subsidies may induce countervailing duties in injured countries. If the injured countries do not either produce or have some potential for the production of a good, then there are no grounds for the imposition of these duties. The relative size of trading partners and their relative openness to trade plays a crucial role. Relatively small countries are more reliant on external trade than larger ones. A small subsidy to an import-competing industry in a large country may have a more distorting impact than a large subsidy applied to a small country's exports (Thirsk, 1985, p. 145).

Preferences for tariffs often are due to compelling political realities. People are used to tariffs, while subsidies personify unfair competition. We cannot force foreigners to eliminate their tariffs on our exports but we may, if we identify their subsidies, make them remove these by the threat of imposing countervailing duties. An international abolition of tariffs would be ignored while a prohibition of export subsidies legitimates retaliation by means of countervailing duties (Wonnacott, 1987, pp. 86–7). This flexible system of instant unilateral retaliation may result in an informal system of international cooperation in the settlement of disputes in trade. This situation is, however, due to the shortcomings of the formal settlement of disputes in trade under the auspices of the GATT. Of course, there are other incentives for the introduction of subsidies. Let us consider them in turn.

Firms invest because of the anticipation of profits in the future. Investments are undertaken because markets are foreseen, costs of production make profits possible, and funds, at acceptable rates, are available. If profit opportunities are fading away, then unemployment may rise. Governments are reluctant to accept such a state of affairs, so they offer subsidies (investment, production and export), among other things, to firms in order to alter unfavourable trends. If a country wants to protect all the firms in an industry, then an outright subsidy may be a better alternative to reduced tax rates. A subsidy might help all firms, while reduced tax rates may help only those that are profitable. Reduced taxes may be preferred if the policy aim is to remove the lame ducks.

A valid case for subsidies can be made if there are significant market imperfections. Unemployment was a cyclical phenomenon in the past. Nowadays, its nature is different. In many cases labour needs retraining in order to be hired. Vocational training may be a valid case for subsidies.

A special type of subsidy may be present in government procurement policies. By discriminating in the award of government contracts, a government may sharpen the competitive edge of an economy, which is very important during the first steps in the development of an industry, commodity or service. A firm's shareholders thus receive income transfers from home taxpayers. If the industry is successful and if sunk costs are high, then late-comers may not enter the market. This strategic pre-emption of the market may provide the firm and the country with super-normal profits from sales on foreign markets. One example is the purchase of defence equipment as a subsidy to high-technology firms. This is the case in the United States' aircraft industry which received (and still receives) indirect subsidies. In Europe, the airbus industry is directly subsidized by the participating governments. It is very hard for potential investors in other regions of the world to compete with firms that combine their forces with national governments in this industry.

If one neglects the possibility of retaliation, intervention can make a country better off. When super-normal profits (rents) from export to foreign countries exceed the cost of subsidies (production and/or export), obviously the exporting country increases its wealth.

A special type of subsidy may also be present in goods and services supplied to firms and citizens by the government. These goods and services are offered at lower prices by government enterprises than by private firms which must pay taxes. When managers of companies start spending more time lobbying for government grants than worrying about the actual operation of their companies, taxpayers and consumers should get nervous (Brander, 1987, p. 28). The long-term prosperity of a country cannot be promoted by subsidies to inefficient firms. By doing so, new wealth is not created, but an extra tax is imposed on the prosperous. In services that are provided by the government and not by private firms, there is at least some subsidy element.

An output subsidy may be preferable to an export subsidy. The rationale is that an output subsidy does not necessarily lead to higher domestic prices of differentiated products as is the case with a tariff or an export subsidy (Flam and Helpman, 1987, pp. 94–5). Output subsidies are often tacitly accepted, while export subsidies are often subject to countervailing duties. An R&D subsidy always expands these activities, more varieties appear and more firms enter the industry. The price of differentiated goods may increase or decline, as an increased number of firms may result in lower output per firm. This R&D subsidy may, therefore, improve or deteriorate welfare, or leave it unchanged.

One of the most obvious expressions of subsidies was the United State's Domestic International Sales Corporation (DISC) which supplied tax benefits to United States' exporters. Initially, the DISC allowed exporters an indefinite postponement of the payment of about a quarter of the income tax on their export profits. This acted as a direct subsidy to capital used in the production for exports. The GATT Council in 1976 found the DISC to be a direct export subsidy programme in conflict with the GATT rules. The current legal embodiment of the DISC, with a similar effect, is the Federal Sales Corporation.

The new theory of strategic trade and industrial policy has identified areas where government intervention can correct certain market imperfections. One of the available policy instruments is subsidies. This policy instrument, however, must be financed either by taxes or by borrowing. Taxes produce distortions because they affect supply of labour, wage costs and/or discourage consumption. Government borrowing increases interest rates and tends to crowd out private investment. These welfare losses are not necessarily larger than the welfare gains obtained from the same subsidies. Governments often prefer to subsidize inputs in the production process. This potentially increases technical productivity in the manufacturing of final goods. This may cause X-inefficiency problems like wasteful use of the subsidized inputs and protection of firms from competition, which reduces pressure on firms to minimize costs. Nevertheless, there is no presumption that the reduced costs from learning-by-doing and economies of scale are more important than the increased costs resulting from the X-inefficiency induced by subsidies. The new trade theorists have chosen to ignore these problems and biased their conclusions in favour of activist industrial and trade policies (de Grauwe, 1989, pp. 70–1).

Finalizing the discussion of subsidies, one comes to the point about present reasons for their public avoidance. Governments dislike direct subsidies because they place the cost within the government's budget, while regulatory measures place the cost on the private sector (Lipsey and Smith, 1986, p. 100). If a government subsidizes, then it must tax elsewhere, borrow and/or reduce supplied benefits. Subsidies are readily measurable and receivers identifiable. Costs incurred by a tariff are spread over numerous consumers and its effects can hardly be measured. A subsidy may be offered on a 'one-shot' basis, but often it becomes a 'multi-shot' commitment which often ends up in the nationalization of a bankrupt firm. Also, in the situation of budget deficits, the governments cannot easily find the necessary funds for subsidies. Therefore, one of the choices for the subsidization of exports may be depreciation of exchange rate.

The costs of financing and disbursing subsidies may be quite high whereas the administrative costs of the implementation of tariffs are relatively low and the proceeds are easy to collect. The administration for the management of subsidies may be formidable and quite difficult to handle (Robson, 1984, p. 53). Sometimes these subsidies are not necessary. If the handling of this instrument is easy, then too many marginal firms will receive support. If an investment is to be taken in any case, then a subsidy for it would be regarded as no more than icing on the cake.

Yet another reason which prevents the introduction of subsidies is international commitment like membership in the GATT. Subsidies may lead to foreign retaliation which would make the trade balance even worse. Some countries may enter into a subsidy warfare with other countries in order to attract investment. This action may induce greater distortions than is the case with tariffs.

Both tariffs and subsidies, as policy instruments, introduce distortions. Therefore, any policy which involves either instrument should be carefully considered. In comparison to free trade, the situation involving imperfect information and either of these instruments is sub-optimal. If a country subsidizes, then it might gain an advantage, but only temporarily. Anything that attempts to supply a country with a disadvantage in exporting in the short run, will cause the adjustment of the exchange rate or factor prices in the long run (Johnson and Krauss, 1973, p. 240). Protection distorts market signals. Even though protection is a second-best strategy, by economic criteria it is a workable and often superior political strategy (Tyson and Zysman, 1987a, p. 53).

General equilibrium model

A partial equilibrium model considers the market for a single good. It assumes that all prices other than that of the good in question are fixed. A general equilibrium model considers all markets. All prices are variable and competitive equilibrium requires that all markets clear. All markets are connected by a chain of inputs and substitutes, information, technology, mobility of factors and goods, income (if one spends more on something, less will remain for other things), etc.

Consideration of the general equilibrium model will start with the 3×2 model. In this case there are three countries A, B and C, as well as two goods (markets) X and Y. Lipsey (1957 and 1960) was the first to study these cases in a customs-union framework. The model included full specialization and constant costs. A small country, A, imports good X from country C which is the foreign supplier with lowest price.

Consider a case illustrated in Figure 2.3, where substitution in consumption is allowed for by smooth and convex indifference curves. There are three countries A, B and C, and two goods X and Y. In the free-trade case, country A trades with country C and achieves indifference curve II. Suppose now that country A introduces a non-discriminatory tariff on imports. The relative price in country A is now AT.

Suppose that this tariff does not give enough incentive to home entrepreneurs to embark upon production of good X. Country A achieves the indifference curve I_1I_1 with equilibrium at point G. If

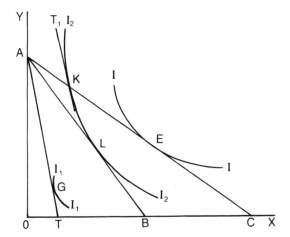

Figure 2.3 Welfare in a trade-diverting customs union

the government either returns all tariff proceeds to consumers or spends the entire amount in the same fashion as the consumers would have done otherwise, then the equilibrium should be on line AC (for country C is the best foreign supplier). The equilibrium point is at point K, which is the point where the line T_1 (parallel to AT which illustrates compensation of consumers) intersects with terms-of-trade line AC. The extent of the rightward shift in the terms-of-trade line depends on how much people are willing to import at these prices and, hence, the volume of tariff revenue to be returned to them. T_1 is deliberately drawn such that K and L lie on the same indifference curve. The tariff has changed the structure of production and relative prices. Consumption of the home good increases, while imports and exports decrease.

Suppose that country A forms a trade-diverting customs union with country B. The terms-of-trade line with country B is illustrated by line AB. Suppose that K and L lie on the same indifference curve I_1I_2. The formation of a customs union has not changed country A's welfare, although the structure of consumption has changed. If the best situation is at point E, then the formation of a customs union for country A is a move from one sub-optimal position, K, to another sub-optimal position, L. Country A is indifferent. If country

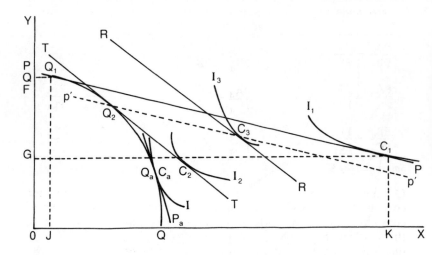

Figure 2.4 Production and consumption in country A before and after tariff

A obtains in a customs union terms of trade which are worse than 0B/0A, then country A is worse off than in the situation with a non-discriminatory tariff. If country A, however, obtains terms of trade which are better than 0B/0A, then a trade-diverting customs union can be welfare-improving for this country. Hence, the classical statement that trade diversion is always a bad thing is rejected.

Lipsey's model may be further developed to a case in which a country produces both goods. This case is closer to reality because substitution in production is allowed for. This is done in Figure 2.4. QQ is country A's production-possibility frontier. In autarky, country A produces at point Q_a and consumes at point C_a. There is a double tangency of the autarky price line P_a with the production possibility curve QQ and indifference curve I at a single point. Suppose that this country opens up for international trade. It is a small country, so it faces a given price ratio PP between good X and good Y. Country A then produces at point Q_1 and consumes at point C_1. The double tangency of production point Q_1 and consumption point C_1 is not required to be at one point. Country A exports quantity FG of good Y and imports quantity JK of good X from country C.

Suppose, now, that country A imposes a non-discriminatory tariff on imports. With the new price line TT, country A's production is at

Table 2.3 Prices in country A and their relation to prices on the international market

Free trade	Non-preferential ad valorem *tariff*	Customs union with country B
$\dfrac{PA_d}{PB_d} = \dfrac{PA_i}{PB_i}$	$\dfrac{PA_d}{PB_d} < \dfrac{PA_i}{PB_i}$	$\dfrac{PA_d}{PB_d} = \dfrac{PA_i}{PB_i}$
$\dfrac{PA_d}{PC_d} = \dfrac{PA_i}{PC_i}$	$\dfrac{PA_d}{PC_d} < \dfrac{PA_i}{PC_i}$	$\dfrac{PA_d}{PC_d} < \dfrac{PA_i}{PC_i}$
$\dfrac{PB_d}{PC_d} = \dfrac{PB_i}{PC_i}$	$\dfrac{PB_d}{PC_d} = \dfrac{PB_i}{PC_i}$	$\dfrac{PB_d}{PC_d} < \dfrac{PB_i}{PC_i}$

Source: Lipsey (1960).

Q_2 and consumption is at point C_2. Both production and consumption points are closer to the autarkic levels. If home consumers are compensated (all tariff proceeds are returned to them), then there will be additional imports. This is shown by the line RR which is parallel to line TT (the distance between the two lines equals tariff revenue), consumption is at C_3. Now suppose that country A enters into a trade diverting customs union with country B, which is a less efficient supplier than country C. If country A achieves a lower indifference curve in this customs union than I_3, then country A is worse off than in the pre-customs union situation. If country A, however, achieves in the customs union a higher indifference curve than I_3, then this trade-diverting customs union is increasing its welfare and is beneficial to this country.

In order to be closer to reality, higher dimensional models are necessary. Consider a 3×3 model in which country A produces commodity X, while it imports commodity Y from country B and commodity Z from country C. Table 2.3 states three optimality conditions between country A's domestic and international prices for this model. In free trade all three conditions are fulfilled. Price ratios for the same commodities in country A and abroad are equal. If country A imposes a non-preferential tariff on all imports, then optimality will be achieved only in the price ratio between the imported commodities. A customs union with country B shifts country A from one sub-optimal position to another, since optimality is satisfied only in one case (between country A's commodity X and country B's commodity, Y).

Three-commodity models of customs union were studied by Meade (1968), Riezman (1979), Berglas (1979) and Lloyd (1982). In the model by Meade, each country exports one commodity while it imports the other two from other countries. Riezman's model permits each country to export two commodities and import only

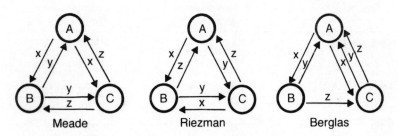

Figure 2.5 Trade flows among countries in models by Meade, Riezman and Berglas

one commodity. The model by Berglas is more complicated. Country A and country B have only one export commodity each. Both countries import two commodities. Country A exports its commodity X to both country B and country C and imports commodity Y from country B and commodity Z from country C. Country B exports commodity Y only to country A and imports commodity X from country A and commodity Z from country C. Figure 2.5 illustrates trade flows in these three models.

The models by Meade and Riezman have very different trade flows, but the two are symmetric as opposed to Berglas' model which is asymmetric (Lloyd, 1982, p. 49). Patterns of trade may be different and more complicated than those illustrated in Figure 2.5. Asymmetry in trade patterns prior to the formation of a customs union has an important impact on the welfare between the countries that form a customs union. The extension from three- to *n*-commodity models ($n > 3$) does not significantly affect the results (Berglas, 1979, p. 317).

Higher dimensional models of trade, like the 3×3 model, are necessary because they offer an important advantage: substitution effects. In a two-commodity model, one must be an export and the other an import commodity in each country. Higher dimensional models permit various restrictions on trade among different countries. The weakness of the models is that they assume that the commodities are final goods. Any reduction in impediments to trade on semi-processed goods may have a different impact on national production than a reduction of barriers to trade on final goods. A relatively high tariff on imports of final goods encourages this kind of production domestically. However, a relatively high tariff on imports of final goods in country B, induces country A to expand the production and export of semi-processed goods.

Conditions for a welfare-improving customs union

In a world with many distortions to trade, any customs union is just a second-best solution. On these grounds, a prescription for a welfare improvement along the neo-classical lines is not possible. Trade creation in a customs union, however, will predominate if the following six conditions are met in full or, at least, in part:

- The height of tariffs (as well as other impediments to trade) personifies a country's uncompetitiveness. In an extreme situation when country A has a prohibitive tariff and if domestic production is impossible, then there will be no home consumption of the good in question. Any reduction in this tariff has a potentially beneficial welfare effect on consumers in country A. Figure 2.2 illustrates the case in which the higher is the pre-customs union tariff in country A, the higher is the trade creation in a customs union with country B. Of course, the common external tariff must be lower than the pre-customs union tariff. The lower the tariffs in country C on exports from country A, the lower will be export diversion towards country B. The lower the common external tariff, the smaller is the probability that the union partner will replace the most efficient supplier, which is country C. A relatively low common external tariff permits some competition from countries which are outside a customs union. A partial reduction in tariffs potentially brings greater benefits than the creation of a customs union, because it inhibits trade diversion. The lower the pre-customs union tariffs the lower the potential benefits from a customs union. All these effects, however, depend on the elasticity of trade flows to the change in tariffs.
- The flatter the demand and supply curves in relation to the quantity axis in Figure 2.2 (elasticity must be greater than unity), the greater the areas 2 and 4 which embody trade creation.
- The lower the demand for country C's exports and the greater the demand for goods produced by partner countries in a customs union, the greater the trade creation.

- The larger the number of countries that participate in a customs union, the smaller the probability of trade diversion. An incentive to form and enlarge a customs union persists until the world becomes a customs union, that is, until the creation of free trade. A customs union among all countries of the world will have only trade creation as a consequence (Kemp and Wan, 1976).

- The more inelastic the supply from third countries, the more these countries lose while the customs-union partner countries gain. Trade diversion is preferable to trade creation for the preference-granting country, for it does not entail sacrifice of domestic industrial production (Johnson, 1973, p. 89). This is a reinforcement of the second-best character of the theory of customs union.

- Commodities of different countries are competitive if these countries have similar costs of production for the same commodity. The gain from integration is, then, potentially greatest. If the same countries have different costs of production for the same commodity, they have complementary economic structure.

Trade among countries which have different costs of production for similar commodities and different factor endowments, may often be characterized by inter-industry trade, while trade among countries with similar costs of production for similar commodities, with similar factor endowments and similar consumer preferences (tastes) may be characterized by intra-industry trade. Competition between countries with complementary economic structures in a customs union will ensure that the most efficient producer supplies the customs-union market which ensures a welfare gain. In a multi-country and multi-commodity case, however, country A may be the most efficient producer of good X, while country B is the least efficient producer of the same good. Also, country B may be the most efficient producer of good Y, while country A is the least efficient producer of this good. So, with respect to goods X and Y, these two countries have complementary production structures. A customs union between these two countries, which will cover just two sectors of production, commodities X and Y, may be welfare-improving.

If countries that contemplate the creation of a customs union have competitive structures prior to customs union, but achieve complementarity after entry into the customs union, then an increase in welfare might be the outcome. All these (im)possibilities represent reinforcements of the second-best character of the theory of customs unions.

The introduction of terms like complementarity and competitiveness are not necessary. The most important condition for a welfare-improving outcome from the creation of a customs union is that a customs union stimulates competition within its boundaries and that the common external tariff is not erected primarily for protection against imports from outside countries (Lundgren, 1969, p. 38).

DYNAMIC MODEL

The classical theory of customs unions assumes that the static effects of resource reallocation occurs in a timeless framework. If one wants to move the theory of customs unions towards reality one must consider dynamic effects. Instead of considering only the possibility of trade in commodities, dynamic models analyse the possibility of allocations across time. The static effects of international economic integration have their most obvious and profound influence in the period of time immediately following the creation of, for example, a customs union. Gradually, after several years of adjustment, the dynamic effects will increase in importance and become dominant.

Current flows of trade may not remain constant, but rather they may change over time. Changes in the equilibrium points in, for example, Figure 2.2 are described as instantaneous changes. Such changes in equilibrium points, however, may not always be possible. Delays in reaction on the part of countries and consumers in a customs union could be caused by their recourse to stocks of inventories. Hence, they do not immediately need to purchase those goods whose price has decreased as a consequence of the formation of a customs union. They also may have some contractual commitments that cannot be abandoned overnight. Finally, and nowadays less likely, consumers may not be aware of all the changes. Up to the nineteenth century, state intervention was negligible, but markets remained disconnected because of imperfect information and relatively high transport costs. A time interval between the implementation of a policy change (creation of a customs union) and its favourable effects may include an initial period of economic deterioration in certain regions, which may be followed by improvements due to the J-curve effect. Let us study each of the dynamic effects in turn.

The change in the efficiency of the use of factors due to increased competition (antitrust policy)

Introduction

Perfect competition provides the widest opportunities for everybody. By so doing, it stimulates efficiency of economic activity. Competition policy is a mixture of two irreconcilable impulses. On the one hand, there is an argument for concentration which rationalizes production and benefits from large-scale production. On the other hand, there is a case for antitrust policy which prevents monopolization, thus increasing competition which increases welfare.

Concept

Sometimes, like Article 86 of the Treaty of Rome, the law does not prohibit the possession of a dominant position in the market (monopoly or monopsony), but rather the use or, as this Article states, the abuse of this dominant position. This means that the big firms are permitted to have market power, but they are forbidden to exercise it. This is romantic. Whoever gets the power will behave as a monopolist. This temptation is hardly avoidable. Anyway, this legal formulation recognizes that the need for a certain level of concentration in some industries is inevitable for the attainment of the efficient scale of production, both for home and foreign markets. Otherwise, protected and inefficient national firms, which have higher costs of production than foreign firms, will continue to impose welfare losses on consumers. That is the reason why many European countries have relaxed their antitrust policies. Concentration of production is a barrier against foreign competition on the home market and a springboard for penetration into foreign markets.

The most common indicator of market structure or the degree of competition is the proportion of industry output, sales, investment or employment attributable to a subset (usually three to ten) of all firms in the industry. If this ratio is relatively high, then it illustrates that market power is concentrated in relatively few firms. It is important to be cautious in dealing with these ratios. While an employment concentration ratio may show a monopoly situation, a sales concentration ratio may not. Competitiveness is not only linked to market shares, but as a dynamic phenomenon, to the relative growth of productivity innovation, R&D, management and operational control, success in shifting out of sunset industries, training of labour, incentives and the like. Anyway, this ratio is the barometer of the oligopolistic restriction of competition.

Integration may provoke several scenarios. On the one hand, increase in industrial concentration may be the consequence of the firms that take advantage of economies of scale. Economies of scope may increase concentration because they favour diversified firms which are often large. On the other hand, small firms may benefit, as in Japan, because they may be included in the network of large firms. Also, reduced cross-border transaction costs makes it easier for smaller firms to penetrate the markets of partner countries. This may reduce concentration. Strategic alliances among firms may not markedly increase concentration. In this case, however, boundaries of the firms are becoming obscure.

Apart from raw materials and semi-finished goods, firms compete in product differentiation, quality, R&D and advertising, as well as in price. Major changes in the capacity of a firm which are linked to big sunk costs do not happen frequently. It is more difficult, however, to test the impact of non-price rivalry (like competitor's R&D or design activities) and non-technical matters (like management and marketing) than to test the impact of their prices. It also takes a longer time to retaliate along these dimensions than to change prices (Schmalensee, 1988, p. 670).

The impact of competition is not restricted to prices and costs. Competition also yields other favourable effects. It stimulates technical progress, widens consumers' choices, improves the quality of goods and services, as well as rationalizes the organization of firms.

Innovation is an important economic impulse. There is no simple answer to the question of whether international economic integration stimulates or prevents innovation by firms. There are two opposing views. Firstly, a monopolist faces a secure market for the output. It can anticipate normal or super-normal profits from an innovation and can also reap all of the profits from its implementation. It is therefore easier for such a firm to innovate than it is for a firm which does not have such a market foresight and influence. On the other hand, without the pressure from competition, the monopolist may not feel a need to innovate. The impression of long-term stability favours a conservative way of thinking which restricts innovative activity. Monopolists may not wish to 'rock the boat' and can prevent or delay the implementation of innovations either in their own production or in the production activity of others.

Empirical studies draw attention to the fact that monopolization or concentration is not the main factor explaining innovation. Also, innovations are more numerous in industries which are less concentrated and where there are no serious barriers to entry. New entrants have more impetus to test and develop new products and technologies than the already established producers. In many industrialized countries, the average size of firms is becoming smaller not bigger. However, the sectors with the most advanced technology are often the most concentrated, the most profitable and the largest.

If the impact of new technology is not isolated in empirical studies, then there is a tendency to overestimate the influence of innovation on the degree of concentration, profitability and market size (Emerson *et al.*, 1988, pp. 126–9). A positive effect on innovation (creation of technology) is anticipated from the completion of the EC internal market after 1992. An enlarged market will stimulate competition which will give an incentive to innovation which will promote competition to the benefit of the consumers. If corrective measures in support of trade or industrial policy are added, they do not necessarily violate a free-trade system in the long term. They may simply add an adjustment mechanism to the already highly imperfect and sub-optimal situation.

The new theory of trade and strategic industrial policy argues that, in the situation with imperfect competition, firms will be able to make rents. Intervention in trade and industry may, under certain conditions, secure those rents for the domestic firms. Such trade policy of beggar-thy-neighbour or 'war' about economic rents may look like a zero-sum game where everybody loses in the long term. However, there is at least one good case in favour of intervention. With externalities and spillovers, the governments may find reasons to protect some sunrise and high-technology industries. Sunk costs, as well as R&D, may be supported by the governments since the positive effects of introduction of new technology are felt throughout the economy and beyond the confines of the firm that introduces it. The whole world may benefit, in some cases, from new technology whose development was supported by government intervention. Therefore, the new theory says, that with externalities, intervention may be a positive-sum game where everyone potentially gains in the long run.

In a situation without trade, and where a monopoly in country A produces good X while there is free competition in country B in the market for the same good, one can expect that prices for good X will be lower in country B. If free trade is permitted, country B will export the good to country A. This shows that the difference in market structure between countries may explain trade, even though the countries may have identical production technologies and factor endowments (Brander, 1987, p. 13). The characteristics of trade protection determine the conditions for competition within a market.

One needs to distinguish between comparative advantage and competitive advantage. The former is the relative export strength of one sector compared to other sectors in the same country, while the latter is the export strength of firms of one country compared to firms in other countries selling in the same segment of the international market (Tyson and Zysman, 1987a, p. 28).

Perfect competition eliminates inefficient firms from a market, but at the same time rewards the efficient ones (creative destruction). If inter-country factor mobility is allowed for, the supply of factors (labour, capital, land, technology, organization and entrepreneurship) increases. Competition probably operates best when a firm believes that it is in the process leading to it becoming a monopolist (at best), or an oligopolist (at least). Consumers may be made worse off if the equilibrium industry structure is monopolistic or oligopolistic. This would be tempered somewhat if oligopolistic firms introduce the most efficient innovations as rapidly as perfectly competitive firms would.

Reliance on various foreign technologies is an inevitable fact for small, open economies. Such countries often do not have the resources to develop basic technologies for all lines of production. If this situation is regarded as detrimental, then a customs union may increase the pool of resources (human, technological and financial) for innovation and development of new technologies, products and inputs, which may mitigate the disadvantage of smallness.

In a relatively integrated area like the EC, one would expect that prices of similar goods in different countries would be similar, due to competition. The larger the competition, other things being equal, the smaller the differences. Pre-tax prices for the same goods may differ due to transportation and handling costs. Evidence does not substantiate this expectation. The EC is aware of the barriers to competition other than tariffs and quotas, so it has an ambitious programme to create a genuine internal market by the end of 1992.

There are, however, various regional factors that prevent full equalization of prices. In some regions there may be a small market for certain goods, so, in order to do business there, firms may price their goods relatively higher there. Due to special requirements about ingredients in some countries, the same basic good (for instance, chocolate) may be priced differently. If there are close local substitutes, then foreign suppliers may modify the price of their output accordingly. Some goods may be regarded as luxuries in one country and be taxed accordingly, while in another country, they may be regarded as basic necessities. This widens the price gap for the same goods in different countries. For goods in a perfectly competitive market, free competition, together with free entry and exit, ensures equality of prices and drives profits to zero. In imperfectly competitive markets there is room for differences in price and, therefore, for greater profits.

Intra-industry trade

While increased competition offers potential gains with respect to the efficient allocation of resources in production and in increased consumption, there is nothing to ensure that these gains will be realized in practice. If a government has this pessimistic view, and if it believes that the domestic production will be wiped out by foreign competition, then this government may pursue a policy of protection on the grounds that it is better to produce something inefficiently at home than to produce nothing at all. This disastrous scenario has not been identified in reality. The very existence and continuous enlargements of the EC is the best example of this. Firms in different EC countries have not been thrown out of business by competition from firms in partner countries. Instead, many of them have continuously increased their business. They have specialized in certain lines of production which are supposed to satisfy distinct demand segments throughout the EC. Trade takes place in these differentiated products. This is known as intra-industry trade.

There are also other examples. Successive rounds of negotiations within the GATT reduced tariffs. The ensuing intra-industry adjustment in trade and specialization among developed countries occurred relatively smoothly. Contrary to the expectation of the factor-endowment theory, this kind of adjustment prevailed, and it carries fewer costs than inter-industry adjustment. Even if there were fears that the foreigners would eliminate domestic firms through competition, exchange rates may act as an important safety valve. It may prevent this outcome and ease the process of adjustment.

The variety of goods produced in a country, as the new theory suggests, is limited by the existence of scale economies in production. Thus, similar countries have an incentive to trade. Their trade may often be in goods that are produced with similar factor proportions, and such trade does not involve big adjustment problems and the income distributing effects characteristic for more conventional trade (Krugman, 1990, pp. 50–1).

With the growth of income, consumers are not satisfied with identical or standardized goods. They demand and pay for varieties of the same basic good, often tailored to their individual needs. Intra-industry trade refers to trade in differentiated commodities. It happens when a country simultaneously exports and imports goods which are close substitutes in consumption. Differentiation of goods begins when various characteristics are added to the basic good. The neo-classical, international-trade and customs-union theory refers to two goods. Therefore, it can not consider preference diversity and intra-industry trade in a satisfactory way. The neo-classical theory's 'clean' model of perfect competition cannot be applied here. The potential for intra-industry trade increases with the level of economic development, similarity in preferences (tastes), openness to trade and geographical proximity which reduces costs of transport/service. A significant part of trade among developed countries consists of intra-industry trade which is caused by economies of scale. Preferences may be such that variety is preferred to quantity, so that trade is not due to different factor endowment as to different preferences.

There is a finding that incentives for intra-industry trade come from the relative height of per capita income and country size, product differentiation, participation in regional integration schemes, common borders, as well as similar language and culture. Negative influence on this type of trade comes from standardization (which reduces consumers' choice), distance between countries (increases the cost of information/service necessary for trade in differentiated goods) and trade barriers which reduce all trade (Balassa and Bauwens, 1988, p. 1436).

Intra-industry trade refers to trade within the same trade classification group. It is relatively high among developed countries. One may wonder if intra-industry trade is a statistical rather than an authentic phenomenon. Also, it may be argued that two varieties are not always two distinct goods. The criteria for aggregation in international trade statistics (SITC) are similarity in inputs and substitutability in consumption. They often contradict each other. Many of the three digit groups in SITC include heterogeneous commodities. SITC 751 (office machines) includes typewriters, word-processing machines, cash registers and photocopying machines, while SITC 895 (office and stationery supplies) includes filing cabinets, paper clips, fountain pens, chalks and typewriter ribbons. On these grounds one may believe that intra-industry trade is a pure statistical fabrication. This is hardly so. If one studies more than three digit groups, differences may appear. The index of intra-industry trade (IIT) in a country is represented by the ratio of the absolute difference between exports and imports in a trade classification group to the sum of exports and imports in the same classification group.

$$\text{IIT} = 1 - \frac{|X_j - M_j|}{X_j + M_j} \qquad (2.2)$$

That index is one for complete intra-industry specialization (a country imports and exports goods in a group in the same quantity) and is zero for complete inter-industry specialization. The expectation that trade liberalization will shift the index closer to one in the case of developed countries has been substantiated in numerous studies surveyed by Greenaway and Milner (1987).

Some goods from the same classification group may be perfect substitutes, that is, may have identical end-uses (e.g. plates). But plates may be made of china, glass, paper, plastic, wood, metal or ceramic. Every type of this end-product requires different factor inputs and technology. Similar examples may be found in tableware, furniture, clothing, etc. These differences among goods that enter a single SITC group may not be important for statistical records, but they are often of crucial importance to consumers. With an increase in income there is an increase in demand for a variety of products. Increased income gives consumers the possibility to express variety in taste through, for example, purchases of different styles of clothing. A customs union may change consumers' preference ordering since the choice of goods in the situation prior to a customs union or reduction in tariffs may be different.

Integration in the EC increased intra-industry trade within this group of countries, while integration in the Council for Mutual

Economic Assistance (CMEA) had as its consequence greater inter-industry trade (Drabek and Greenaway, 1984, pp. 463–4). Preferences in the centrally planned economies are revealed through plan targets. They are different in comparison to economies in which market forces reveal consumers' preferences. In market economies competition takes place among firms, while competition in centrally planned economies occurs among different plans which are offered to the central planning body.

A free-trade area between the United States and Canada may not crucially alter the pattern of trade between these two countries. One reason is that the last reduction in tariffs agreed in the Tokyo Round of the GATT negotiations took place in 1987. After this reduction, trade between these two countries is largely free, that is 80 per cent of trade is duty-free while a further 15 per cent is subject to a tariff which is 5 per cent or less. Another reason is that there is greater similarity in consumers' tastes in North America than in the EC.

Since a large part of trade among developed countries has an intra-industry character, this may lead to the conclusion that the Heckscher–Ohlin (factor proportions) theory of trade is not valid. Intra-industry trade among countries is not based on differences in factor endowments among countries. Countries tend to specialize and export goods which are demanded by the majority of domestic consumers. It is the demand which induces production, rather than domestic factor endowment. Countries have a competitive edge in the production of these goods and thus gain a competitive edge in foreign markets, while they import goods demanded by a minority of the home population (Linder, 1961). The United States, Japan and the Federal Republic of Germany have the greatest comparative advantage in goods for which their home market is relatively big. These are standardized goods for mass consumption.

Intra-industry trade may be described in terms of monopolistic competition and product differentiation. Perfect competition is not a realistic market structure, so perfect monopolistic competition is the most perfect market structure in a situation with differentiated goods (Lancaster, 1980). Armington's assumption states that products in the same industry but from different countries are imperfect substitutes (Armington, 1969, p. 160). In other words, buyers' preferences for different(iated) goods are independent. This assumption may overestimate the degree of market power of a particular producer.

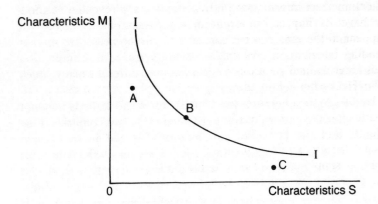

Figure 2.6   Characteristics of computers

Instead of taking goods themselves as the basis for analysis, 'address models' of goods differentiation take characteristics that are embodied in goods as their starting point (Lipsey, 1987b). A good like a computer may be considered as a collection of different attributes like memory, speed, print, graphics and the like. Figure 2.6 illustrates two characteristics of a set of goods (computers).

Each good (computer) A, B and C, respectively, has a certain combination of characteristic S (speed) and characteristic M (memory). Each good is defined by its location in the continuous space of characteristics, hence it has a certain address. Consumers' preferences are defined over characteristics, not goods. Some consumers prefer memory over speed, while others have opposite tastes. Under the assumption that all three goods have the same price in Figure 2.6, let a consumer have tastes embodied in the indifference curve II. This consumer maximises utility with the purchased good B. Each good in this model has close and distant neighbours. There are many goods and many consumers. Everyone attempts to attain own highest indifference curve which, because consumers have different preferences over memory and speed, gives rise to intra-industry trade. Address models of localized (monopolistic) competition may be an important part of the explanation of intra-industry trade.

Intra-industry trade is connected to imperfect product markets (monopolization, foreign direct investment) and consumers' demand for a variety of products. Economies of scale may be an important part of the explanation of trade in differentiated goods because, for this reason, countries with similar endowment of factors will still trade. Imperfect information on the part of consumers about goods may have its impact on intra-industry trade, but its effect will disappear in the long run because of advertising and other ways of spreading information. All explanations of trade in differentiated goods refer to final goods in trade among developed countries.

The Heckscher–Ohlin theory gave students the impression that the factor proportions theory is orthodoxy. Linder's theory tended to be less rigorous and thus has not made the same impression on students. Still, Leamer (1984) found evidence which supports the classical theory. Linder's theory does not reject factor proportion theory, it simply explains that factor proportions are not the only cause of trade. One may conclude that the factor proportion theory determines trade and specialization among different SITC classification groups, while economies of scale and diversity in tastes determine production and trade within SITC classification groups.

European Community

Competition policy requires skilful handling in a scheme which integrates countries like the EC does. Breaking up a price-fixing cartel is obviously a competition issue. However, deciding how many big chemical or car companies the EC should have is a political question. There should be control over mergers with an EC dimension. The EC Commission has a say if a bid crosses each of the following three thresholds: if annual worldwide turnover of the new (merged) company is above ECU 5 billion; if sales of each party in the EC are more than ECU 250 million; and if each party makes more than 66 per cent of sales in any of the EC country. If the proposed merger has a dominant position which may restrict competition (if the new firm can increase prices by, for example, 10 per cent without losing market share), the Commission will have the authority to stop the deal.

In the classical model of perfect competition, state aid can do greater harm to competition than can the most malicious merger. However, there are cases like industrial and regional policies which justify the existence of state aids. Article 92 of the Treaty of Rome regulates state aid. It prohibits any aid which distorts competition among the member countries. A few exceptions permit aid to the regions affected by calamities, projects which are in the EC's interest and some regional development aid. The governments can

Table 2.4   Total average annual aid in the EC countries, in 1987 prices

Country	% of GNP		ECU/employee		ECU billion	
	1981–86	*1986–88*	*1981–86*	*1986–88*	*1981–86*	*1986–88*
1 Luxembourg	6.0	4.1	1,620	1,283	0.3	0.2
2 Belgium	4.1	3.2	1,243	1,061	4.4	3.9
3 Italy	4.0	3.1	1,188	998	24.2	20.6
4 Greece	2.5	3.1	449	362	1.6	1.3
5 Ireland	4.0	2.7	891	662	1.0	0.7
6 FR Germany	2.5	2.5	817	942	20.5	23.9
7 Spain	—	2.3	—	521	—	5.9
8 Portugal	—	2.3	—	175	—	0.7
9 France	2.7	2.0	906	726	19.1	15.3
10 The Netherlands	1.5	1.3	451	454	2.3	2.4
11 United Kingdom	1.8	1.0	455	261	10.8	6.6
12 Denmark	1.3	1.0	406	334	1.0	0.9
European Community	2.8	2.2	791	687	85.2	82.3

Source: *The Second Survey on State Aids* (1990), EC: Brussels.

still disguise industrial aid as regional aid. It is difficult to trace such support if companies make losses. R&D aid can similarly be abused. A state can finance basic and applied research according to the agreed sliding scales. The State-aid Department of the EC Commission has a staff of only 30, and they cannot be expected to examine every state aid, especially if one bears in mind that every region in each member country has the staff (often significantly more numerous than the Commission's) to dispense aid. Therefore, the Commission's priority is the prevention of the biggest and most competition-distorting examples of aid. All these formidable issues linked to competition are increasingly becoming a paradise for lawyers.

Table 2.4 shows state aids in the EC. The amount includes aids to manufacturing (40 per cent of total aids) agriculture (13 per cent), railways (31 per cent) and coal (16 per cent). Although state aids in the EC countries have on average a declining trend in the last decade, their mere magnitude is so high that they may have a negative impact on the completion of the internal market.

Table 2.5 Total average annual aid to the manufacturing industry (excluding steel and shipbuilding) in the EC countries, in 1987 prices

Country	% gross value added		ECU per employee	
	1981–86	*1986–88*	*1981–86*	*1986–88*
1 Greece	13.9	16.4	—	3,721
2 Portugal	—	8.1	—	701
3 Italy	8.2	6.5	3,791	3,077
4 Ireland	7.3	6.2	2,551	2,551
5 Belgium	4.5	4.6	1,533	1,693
6 Luxembourg	3.5	4.4	1,119	1,812
7 Spain	—	3.7	—	1,067
8 France	3.6	3.5	1,399	1,371
9 The Netherlands	4.1	3.5	1,442	1,528
10 FR Germany	2.9	2.7	1,010	1,139
11 United Kingdom	2.9	2.5	869	723
12 Denmark	2.8	1.6	700	643
13 European Community	4.0	3.8	1,474	1,439

Source: *The Second Survey on State Aids* (1990), EC: Brussels.

State aids, as presented in Table 2.5, to the manufacturing industry (excluding steel and shipbuilding) do not have a clear and obvious declining trend in the past decade. The decline is noteworthy only in the cases of Denmark, Italy and Ireland. Objectives of aids (employment, R&D, regional development), as well as their forms (grants, subsidized loans, loan guarantees, etc.) vary among the member states. Entrenched interests in the manufacturing industry were quite hard to break, and present a serious threat to the 1992 Programme whose stated aim is an increase in competition on the internal EC market and contribution to an undistorted system of internal trade in the manufactured goods and services.

Conclusion

Increased competition will, without any doubt, put a downward pressure on prices and costs. This outcome will enable economic growth with a reduced inflationary pressure. It is not clear, however, how this will happen in practice. Competition may reduce prices (inflation) of goods and services. It may increase output, but keep prices (inflation) constant. In this case a reduction in prices is offset by an increase in demand. Also, and most likely in practice, competition will result in a blend of benefits which accrue from increase in output and decrease in prices.

Specialization and returns to scale

Returns to scale refer to the relation between input requirements and output response with its impact on costs. Returns or economies of scale comprise a number of things, from simple technical scale to phenomena like processing complex information; direction, control and improvement of independent activities; and experience. If a firm's output increases in the same proportion as its inputs, then that firm's technology exhibits constant returns to scale or, one may say, that a firm has constant marginal costs. If a firm's output increases by a greater proportion than inputs, then this firm's technology has increasing returns to scale or it enjoys decreasing marginal costs (or increasing marginal product). If a firm's output decreases by a smaller proportion than input requirements, then the firm suffers from decreasing returns to scale or increasing marginal costs.

Suppose that a firm uses a set of inputs X in the production of a good Y. Constant, increasing and decreasing returns to scale may be defined for homogeneous production functions. A function is homogeneous of degree k if:

$$f(tx_1, tx_2) = t^k f(x_1, x_2) \tag{2.3}$$

$t > 0$ and k is constant. If the set of inputs X is increased by t, output is increased by t^k: $k = 1$ implying constant returns to scale, k > 1 increasing returns to scale and $0 < k < 1$ results in decreasing returns to scale. These can also be presented graphically.

Figure 2.7 illustrates technologies with various returns to scale. A firm's technology has constant returns to scale in case (a) where isoquants for output for quantities 1, 2 and 3, respectively intersect the path from the origin at equal distances, making $0A = AB = BC$. In the increasing returns to scale, case (b), isoquants are closer together $0A > AB > BC$. The third case (c) describes decreasing returns to scale. Isoquants are farther away from each other, $0A < AB < BC$.

Figure 2.8 illustrates the cost behaviour of different technologies.

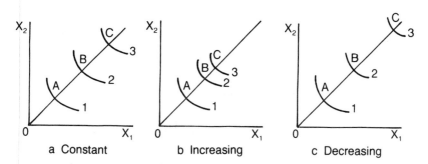

Figure 2.7 Technologies with constant, increasing and decreasing returns to scale

With constant returns to scale, marginal cost per unit of output Y is unchanged. With increasing returns to scale, as output increases, costs per unit of output are decreasing, while with decreasing returns to scale as output increases, costs per unit of output are increasing too. Decreasing returns to scale describe a situation in which there are some inputs (like land) in fixed supply. With increasing returns to scale in industry Y, the ratio at which the two commodities exchange in the market differs from the ratio in which they can be converted into one another through production. When factors are shifted to the increasing-returns-to-scale industry, the gain in production in that industry is greater than the loss of output in the other, so there is a net increase in output. This increases real wages, average standards of living and gross national product (GNP).

The pure theory of international trade is concerned mostly with perfect competition. In a situation in which the minimum efficient scale is relatively large, only a few firms may exist simultaneously. Competition in such markets is not perfect. When markets are enlarged by either a customs union or by other types of international economic integration which increase competition, firms may expand their production in order to achieve lower costs (economies of scale) and specialization or they may leave this business.

The existence of internal non-tariff barriers to trade is the cause of unexploited economies of scale in the EC market. An empirical study of potential economies of scale in the industry of the EC reports that in more than a half of all branches of industry, twenty

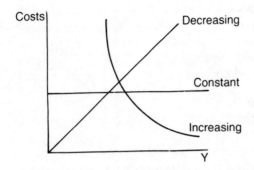

Figure 2.8   Cost curves with constant, increasing and decreasing returns to scale

firms of efficient size can co-exist in the EC market, whereas the largest national markets can support only four each. The EC internal market can offer the potential for efficiency and competition. Twenty efficient firms are more likely to assure effective competition than four firms (Emerson *et al.*, 1988, p. 18). This finding ignores the logic behind the role of concentration in modern industries and the contribution which a few oligopolies, exploiting economies of scale and carefully monitored by appropriate regulatory authorities, can and do make to economic welfare. Besides, there may be fierce competition even among the four firms (take a look at competition in the United States' long-distance-telephone-call business).

The United States' economic system is created in such a way that it is open to internal competition. Antitrust legislation is very strong. Nevertheless, the President's Commission on Industrial Competitiveness (1985, Vol. 2, pp. 192–3) recognized the potential efficiency gains which may come from concentration of business in certain industries. Without the prospective reward of temporary monopoly, firms may not have big incentives to innovate. A temporary departure from free competition may be desirable, in the sense that it is better to allow the establishment of temporary monopolies as a way to induce innovation, than to seek static efficiency at the cost of technological progress (Krugman, 1990, p. 173).

Changes in technology exert a continuous pressure on the efficient size of plant. Hence, the minimum efficient size of plant changes over time. Large-scale production is profitable only if there is secure access to a wide market. It is reasonable, therefore, to argue that firms which operate on a wide market are likely to be closer to the minimum efficient plant size than ones which act within a more restricted framework. Recent developments in technology are diminishing scale economies associated with mass production in large plants. Modern technology increases the role of smaller, but highly specialized plants.

Economies of scale are largest in transport equipment, electronics, office machines, chemicals and other manufactured products. These are the sectors in which demand has the highest growth and where technology changes fast. The common element to these industries is the vast investment required to produce even a small amount of output. Advanced technology is not necessary for increasing returns to scale, but increasing returns to scale are frequently in high-technology industries. Also, these sectors are, just as many others, under continuous pressure from international competition. Sectors with relatively smaller returns to scale are the ones with stagnant demand and relatively low technology content. They include the food, textile, clothing and footwear industries.

Adam Smith pointed out that specialization is limited by the extent of the market. A customs union increases the market area for firms in the participating countries, hence it increases the opportunities for specialization. By trade, countries may gain not only from exchange, but also from specialization and a wider choice of goods. Trade increases the bundle of available goods in relation to autarky, while by specialization and change in the output mix a country may reap the full advantages of its factor endowment. A country may also gain from economies of scale which form the basis for trade independent of other sources of comparative advantage.

Economies of scale may be internal to individual firms. It may also be external to these firms (this is the case when the whole industry grows and when all the firms in that industry enjoy the fruits of this growth). The attention here will be focused on technical (as one of the types of) economies of scale. The importance of economies of scale is that they are not consistent with perfect competition. With an imperfect market structure many welfare outcomes are likely to happen. A perfectly competitive firm takes the price for its product as given. A firm with increasing returns to scale in such a market will find it profitable to produce one more unit of output since it can do so at less than the prevailing

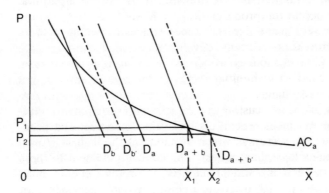

Figure 2.9 Economies of scale and their impact on the price in exporting country A

price. In so doing it would tend to increase output until it dominates the market and efficiency sets the price for its output.

Consider the case in Figure 2.9 which illustrates the impact of economies of scale on the price in exporting country A. The vertical axis shows the price in country A for good X. Increasing returns to scale are implied by the downward-sloping AC_a curve. The producer of this commodity has a monopoly position in the domestic market. There is no producer in country B, but this country has a tariff on imports of good X for fiscal reasons. Domestic demand in country A is represented by the curve D_a and the demand for the product in country B is represented by the curves D_b and $D_{b'}$. The former is the demand curve incorporating a tariff in country B on imports of good X, while the latter reflects demand for this good if no tariffs were levied.

The initial equilibrium in this market is represented by the intersection of the joint demand curve D_{a+b} and the AC_a curve as implied by the monopoly position of the country A producer. If countries A and B enter into a customs union, then the tariff on imports of good X into country B will be eliminated, increasing the demand for this good. Thus, the curve representing demand in country B is $D_{b'}$ and the joint demand in the customs union is $D_{a+b'}$. Faced with this increased demand, the producer in country A will expand output. With increasing returns to scale this output expansion lowers the marginal and average costs of production and leads to a fall in the equilibrium price from P_1 to P_2. The elimination of the tariff here has an unambiguously positive effect: all consumers can purchase a greater quantity of good X at a lower price and profits to the producer have increased.

This effect is called the *cost-reduction* effect (Corden, 1984, p. 123). It is distinct from trade creation since the existing supplier reduces the price for the good X. There is an additional effect: suppose that there was an initial tariff on imports of good X, but it was insufficient to induce domestic production of X in country A. After the creation of a customs union with country B, the market area for country A is increased. Costs of production may fall, hence production of good X may begin in country A, replacing imports into both customs union partners from country C. For country A this is *trade suppression*, while for country B this represents trade diversion. While learning by doing, country A may become a more efficient producer of good X than country C, so in the longer run, this policy may pay off. The country in which production with increasing returns to scale occurs gets double gains (employment and increased production). Governments in the customs union may cooperate in order to evenly distribute the industries with increasing returns to scale, otherwise they may end up in an investment subsidy war to attract such industries.

In perfectly contestable markets price equals marginal cost (firms just cover production costs of the last unit and profits are zero). Economies of scale introduce imperfection into the market system since firms set prices at average cost and make profits. Therefore, economies of scale lead to more specialization compared to the situation with constant returns to scale. The existence of these firms is protected by barriers to entry to increasing-returns-to-scale industry. The major barriers to entry in most industries are sunk costs and capital requirements.

Investments in market penetration and some of the investments in plant and R&D are not recoverable. They also often have little market value. Large sunk costs make firms reluctant to enter an industry if long-term access to wide markets is not secure. Expectations about the future play a key role. This restricted or blocked entry results in a smaller number of firms in the industry than would be the case under free entry. Sunk costs provide advantages to the first entrants. Substantial rents may be earned from being at the frontier of technological change, where standards are determined for future products and processes, and where, once standards are established and industries matured, new entry becomes difficult (Tyson, 1987, p. 74). A defensive strategy to counteract such developments would be to respond to the competitor's action in order to keep market share, while an offensive strategy would be the development of new goods or services in order to enter new market segments and/or weaken the competitor.

Market pre-emption places potential competitors at a disadvantage. It increases the possibilities for rents, but also bears great risk of failure. New technologies may not remain clandestine for ever. If a monopolist makes a profit, other firms will try to enter the industry. Imitators may appear so that the firm's advantage and rents may be eroded. The longer the time lag for imitation, the greater the possibility for the firm to reap rents as the reward for risk and the right choice of investment.

There must be a barrier to entry for a monopolist to keep its present position. Apart from sunk costs and minimum efficient scale, the monopolist may use predatory pricing and/or aggressive advertising of its brand in order to discourage potential entrants.

Predatory pricing means charging unprofitably low prices in order to eliminate an existing or potential competitor from a market. This strategy is backed either by the home government's support or by charging the domestic consumers high prices in a protected market or both. This strategy may, in fact, be unprofitable in the long run. The predator's losses may exceed the prey's since the prey can shut down temporarily, while the predator must make substantial sales to keep prices low. If the prey goes bankrupt, the predator may need to acquire its assets in order to prevent a new rival from buying them up. It will often be less costly to merge with the prey at the outset than to drive it out of business by a predatory strategy (Schmalensee, 1988, p. 665).

Retaliation against predatory pricing can be anti-dumping duties. The existence of such kind of dumping is not that easily proven in practice. Even the GATT rules do not take into account volatile exchange rates, continuous shortening in the life-cycle of high-technology goods and the complexity of modern marketing arrangements.

A mature technology often means that factories for standardized goods are often similar in size, hence countries may differ in the number of plants because of different market size. This is the lesson for small countries as well as for LDCs. They ought to pool their markets and resources in order to overcome these barriers to entry and to reap the benefits of economies of scale.

After a certain level of output, some costs – in particular depreciation of equipment – may increase disproportionately in relation to output, and partly offset the reduction in costs that accrues from increasing returns to scale. For example, the ends of the blades on a very large turbine move at a speed that can be close to that of sound. At such a speed metal fatigue increases disproportionately in relation to a turbine's capacity.

If one takes a look from the side of production, it can be noted that economies of scale may require some level of standardization which may restrict product variety and consumers' choice. Standards are technical regulations which specify the characteristics of goods. They can be quite different among countries. To harmonize standards in a customs union for trade and consumption purposes would be a difficult task. Mutual recognition of standards can be a promising strategy in the short term. This would place traders in different countries on an equal footing and eliminate disadvantages to some of them which accrue from non-tariff barriers. But trade in general, and intra-industry trade in particular, may increase product variety in relation to autarky. Product differentiation may reduce export opportunities for small, open economies like Belgium. These countries have little influence on foreign tastes and tend to enjoy comparative advantages in semi-manufactured goods (Gleiser, Jacquemin and Petit, 1980, p. 521).

For example, in the United States and Japan, the market for consumer durable goods is dominated by a single brand which takes advantage of economies of scale. The situation in the EC member countries is different. Almost every country has its domestic producer. But the United States' or Japanese formula will not easily be implemented in Europe. This is due to diverse and deeply rooted national preferences. While the Britons want to load their washing machines from the front, the French prefer to do so from the top. The Dutch prefer high-powered machines which can spin most of the moisture out of the washing, the Italians like better slower spinning machines and let the southern sun do the drying. This situation has its impact on the protectionist pressure against third-country suppliers. Yet, there are other goods where preferences among countries are identical. It is likely that the German car producers are going to look for the same qualities in a photocopier as would Italian wine exporters.

The neo-classical theory of international trade argues that countries should specialize in the production of those goods for which they had a comparative advantage. Modern theories are questioning this way of reasoning. International specialization and trade are due to other factors as well. Economies of scale stimulate specialization in production for a narrow market niche, but on a wide international market. This may entail only reallocation of resources within the same industry or sometimes within a single company. Modern footloose industries are not linked to any particular region. A country's comparative advantage is therefore created by the deliberate actions of firms, banks and/or governments.

Consideration of returns to scale would be incomplete without referring to services. The impact of returns to scale on costs in the manufacturing sector is obvious indeed. It is less capable of significantly reducing costs in the services sector, although experience and competition can increase productivity in this sector too. Banking, insurance, transport and forwarding are those sectors which are most affected by international competition. But there are serious methodological limitations in the quantification of returns to scale in the service sector (for example, how to measure the output of an insurance company).

Returns to scale have not been thoroughly studied in the theory of customs unions because it is difficult to model them. Therefore, one should be very careful while using the classical theory either as a description of what is likely to happen in a customs union or as a guide to policies that will ensure that such a union fulfils expectations. Another important fact is that a substantial part of production is linked with economies of scope rather than scale. While economies of scale imply a certain level of standardization in tastes and production, economies of scope deal with product or process diversity. Economies of scope allow firms to respond swiftly to changes in the supply of inputs and shifts in demand because they come from common control of distinct, but interrelated, production activities. (For example, the same kind of fabric can be used in the production of various goods.)

Economies of scale are coupled with market imperfections which make possible various welfare outcomes. Distortions, like deviation from marginal cost pricing or the existence of barriers to entry mean that the creation of a customs union does not necessarily either improve or worsen welfare. With economies of scale and other distortions, the welfare effects of customs union creation and the pattern of trade are much more affected by government policy than they are in the neo-classical theorists' world of comparative advantage and factor proportions.

Terms of trade

The terms of trade is the ratio of the quantity of imports that may be obtained in trade for a certain quantity of exports or, alternatively, it is the relative price of imports to exports. If home demand for good X is elastic, then the home country's tariff on imports may reduce both consumption and imports of this good. If this country can act as a monopsonist, it may turn prices on the international market in its favour – which improves its terms of trade. The same powers may be wielded by a customs union. Third countries may not only lose exports by the possible trade diversion, but may also have to increase their effort in exports to the customs union in order to mitigate the impact of adverse terms-of-trade changes.

If a customs union is large enough to influence its terms of trade on both the export and import side, then the customs union sets the international prices for these goods. Other countries, supposedly small ones which are the price-takers for the standardized goods, must accept the prices which prevail in the customs union less the common external tariff and less the cost of transport if they want to sell in the customs-union market. A big customs union may exercise its monopoly and monopsony powers at the expense of third countries' consumers who pay domestic tariffs and producers who pay the customs union's common external tariff.

Monopoly power is not without its disadvantages. If a customs union is large enough to influence prices on international markets, then in the absence of offsetting changes in the rest of the world, an increase in the customs union's supply of good X would simply decrease the price of that good. On the side of the customs union's demand for good Y from abroad, an increase in demand would increase the price of good Y. The greater the demand in the customs union for good Y and the greater the supply of good X and the greater the trade of the customs union, the greater will be the deterioration of the customs union's terms of trade. With both monopoly and monopsony powers, and without changes in the outside world, the customs union is made worse off by its desire to increase trade. This situation may be called immiserizing the customs union.

Terms-of-trade effects of a customs union do not only have an external dimension. It also has an internal meaning. Trade flows among the member countries are also affected. The unionized partners are not only allies in their relations with off-shore countries, but also competitors in the customs-union internal market. The elimination of tariffs and quotas on trade in a customs union has a direct impact on internal trade and prices. A union member country may gain from an improvement of customs-union terms of trade with third countries, but this gain may be reduced by worsened terms of trade with the customs-union partner countries.

The countries which are in a customs union may experience a shift in productivity due to increased competition and the rapid introduction of new technologies. If one excludes all demographic changes, then any increase in labour productivity has a direct effect of increasing real income under the assumption of unchanged quantity and velocity of money. This has a direct impact on the terms of trade because prices of home goods fall.

The bargaining power of the countries that have entered into a customs union is greater than the power they exert as individuals prior to entering the customs union. What matters here is not absolute, but rather the relative size of the union against its trading partners. The improvement of the terms of trade is not only the principal effect, but also one of the major goals of integration of trade in manufactures in western Europe. The reason for the official silence on the issue is the possible charges by the injured trading partners (Petith, 1977, p. 272). The statement that improvement in terms of trade (beggar-thy-neighbour) is the major goal of integration in trade in manufactures in western Europe is difficult to reconcile with what is happening there. Neither firms nor governments think in these terms.

The EC is often advised by third countries, especially the United States, to adopt more liberal trade and investment policies, as well as to resist the temptation to build 'Fortress Europe'. The capacity and willingness of the EC to accept such advice depends, at least in part, on similar actions by its major trading partners: the United States, Japan and, increasingly, by developing countries like Korea and Taiwan.

Increase in earnings from exports

Suppose that countries A and B, respectively, form a customs union. Country B imports good X from country A. Country A may expect an increase in export earnings from trade with the customs union partner because tariffs are no longer applied to their internal trade. Under similar assumptions country B may expect an increase in export earnings from trade with country A. The assumption made is that the adjustment is costless. Whether this short-term increase in export earnings will be sustained in the long run depends on the shift in the pattern of consumption in both countries. If one introduces costs of adjustment, then in the long run both countries have to generate income and production that will continue the short-run pattern of trade. It also depends on the development of substitutes and the height of the common external tariff which may (not) prevent imports from the outside world.

Public goods

Consideration so far has referred to the effects of the formation of a customs union on final private goods. Let us introduce public goods, which are consumed by everybody in a country and which enhance welfare just as the consumption of private goods does. Those who want to consume many of these goods may not be prevented from their consumption, nor will they be forced to pay the full price for these goods (or services). There are many free riders.

Without government support, free markets would provide few of the public goods, such as: defence; flood, fire and police protection; a system of contract law and a mechanism for its enforcement; arts; statistics; weather forecasting and the like. Many countries feel public pride because they develop production of something that they have previously imported, but without mentioning either the price for this or the final good's import content. In doing so, they create a 'psychological income' of a nation. Income maintenance and the provision of private goods (or services) at prices below costs, like education and health, still take a significant part of state activity.

Exact direct and indirect prices of each public good are not readily available to each consumer. If the consumers and taxpayers were informed, as well as aware, of the full cost of these goods and services, they might not be very keen on supporting their production. If there are similar propensities for the production and consumption of these goods in the countries in a customs union, then the cost per unit of public good may be reduced by international economic integration if countries can produce and consume these goods jointly.

In the situation where there exists a preference for public goods (for example, a kind of industrial and/or agricultural production) the creation of a customs union may be a more efficient way of satisfying this preference than a country's individual non-discriminatory tariff protection. The classical theory suggests that a direct production subsidy, rather than a customs union is the most efficient protective means. The rationale for this suggestion is that this policy avoids the consumption costs which are the consequence of a tariff. On these grounds, the economic rationale for a customs union can be established on the public-goods case only if political or other constraints rule out the use of direct production subsidies (Robson, 1987, p. 53).

A country's international commitments (e.g. membership in the GATT) rule out, or severely restrict, the use of subsidies or discriminatory tariff treatment. In this case, the formation of a customs union seems to be the only feasible way for reaping the benefits of increased economic freedom. In most cases, international schemes which integrate countries are among countries whose preferences for public goods are similar (Robson, 1987, p. 54). But the fact remains that non-economic reasons play a prominent role during the creation of customs unions.

Adjustment costs

Attention hitherto has mostly been directed to the welfare effects of a customs union due to increases in product variety and consumption. It was assumed, along the lines of a neo-classical model, that adjustment of production (shifts from unprofitable into profitable activities) is instantaneous and costless. That may be a significant weakness of this approach. External shocks like improvements in technology or trade liberalization have their immediate impact in increases in efficiency and income. Employment of labour may be generated at a later stage. Adjustment to these shocks may require both time and government intervention. To get a full picture of the welfare effects of a customs union, gains from shifts in trade and production in a customs union should be reduced by the cost of adjustment.

Adjustment costs may be quite high. National governments may therefore be tempted to transfer these costs abroad. Private adjustment costs include reduction in wages, losses in the value of housing and depreciation of the value of firms' capital. Social costs include forgone output from unemployed capital and labour.

The common external tariff may discriminate against imports from third countries, which may adjust swifter than otherwise. In order to avoid the common external tariff, their governments may, among other things, respond by shaping their comparative advantage in higher lines of production to gain a competitive edge in advanced products and export them to the customs union. The dynamic models are not as simple, smooth and straightforward as classical models of trade and adjustment, but they are much closer to real life.

Experience in the EC, EFTA and successive rounds of tariff reductions under the GATT, have shown that the adjustment takes place relatively smoothly. In the case of the EC these cost were so much smaller than expected that the elimination of tariffs has advanced at a much faster pace than anticipated in the Treaty of Rome. There were intra-industrial adjustments, rather than inter-industrial. The disastrous scenario of throwing out home business on a large scale has not materialized. The buffer against such a scenario, as well as the means for the mitigation of adjustment costs, may be found in increased capital mobility and flexible rates of exchange.

One has to be careful here. The fact that the adjustment occurred 'relatively smoothly' in the 1960s and early 1970s in the EC and EFTA, in conditions of exceptionally rapid growth and full employment, does not necessarily mean that this will always be the case. The capacity to respond flexibly to increased opportunities introduced by economic reforms in eastern Europe and the USSR, may be jeopardized by the hangover from the centrally planned system, heavy interventionism, inward-looking economic strategy and old ways of doing business.

If freeing trade does not produce pain in the form of pressure and cost of adjustment, it probably produces no gain either. The compulsory reallocation of resources is the source of gains. The adjustment cost is a finite, once-and-for-all investment. The gains from improved resource allocation present a continuous flow over time. Therefore, there are reasons to believe that the 'pain' is much exaggerated (Curzon Price, 1987, p. 16). Trade liberalization accelerates competition in the participating countries. For that reason, the expectation that international economic integration is beneficial in the long run can be accepted with much confidence. Economic adjustment is a necessary condition if countries want to keep the growth of the economy in circumstances of high-risk choices, where technology and the situation on the market changes fast. They will have to learn how to live with change.

Adjustment cost – that is, shifts among economic activities –

means that labour will have to be reallocated. Positions will be lost in some business activities, while they will be created in others. Structural funds for social, regional and industrial issues can act as built-in stabilizers which help the initial losers to recover.

An economic policy of non-interference with market forces has obvious advantages because competition and efficiency are stimulated, consumers' tastes are satisfied and there is a reduction in the costs of government administration and intervention. On the other side of the coin, government intervention may be required because markets are imperfect, private firms seldom take into account social costs of production (externalities) and adjustment, and market forces may increase inequality in the regional distribution of income. However, intervention meant for the smoothing of adjustment problems may develop into deeply rooted protectionism, which increases costs to everybody. Hence, neither a pure market system nor a paramount government intervention can take account of all private and social costs and benefits of adjustment. While intervention may solve major economic issues, market forces may be more successful in the fine tuning of the economy.

A country's comparative advantage is a dynamic concept. It may shift over time. Countries may not be sure that their comparative advantage will remain unchanged in the years to come. International economic integration may be a way for a country to secure markets for the widest range of home goods and to secure sources of supply in the future. Geographical proximity of the partner countries ensures that gains from trade, specialization and wider choice of goods are not wasted on costs of transport. This leads us to the issue of optimum partners for a customs union.

OPTIMUM PARTNERS FOR A CUSTOMS UNION

International economic integration has been exercised in all parts of the world. All these efforts were not always successful. Most of these attempts since the end of the Second World War have failed or achieved very little. The reasons for these results include: a great dependence on countries outside the grouping (the case in all schemes which integrate LDCs, even the EFTA up to an extent); too small an internal market to support more than a modest industrialization (the Central American Common Market); high costs of transportation and poor communication (the Latin

American Free Trade Association, schemes in Africa); and the central planning system of economic integration in the CMEA which avoids market signals and prevents spontaneous integration (Panić, 1988, p. 6).

A large volume of trade between countries is a condition which may induce countries to contemplate integration. If trade is of minor importance for country A, this country may not be interested in entering a discriminatory trade arrangement with another country.

Common technical standards in areas of traffic, telecommunications and electronics produce relatively efficient operation of international grids without any form of integration. If this operates smoothly, then the potential partner countries may look for some other economic fields which may operate as well, but which ask for a customs union or other type of formal international economic integration arrangement.

Consider the two countries, A and B. Country A is big and country B is small. Assume next that country A is diversified in production. If both countries are at the same level of economic development measured by income per capita, then it is likely that the structure of imports of country B consists of a larger number of items than the structure of imports in country A. Country A may satisfy most or all of her demands from domestic sources and this may influence her terms of trade. Country B has to accept the world market prices (country A's) for all products other than those in which it efficiently specializes. Country A sets most of the international prices. If small country B wants to sell a standardized good in country A's market, then country B has to accept country A's domestic price less the tariff and cost of transport. Hence, big country A's tariff may bring greater cost to small country B's welfare, than are the benefits from country B's own tariff on imports.

In Figure 2.10, QQ' illustrates country B's linear-production possibility frontier. The price line coincides with the production-possibility frontier in autarky. With the indifference curve I, home production and consumption is at point C. If the price line changes to P_1 due to trade, one gets the corner solution. Country B becomes completely specialized in the production of good Y at point Q. With the indifference curve I' consumption is at point C_1, that is the point where the indifference curve is tangent to the price line. If the price line changes, and if one joins production and consumption points, one gets a kinked offer curve QCB for country B. The construction

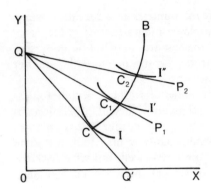

Figure 2.10 Offer curve in country B with a linear production possibility frontier

of the offer curve for country A is similar, but the production-possibility frontier for this country is shifted outwards from QQ' and it also has a different (flatter) slope.

Consider the situation in Figure 2.11 with trade in two commodities, X and Y, and two countries, A and B, where country A is big and country B is small. 0A represents big country A's offer curve, while 0B represents small country B's offer curve. The offer curves for both countries are constructed in the manner described in Figure 2.10. The longer linear portion of 0A relative to 0B is due to the longer production possibility frontier of big country A. The equilibrium point between the two offer curves is where they intersect. That is point E. Between the origin of the figure and the equilibrium point may be pencilled in the equilibrium price line. The equilibrium point is on the straight portion of big country A's offer curve. The price line coincides with offer curve 0A. The small country B must accept country A's price if it wants to trade. The small country cannot change this situation at all. If one keeps in mind that the offer curves are concave toward the import axis, one finds that at price line 0E, country B is specialized in good Y and imports good X, while country A produces both goods and is indifferent to trade.

Suppose another case with many countries and where a large country A and a small country B form a customs union. An increase in country B's demand for country A's good may be relatively easily

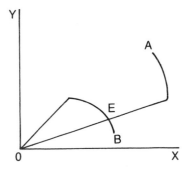

Figure 2.11 Terms of trade between a big and a small country

satisfied by country A, either from stocks or from a marginal increase in the use of existing capacity. An increase in country A's demand for country B's product may not be satisfied immediately if country B does not have free capacity or stocks. Country B's capacity may be limited by non-specialized, short production runs. In the case that some reallocation of resources in the economies of these two countries is necessary, the assumption is that due to its less specialized technologies the rate of transformation in country B is smaller than in country A, so country B can more easily shift her resources and direct them to the production aimed at country A's market, than the other way around. If small country B cannot reallocate resources towards the production of goods which are in demand in country A, then trade cannot take place between these two countries, unless country A transfers a part of her income to country B which the recipient country then spends on imports from country A.

To operate in a large market, a small country should undertake substantial investment in production and marketing. Failure in the customs-union market for a small country would mean the loss of most of its market. Investment expenses would not be recovered. The failure of a big country's exports to a small country's market would mean relatively smaller losses than the ones experienced by a small country in the same situation. The creation of a customs union is a much riskier enterprise for the small country than for the large country.

Government intervention in the form of subsidies is often needed for the capitalization and operation of some industries. When a small country subsidizes an activity, it most often has exports in mind. When a big country subsidizes home production it has in mind import substitution. On these grounds part of the small country's exports may be subject to countervailing duties by country A. Due to the asymmetric size of their respective markets, the big country may not regard the opening of the small country's market as an adequate compensation for the opening of it's own larger market. If there are many countries and if country B trades heavily with country A, then the trade relations with the external world for country B are almost bilateral. The trade relations of country A may be more evenly distributed among various countries. On these grounds, country A would request further concessions from country B.

A sad example is the United States' annexation of Hawaii. It all started with sugar. Very sweetly. Sugar was grown in Hawaii and exported to California as early as 1827. Exports were growing continuously. Hawaii initiated a treaty on the reciprocal trade with the United States in 1848. The treaty was signed in 1855 but the US Senate has not ratified it. The same happened with another treaty of 1867. Finally, a new treaty of 1875 was signed and approved by the US Senate. It provided reciprocal duty-free trade. The treaty was supposed to be an economic success for Hawaii, in particular for its exports of sugar. In 1890 the United States passed a tariff bill which removed the United States duties on sugar from all other countries. Thus Hawaii lost its privileged position in the United States market. In this situation, annexation could be the solution for the problem of Hawaii. Also, Hawaii had political problems. The taxation system was inequitable and the government was not fully representing the will of the people. Various machinations, including a small revolution, followed – with the aim of annexation. But these efforts failed. Nevertheless, by a resolution of the US Congress in 1898, Hawaii became a part of the United States. The Hawaiians, however, were given no vote in the matter. This change caused little disturbance in Hawaii. After all, this country was so dependent on the United States that annexation seemed to be the best way to have continued free access to the United States' market (Wilkinson, 1985). Luckily, this unpleasant example belongs to the past century.

The position of small countries in negotiations about a customs union has disadvantages, but it is not hopeless. Of course, there are other factors apart from the relative size of countries that influence negotiations. If she is to choose, a small country has her own trump cards. This country may look for partners elsewhere and/or leave the customs union if she thinks that this arrangement with the big country brings losses. If a small country has a genuine resource, geographic location, and/or if she may specialize in certain production niches, this country may influence negotiations and her terms of trade with a big country. Integration between countries at different levels of development remains problematic, however, unless there is a probability of success in finding political solutions for the compensation of those with disadvantages.

The greater the similarity between the countries which contemplate integration, the easier the negotiations and the smoother the adjustment and operation of the final arrangement. Optimum partners for the creation of a customs union are those of equal economic size – as France, the Federal Republic of Germany and possibly Italy were at the time of the establishment of the EC (1957). This condition of optimum partnership (political conditions aside) does not give any country the possibility of blackmailing other countries on economic grounds. The (intra-industry) adjustment to the new circumstances is easier and smoother in countries which are similar with respect to income levels and factor endowments. Inter-industry adjustment in different economies is relatively hard. However, the existence of relatively small and backward countries in the EC is evidence that there are various possibilities for countries to participate in a customs union and other types of international economic integration.

Medium-sized countries like Canada (wheat), Saudi Arabia (oil) and Brazil (coffee) may influence the price of their primary products. While income elasticities of demand for manufactured goods (traded on the oligopolistic markets of developed countries) are relatively high, the elasticities for primary goods (traded on competitive markets) are relatively low. Hence, smaller countries' exporters of primary goods generally have weaker bargaining positions than countries whose products are sold in oligopolistic markets.

The removal of tariffs on trade among countries may have substantive effects only if the integrated countries have, or can create, a base for the production of various goods and services which are demanded in the partner countries. This is of particular importance for the LDCs. These countries are at relatively low levels of income, they have similar structures of production (often goods and services for subsistence which do not enter into international trade) and relatively high concentrations of one or a few commodities in their production and in exports. These countries do not have much to integrate. Their current economic structure does not permit them to trade even on a modest scale. The level of internal trade within the organizations which integrate LDCs seldom

Table 2.6   Intra-trade of developed and developing countries

Economic grouping	Share of intra-trade in total group export in %				
	1960	*1970*	*1975*	*1985*	*1988*
EC (12)	—	51.6*	52.5	54.7	59.9
EFTA	15.7	23.2†	—	—	—
CMEA	62.3	59.4	57.4	53.7	56.8
ASEAN	21.7	14.7	13.9	16.7	17.5
UDEAC[1]	1.6	3.4	3.9	3.0	3.6
CACM[2]	7.5	26.8	21.6	17.7	14.4
CARICOM[3]	4.5	7.3	6.7	5.4	3.3
LAIA[4]	7.7	10.2	12.8	11.5	10.7
CEAO[5]	2.0	9.1	6.7	6.5	10.5
ECOWAS[6]	1.2	2.1	3.1	3.2	4.9
CEPGL[7]	0.0	0.2	0.1	0.6	0.7
MUR[8]	0.0	0.1	0.2	0.4	0.6

Source: UNCTAD (1990).
Notes:

* 1973
† 1972

[1] Customs and Economic Union of Central Africa (1964)
[2] Central American Common Market (1960)
[3] Caribbean Community (1968)
[4] Latin American Integration Association (1980), (formerly LAFTA, 1960)
[5] West African Economic Community (1974), (formerly West African Customs Union, 1959)
[6] Economic Community of West African States (1975)
[7] Economic Community of the Great Lakes Countries (1976)
[8] Mano River Union (1973)

exceeds 10 per cent of total foreign trade, as is obvious from Table 2.6. These countries compete on the same international markets with primary goods and do not have many goods and services to offer each other.

Reallocation of home resources in these countries, together with the discovery and commercial use of raw materials coupled with foreign aid and loans, may help them to produce differentiated goods and offer a variety of products to partners in trade. Just a simple liberalization of trade within a group of LDCs, as the neo-classical school suggests, will not be enough. A more positive approach (intervention) in the shaping of comparative advantage and imports of technology and capital from outside the block will be needed.

For a successful international economic integration the necessary condition is a certain minimal level of economic development. With an increase in development, the presumption is that product variety in the national output mix will increase. This may give an impetus to trade. What that minimum level of economic development is, depends on the ambitions of the countries involved. Do these countries intend to increase their bargaining power by the formation of a customs union or do they wish to use it as a means to increase or foster economic prosperity? In the second case the required level of economic development is relatively higher than the level required in the former situation.

An important role is played by the timing of the creation of a customs union. During times of economic prosperity it is easier to find gains for the participants than during a recession. A period of prosperity makes negotiations easier because every participant may expect and obtain gains. The highest rates of growth, however, are not necessarily optimal for international economic integration. On the one hand, entry into a customs union introduces changes which do not necessarily have to be efficient because there is not sufficient capacity in the economy to accept them. The economy may be 'overheated' and the creation of a customs union may increase production (marginally), but it may also increase inflation. On the other hand, during recession, an entry into a customs union may mitigate the effect of economic crisis.

In conclusion, a customs union, and other types of international economic integration, are not suitable for all countries. For different countries some types of international economic integration are more suitable than others. There are several conditions for the success of a customs union: its size, height of tariffs, level of development, market structure, achievement of the dynamic effects and the like. The potential partners for a customs union should check if they meet these conditions or if they may achieve them by means of international economic integration.

FREE TRADE AREA

Both free trade areas and customs unions yield similar results to an economy differing only in detail. Free trade areas tend to produce more trade creation and less trade diversion than a tariff-averaging customs union (a union where the level of common external tariff is the average of tariffs of the participating countries). A tariff-averaging customs union increases the level of protection of those countries which previously did not have tariffs or whose tariffs were below the level of the common external tariff. As such, free trade areas place a much lower cost on third countries than tariff-averaging customs unions.

If one assumes that the level of the common external tariff is equal to the lowest tariff of a member country in a customs union, then there is no theoretical difference between a free trade area and a customs union (although at least one member's external tariff will fall in a customs union). Effects of both types of international economic integration are the same. Of course, countries in a free trade area still negotiate in international negotiations about trade and tariffs on their own, while countries in a customs union negotiate as a single unity.

Rules of origin are the bases of a free trade agreement. These rules prevent trade deflection. This effect of free trade area formation refers to the import of goods from third countries into the area by country A (which has a relatively lower tariff than the partner country B) in order to re-export the goods in question to country B. These speculations do not depend only on the difference in the height of tariffs, but also depend on transport, storage and insurance costs, as well as on the quality (perishability) of goods. Without rules of origin in a free trade area, only the lowest tariffs will be effective. Trade deflection problems do not exist in customs unions due to the common external tariff.

The agreement among the member countries specifies which goods can qualify for tariff-free treatment within a free trade area. These goods include items which are produced entirely in the area and goods which are imported from external countries as inputs and which are, then, transformed in such a way (according to a 'sufficient material transformation' rule) that they are treated as different commodities. A liberal and widely accepted definition of origin states that goods originate from where they undergo their last substantial transformation. The implementation of such a definition is in practice 'supplemented' by a number of precise regulations about the necessary 'local content', usually expressed in percentage of value added. These goods change their classification for customs purposes. Free trade areas in practice usually include manufactured goods but exclude agricultural goods. This is because countries want to maintain national agricultural policies. It is another matter how smart this policy choice is.

Rules of origin can be restrictive or liberal. If the required value added within the area is, for example, 90 per cent, then very few commodities would qualify for duty-free treatment. Liberal rules of origin require that just a minor part of the value of goods should be added within the area. Commonly, rules of origin require that 50 per cent of value added should be within the area in order that goods receive a tariff-free status (for example, EFTA, Canada–United States Free Trade Agreement).

An important issue is the basis for the application of, for example, a 50 per-cent value-added rule. The choice is between the application of this rule to direct manufacturing costs or to invoice values which includes overheads. Consider the following example. The direct cost of manufacturing good X in country A is 75 dollars while overheads and profits are 25 dollars which make a total invoice value of 100 dollars. For good X to be exported without tariffs to the free trade area partner country B, the 50 per-cent direct-cost rule allows 37.50 dollars worth of imported components, while the 50 per-cent of invoice-value rule allows 50 dollars worth. The former rule offers a higher protection against the use of out-of-area inputs than does the latter rule. The EFTA uses the invoice-value rule, while the Canada–United States Free Trade Agreement uses the direct-cost rule (Lipsey and York, 1988, pp. 31–3).

Rules of origin can be criticized on the grounds that they are open to much abuse (simple change of packing), can be avoided by unscrupulous traders (fake origin statements and marks on the goods) or that the cost of monitoring the system are too high. The experience of the British Imperial preference scheme offers evidence that the operation of the system may be smooth. In this case the parties were geographically separated, but it would be difficult to prevent smuggling along a reasonably open continuous land frontier (Curzon Price, 1987, pp. 22–3). Luckily, free trade in manufactured goods between the EC and EFTA countries operates easily. This is due to similar and low tariff rates between the parties. Therefore, rules of origin in this case do not play an important role.

The main purpose of rules of origin is to prevent the third countries from using intra-area tariff preferences. The implicit intention is to divert trade from non-member sources. The minimum area content requirement can be criticized on the grounds that it shifts the production-factor mix away from the optimal one, it reduces rationalization in production and may reinforce market rigidities.

Hitherto, the analysis dealt with tariffs on final goods. If tariffs are introduced on raw materials and semi-manufactured goods and if one supposes that production functions are identical in all members of a free trade area, all other things being equal, production will be located in the member country which has the lowest tariffs on inputs. Such a situation where 'tariff factories' are created distorts investment decisions and the location of production. All this increases both the prices paid by consumers and the possibility of retaliation from abroad. A solution to the problem may be found in the liberal rules of origin which encourage trade creation and reduce misallocation of resources, rather than restrictive rules which generate trade diversion.

DISTRIBUTION OF COSTS AND BENEFITS

After the establishment of a customs union the welfare of the participating countries may change. The enhanced market forces will not necessarily result in acceptable results in the distribution of costs and benefits of integration. Some member countries may reap more benefits than others. The most efficient producers in some member countries may increase sales, employ more factors, introduce large-scale production and generate government revenue. Other countries in the customs union purchase from their partners, who may not be the most efficient suppliers in the world, but who are protected by the common external tariff. These importing countries lose tariff revenue and they pay a higher price for the goods which their customs-union partners produce less efficiently than the third countries' suppliers. These countries, whose destiny would be to lose in a customs union without being compensated, would never enter into this arrangement. Although the establishment of a customs union may make some countries worse off than in the situation prior to a customs union, if compensations from gainers to losers is possible, a customs union may potentially make everybody better off. For a successful integration scheme, member countries must all remain satisfied with the distribution of the costs and benefits.

There are three possible cases: all countries in a customs union reap equal benefits which accrue from the establishment of a customs union; all countries gain from customs union, but benefits are distributed disproportionately among them; and some countries gain while others lose.

If the criterion for the distribution of benefits in a customs union is the equality of income per capita, then there are the following possibilities. The first case may not require any action because everybody increases their income in proportion. The second case is harder. Is compensation necessary? Countries may assess before the creation of a customs union if some of them may gain more than others and under which conditions. In the third case, if gains are larger than losses, compensation is necessary in order to convince the losers to take part in a customs union. One must always keep in mind that one country's gains from integration does not imply similar losses for other countries in the arrangement. The question is: up to which point should one compensate? Should one compensate only up to the point where losses are removed and give the rest of the benefits to the gainers? Should one compensate only up to the point where one may convince the losers to participate?

If a move increases welfare then those who gain from this move may compensate those who lose. This is called the compensation test. The second test, called the bribery test, is one in which the potential losers remain better off by bribing the potential gainers not to make the move. If the gainers are allowed to make the change, the move will take place, unless the potential losers are able to persuade the potential gainers to stay where they are. Any change which passes the compensation test increases the size of the economic pie. If these moves are continuous, the pie grows continuously. With compensation, it is unlikely that a player's share will always go on falling. On the other hand, changes which do not pass the compensation test lower the size of the economic pie, so in the long run everyone is made worse off.

Compensation to the losers may be *ex ante* or *ex post*. In the former case uneven results of international economic integration for the member countries are foreseen in advance, while the latter way of compensation is necessary if compensation is to be in full. There is always a danger of systematic losses. The losers may blame international economic integration for their troubles and ask for compensation. The successful entrepreneurs may be discouraged to carry on along these lines, for their fortunes may be taxed by endless transfers to the losers.

Compensation to the losers may be paid in different ways. It may be a mere transfer of funds. If unconditional, this transfer may destroy incentives to adjust. Compensation may be given in the form of development of infrastructure, education and training of labour, marketing studies which help the development of the local spirit of enterprise and so on.

One criterion for fiscal compensation is often stated. It is the loss of a part of customs revenue which is the consequence of the creation of a customs union and the purchase of goods from the partner countries. This problem may be solved by direct transfers of funds from suppliers-countries' treasuries to buyers-countries' treasuries. The country which received full compensation of the customs-revenue losses has not changed its government proceeds in relation to the pre-customs-union situation. This country may shift its resources to the profitable production of goods which are demanded in partner countries and obtain production gains. But full and exclusively fiscal compensation has not been accepted as the sole means of compensation to the countries which appear to lose in any type of international economic integration.

Proceeds from the common external tariff are expected to belong to the customs union. They depend not only on the relative height of the common external tariffs, type of goods, their volume and value, but also on the preferential trade arrangements of the customs union with the off-shore countries. The distribution of these proceeds may be a complex problem. Countries which traded with many partners and which obtained a significant part of their revenue from tariff proceeds, do not have the right to dispose of these funds freely in the customs-union framework. There are several keys for the distribution of these proceeds. They may be spent on the common activities of the customs union, distributed to the member countries, given to third countries as a compensation for trade diversion, saved as a reserve or distributed among all these choices.

The manipulation of the height of the common external tariff may be of interest. The height of the common external tariff may be set as the average height of tariffs of the customs-union member countries prior to the customs union. If a customs union wants to eliminate some internal monopolies, it may set the common external tariff at a lower level in order to allow a certain level of foreign competition. If the height of the common external tariff does not reduce trade with the rest of the world, then there will be no trade diversion.

A reduction in the level of the common external tariff may be not only the most elegant, but also the least harmful way of compensation to those who are felt to be losers from trade diversion in a customs union. If fiscal transfers are required between the countries which are in a common market or economic union, these transfers may be implemented through regional and social policies. Economics is the science which (among other things) studies the reasons for differences in efficiency among various agents. The distribution of the results on (un)equal parts is a matter to be studied in politics.

NON-TARIFF BARRIERS

During the post-war period the GATT was quite successful in the continuous reduction of tariffs on industrial goods. Unfortunately, on the reverse side of these achievements, non-tariff barriers have mushroomed, and eroded the beneficial liberalizing effects of tariff cuts. Non-tariff barriers are all measures other than tariffs which reduce international trade.

While tariffs add to costs of goods like transport costs, non-tariff barriers act like import quotas, but do not generate revenue to the government. Non-tariff barriers present nowadays the most important and dangerous barriers to trade which fragment markets in a more successful way than tariffs have ever done. Tariffs were reduced under the auspices of the GATT to relatively low levels, of course on the average, so that they represent no more than a fig leaf on the economic inefficiency of a country. Still, the national administrations try to obtain short-term political gains through protectionism at the expense of long-term economic cost. Hence, non-tariff barriers are high on the agenda for all international actions to liberalize trade.

Regional trading arrangements involve more than a third of international trade. Trade within these groups of countries has a greater degree of freedom in relation to trade with off-shore countries. In many cases tariffs on internal trade are eliminated, or at least substantially reduced. Many non-tariff barriers can still exist, however, and the consideration, reduction, harmonization and even elimination of the non-tariff barriers are therefore important, not only for the international schemes which integrate countries but also for the strengthening of the multilateral trading system.

Consideration of non-tariff barriers has always been difficult. One reason is the creativity of their authors but also, and more importantly, the lack of data. Administrations either do not record the use of non-tariff barriers or if they do, this is done only partly. It comes as no surprise that the reported impact of the non-tariff barriers can lead to considerable under-estimations. Our classification of non-tariff barriers is presented in Table 2.7.

The greatest concern which stems from a growing use of non-tariff barriers is their transparency; hence they are prone to much abuse, which increases uncertainty about the access to foreign markets. Tariffs are economic policy measures which are obvious. Market forces can thus react to this instrument through adjustment measures. The operation of the non-tariff barriers asks for monitoring measures. This procedure requires increased 'policing'

Table 2.7 Classification of non-tariff barriers

Major group	Type
1 Government involvement in international trade	a. Subsidies (production, export, credit, R&D, cheap government services)
	b. Procurement of public bodies (local, regional, central)
	c. State monopoly trading
	d. Exchange rate restrictions
	e. Tied aid
2 Customs and administrative entry procedures	a. Customs classification
	b. Customs valuation
	c. Monitoring measures (antidumping and countervailing duties)
	d. Rules of origin
	e. Consular formalities
	f. Import licensing
	g. Calendar of import
	h. Administrative controls
3 Standards	a. Technical
	b. Health
	c. Environment
	d. Testing and certification
	e. Packing, labelling, weight
4 Specific limitations	a. Quotas (tariff-free ceilings)
	b. Export and import licensing
	c. Tax remission rules
	d. Variable levies
	e. Bilateral agreements
	f. Buy-domestic campaigns
	g. Voluntary export restriction agreements
	h. Self-limitation agreements
	i. Orderly marketing agreements
	j. Multi-fibre arrangements
	k. Ambiguous laws

of the administration, which increases costs. In relation to tariffs, non-tariff barriers are less desirable – for they circumvent market forces and, hence, introduce greater distortions and prevent efficient specialization.

A government at all its levels (local, regional and central) is an important consumer of goods and services. It can use its procurement policies either to protect home business (in particular small firms) and employment, or to support young industries during the first fragile steps in order to help the creation of a country's comparative advantage. Government procurement can also be employed as an instrument for the implementation of regional policy and/or aid to disadvantaged groups of the population (for instance women and minorities).

Apart from the elimination of tariffs and quantitative restrictions in a customs union, government procurement policies may remain as a significant disguised barrier to trade. This is the case when a government specifies technical requirements in such a way that it is hard for off-shore firms to comply. A mutual opening up of public markets in countries belonging to a customs union can increase gains both in the savings of public funds and in the increase of production efficiency. Compulsory publishing of public tenders, at least those whose value is greater than the agreed threshold, and allowing a reasonable time for the submission of bids may be important issues for negotiations.

It is widely accepted that the eligible goods for tariff- and quota-free trade in a customs union are all those with the exception of ones which jeopardize public morality, public security and order, as well as human, animal or plant life or health. An important non-tariff barrier can be found in technical standards (a set of specifications for the production and/or operation of a good). The intention of this hidden barrier to trade is in many cases to protect the national producer, despite the long-term costs, in the form of lower economies of scale and reduced competition.

One of the most famous cases of non-tariff barrier within an integrated group of countries was the case of a fruit-based liquor *Cassis de Dijon* from the 1970s. FR Germany forbade the importation of this French drink on the grounds that liquors consumed in FR Germany should have more than 25 per cent of alcohol while *Cassis de Dijon* had 5 per cent less than FR Germany's threshold. The case was considered by the EC Court of Justice which ruled that the ban on imports of this liqueur was not legitimate. The importance of this ruling is paramount. It created a precedent in the EC for all goods which are legally produced in one member country. These goods cannot be banned for imports to other partner countries on the grounds that national standards differ. The exception is the case in which the imports of a good can jeopardize an important national interest. If differences in the national standards do exist, then the consumers can be protected by a warning on the good which states this difference. This precedent was also used in the case where the EC forced FR Germany in 1987 to open its market for beers from other EC countries, in spite of the fact that those beers do not comply with the German beer purity law (*Reinheitsgebot*) of 1516. This decision has not, in spite of fears, jeopardized this country's beer production.

Another imaginative non-tariff barrier is illustrated by the Poitiers case. The French government wanted to protect the home market (although there was no home production) from imports of Japanese video recorders. It requested, just before Christmas of 1982, that all Japanese videos must pass through customs inspection in the town of Poitiers. This town is in the centre of France, far from all main ports of entry for these goods, while at the time its customs post had only eight officers and was not well equipped. This action has increased costs (transport, insurance, interest, delays) and reduced the quantity of imported videos. Such a measure, perhaps, made some sense in the situation when the government wanted to restrain rising consumers' expenditure, which made a short-term drain on the balance of payments. In such cases, however, a more appropriate measure might be excise duties or high sales taxes. The lesson which should be learned from this case is that in the case of high-technology goods (with scale economies and learning-curve effects), the time to protect is before foreign firms have obtained most of the domestic market (Wilkinson, 1984, p. 54). This case received much publicity in the media, so the government had 'no other choice' except to revoke this measure – after Christmas, of course.

There are, also, cases of non-tariff barriers which deal with technical specifications. Belgium allows the sale of margarine only in square containers, while round ones are reserved only for butter. The standard width of consumer durables in the EC countries is 60 centimetres, while in Switzerland this standard is a few centimetres smaller. The City of London requests that cabs must offer service in such a way that gentlemen are able to sit comfortably with their hats on. All these specifications (non-tariff barriers) do not have a crucial impact on the protection of life and health. Their final effect is to increase the price to the consumers.

The Treaty of Rome required the abolition of tariffs and quotas on internal EC trade. It also required the elimination of all measures having equivalent effects. At the time of the creation of the EC it was assumed that non-tariff barriers have a minor importance in comparison to tariffs. The GATT was successful in the reduction of the level of tariffs but recession provoked a proliferation of non-tariff barriers in subsequent years.

To prevent the use of non-tariff barriers in an integrated market, the countries involved may agree to harmonize their standards and to consult on the introduction of new ones. A solution which may lead to the harmonization of standards is mutual recognition. Goods which are legally produced and marketed in one member country should have a free access to the markets of other member countries even if their standards differ. This measure would be still insufficient for the creation of a uniform EC market and the increase in competitiveness which goes with it. Harmonization may remove such shortcomings even though it can be criticized on the grounds of its over-regulation and the necessarily long time to be implemented.

Harmonized standards for some things, like safety and health, are essential, while mutual recognition may be a solution for the traded goods while being in the waiting room for harmonization. The long-term effect of such a policy is that the firms will face one set of rules instead of twelve different ones. This may increase gains that come from economies of scale, but this can only make sense when the market for the good or service exceeds one member state. For example, consumer preferences for goods like videos, faxes and computers may be similar throughout the EC, but there are a number of differences with respect to foodstuffs and beverages, where preferences are strictly local. Here, an EC standard that does not pay heed to those distinctions may do more harm than good. The member states of the EC are obliged to notify the EC Commission in advance about all draft regulations and standards. If the Commission or other member states find that it contains elements of non-tariff barriers to trade, they may start remedial action allowed in Articles 30 or 100 of the Treaty of Rome.

Rules of origin in general and the minimum local content requirement in particular, can be used as a non-tariff barrier. Governments are free to use rules of origin as policy measures, since the GATT does not regulate them. As a result, there is a variety of practices which create problems for producers and traders. Rules of origin are used to operate preferential tariffs, as well as to implement commercial policy. Preferential rules of origin are used in a trading group to determine which goods are eligible for the agreed preferential tariff treatment within the group. Non-preferential rules of origin take into account the last substantial operation (the one that gave the good a new quality, that is, the one that shifted the good from one customs classification group to another) and the importance of the operation to the whole process of production – which is important in assembly operations. The Kyoto Customs Convention (1973) states that the 'last' substantial process determines the origin of the good.

Once the authority spots a good which may be imported into its territory, it often introduces an anti-dumping tariff. Off-shore exporters can circumvent this barrier by locating the final, often screwdriver stage of production, in the tariff-imposing country. To counter this action, the home authorities may request that the goods produced domestically must have a certain local content in order to obtain the preferential treatment. Once the original supplier of the good meets this requirement, the local authorities may go further, as was the case with the EC control of imports of Japanese semiconductors. Chips which are merely assembled in the EC will not qualify for the domestic treatment. The EC has issued new rules in 1989 which are linking the origin of semiconductors to the place where the essential technology has its source. In this case, the EC defined the origin of the good by the place where the 'most' substantial production process was made.

Non-tariff barriers have continuously irritated international trade relations. The most striking manifestation of international concern about the reduction of the non-tariff barriers can be found in the modestly extended scope of the Uruguay round of tariff negotiations beyond the 'traditional' GATT agenda. On the regional scale, the EC White Paper (1985) and the subsequent Single European Act (1987) intend to complete the internal EC market and create an economic area without frontiers. This ambitious programme intends to reduce substantially or to eliminate the non-tariff barriers which hinder the free creation and operation of economic activities in the EC.

Non-tariff barriers contribute to the costs which accrue from the non-competitive segmentation of the market. They encourage import substitution and discourage rationalizing investment. The anticipated benefits which would come from the elimination of non-tariff barriers include increased competition – with its effects on the improved efficiency, economies of scale and the consequent reduction in costs of production for an enlarged market – as well as increased specialization. The outcome of this process will be an increased average living standard.

A study by Emerson *et al.* (1988) illustrates the possible benefits which may accrue, under certain conditions, from the completion of the EC internal market. The total EC gross domestic product in

1985 (the base year for most estimates) was ECU 3,300 billion for the twelve member states. The direct cost of frontier formalities for the private and public sector may be 1.8 per cent of the value of goods traded in the EC, or around ECU 9 billion. The cost for industry of identifiable barriers, like technical regulations, may be 2 per cent of the surveyed companies' total costs, which makes around ECU 40 billion. The liberalization of the public procurement would bring gains of ECU 20 billion, while the liberalization of the supply of financial services would save further ECU 20 billion. Gains due to the economies of scale would reduce costs between 1 and 7 per cent, yielding an aggregate cost saving of ECU 60 billion. A downward convergence of presently disparate price levels may bring gains of about ECU 140 billion. Under the assumption of a much more competitive and integrated EC market the estimates offer a range of gains starting from ECU 70 billion (or 2.5 per cent of the EC GNP) to ECU 190 billion (or 6.5 per cent of the EC GNP). The same, once-and-for-all gains, for the 1988 GNP would give a range of ECU 175 to 255 billion. These figures are unlikely to be overestimates, for they exclude important dynamic effects on economic performance – such as technological innovation, which is difficult to anticipate. There is no general opposition to the completion of the EC internal market by the end of 1992, for the opponents to the plan cannot offer an alternative strategy which would make up for the forgone losses from preserving the *status quo*.

The level of tariffs and the use of non-tariff barriers may be inversely related to the level of development of a country measured by the level of income per capita. The non-tariff kind of protection has a negative impact on economic growth and employment in the long term at a continuous cost to consumers and taxpayers. Public concern with respect to these long-term costs of non-tariff measures of protection will press this issue high on the GATT agenda for negotiations in the time to come.

CONCLUSION

The traditional (static) model of customs union considers the effect of reduction in tariffs on welfare. It concludes that the lowering or elimination of tariffs increases competition which leads to an improvement in welfare. The new theory pays attention to the dynamic effects of integration. With economies of scale and imperfect competition, there are no unconditional expectations that all countries will gain from integration, even less that they will gain equally. In the absence of adjustment policies – such as industrial, regional and social policies – integration may impose costs on some countries, rather than give them benefits. Therefore, cooperation among countries with respect to the distribution of gains is a necessary condition for successful integration. In any case, integration profoundly changes the economic structure of participating countries which must abandon the established domestic monopolies and autarkic traditions.

The theory of customs union is based on a large number of restrictive assumptions, so the technical modelling may be far from realistic. Various restrictions in a customs union – such as the prohibition on factor movements or coordinated fiscal and monetary policies – can be overcome in common markets and economic unions. They will be discussed in the chapters that follow.

The theory of customs unions studies extreme cases and it is intuitive in nature. All analyses are suggestive rather than definitive. Yet another difficulty stems from the fact that this theory includes simultaneously both free trade within a customs union and protection against third countries in the form of the common external tariff. A customs union reduces tariffs on trade among some countries, so it may seem beneficial in relation to the situation where each country applies its own system of tariffs. In a customs union, tariffs are removed on the internal trade, but the common external tariff is erected. One distortion is replaced by another, so with respect to the final effect on welfare, all things are possible. If free trade is the first-best policy, then a customs union is at best a second-best situation. Hence a universal prescription for the success of a customs union may not be found. But our effort was not in vain, because many things may be learned from the analysis of extreme cases. Dynamic effects are extremely hard to model and quantify rigorously. It is difficult to predict the exact impact of competition on technological innovation. These are intuitive issues, but none the less important for economic integration.

International economic integration increases the potential for significant international improvement in economic welfare. The countries have to organize themselves – that is, adjust individually and collectively – to reap these gains. Specialization and increase in export potentials are the necessary conditions for success. Also, adjustment policies must be intelligent. Incorrect policies can sink all beneficial effects which accrue from an improved access to a larger market.

In the world of rapid change in technology, a country may not be sure that its current comparative advantages will be secured in the future. A country may therefore wish to secure markets for the widest variety of its goods and services. International economic integration is an uphill job but may be an attractive solution to this problem. Integration may be a risky enterprise for a small country in relation to protectionism in the short run, but a defensive policy of protection may generate the economic decline of a small country in the long run. Few countries may accept this as their long-term goal. International economic integration may be the way out of this scenario. A willingness to cooperate with partner countries on the issue of the distribution of costs and benefits that accrue from the creation of a customs union is of great importance for the smooth and beneficial operation, as well as survival, of a customs union. International economic integration may be subject to various disputes. Most of them stem from the existence of non-tariff barriers. An effective dispute-settlement mechanism is a necessary condition for the adhesion of the scheme.

3 Common market

INTRODUCTION

The entire analysis of customs unions applies to common markets too. Due to the free mobility of factors of production in a common market, the effects of a customs union are, however, substantially enriched. The effects of a more efficient allocation of resources (improvements in the locational advantages for business) are due to the free-factor flow from low- to high-productivity business activities within the common market.

Apart from factor mobility, a condition for the integration of factor markets is non-discrimination of factors originating from the partner countries. In this situation, factors respond to signals which include demand, higher productivity and returns within a common market. Integration of factor markets will be encountered as mobility of labour and mobility of capital in the chapters which follow.

MOBILITY OF LABOUR

Introduction

A customs union involves product-market integration. A common market adds factor-market integration. It is expected that the free flow of factors within the bloc will improve the allocation of resources over that achieved in either a free trade area or a customs union. The neo-classical Hecksher–Ohlin trade theory concludes that a country with a rich supply of labour may either export labour-intensive goods or import capital and export labour, under the assumption that technology is the same in all countries. In either case the country is equally well off.

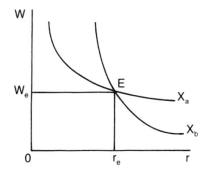

Figure 3.1 Equalization of factor prices

Equalization of factor prices

Assume a model which consists of two countries A and B, two final goods X and Y and two factors of production K and L, respectively. Suppose, further, that factor mobility is perfect within each country but prohibited between countries. If there are no barriers to trade and no distortions, and if technology is the same and freely accessible to both countries, and if production functions are homogeneous of the first degree, both goods are produced in both countries and isoquants intersect only once (there is no factor-intensity reversal), then free trade in goods will equalize relative prices in goods. This will equalize both relative factor prices and their returns between countries A and B, respectively. This stringent situation is illustrated in Figure 3.1.

In Figure 3.1 X_a represents the unit isocost line (combination of factors which keeps output constant) for the good X in country A (production of which is relatively labour intensive), while X_b describes the same cost line for good X which is relatively capital intensive in country B. Equilibrium is at point E where factor prices are equalized through trade at levels $0r_e$ for capital and $0w_e$ for labour. In this model, trade is a substitute for factor mobility. An analogous condition holds in the common market.

The exclusion of balance-of-payments adjustments from comparative statics implies that the adjustment process between the two distant points in time has worked well and that the balance is in equilibrium. In reality, however, such a process may even last a generation. Thus a static model, which usually forgets the adjustment process, can hardly be justified. Capital accumulation, economies of scale and economic growth produce different results in the long run from the straighforward static model (Vosgerau, 1989, p. 219).

A free international trade in goods and factor movements is prevented by the existence of various barriers. In this framework, according to one view, commodity movements are still a substitute for factor movements. An increase in trade restrictions stimulates factor movements, while an increase in restrictions to international factor mobility enhances trade in goods (Mundell, 1957, p. 321).

The assumption has been, so far, that technology was the same in all countries. However, this is not always the case. The difference in technologies among countries enhances, rather than reduces, the possibilities for international capital mobility. LDCs export raw goods in return for foreign investment, which enables them to produce and later, possibly, export manufactured goods (Purvis, 1972, p. 991). Factor mobility, in the case where technologies differ, may increase the volume of trade rather than reduce it. Factor mobility and commodity movements may act in this case as complements.

Substitutability between trade in goods and mobility of factors (Hecksher–Ohlin model) may be the exception rather than the rule. If countries are quite different in relative factor endowments and with weak economies of scale, then individuals who draw their income from factors that are relatively scarce end up worse off as a result of trade. If countries are similar, and trade is mostly motivated by economies of scale (intra-industry trade), then one might expect to find that even scarce factors gain (Krugman, 1990, p. 80).

The basis for trade can be something other than a simple difference in factor endowments. Alternative bases for trade include returns to scale, imperfect competition, difference in production and factor taxes, as well as differences in production technology. In this case free mobility of factors leaves countries relatively well endowed with the factor used intensively in the production of export good (Markusen, 1983, p. 355). International mobility of factors and trade are taken to be complements, rather than substitutes in many occasions. A high concentration of factors (e.g. computer scientists in California) will create an additional comparative advantage which will, in turn, enhance trade.

If factor mobility leads to a reduction in the volume of trade in goods, then factor movements and trade in goods are substitutes. This is the case where there are differences in the prices of goods between countries. If labour moves from country A, in which good X is dearer, to country B, in which this good is cheaper, this decreases the demand for and price of good X in country A and increases them in country B until the two prices are equalized. If relative differences in factor endowments are not the only basis for trade, international mobility of factors and trade may stimulate each other and become supplements (Markusen and Melvin, 1984).

The factor price equalization theorem anticipates that free trade will have as its consequence equalization of wage levels among countries. This need not always be the case. Migration will be a necessary condition for the equalization of wages if the majority of labour in both high-wage countries and low-wage countries is employed in the production of non-tradeable goods. In this case free trade is not a sufficient condition for the equalization of wages between the countries involved.

A study of relative differences in labour rewards in the EC found that there was a convergence in labour costs between the mid-1950s (that is, before the EC was created) until the mid-1960s. From 1968 onwards the trend was reversed. The reasons for convergence may be found in the free trade in goods and the more liberal movements of capital and labour which came from the Mediterranean countries which were not members of the EC (Tovias, 1982). This approach was disputed, for it did not provide an explanation for the converging trend in wages before the creation of the EC or the divergent trend after 1968. There is not even a single wage level within a country because of heterogeneous qualifications and employer demand in each sector. Due to imperfect mobility of labour, trade may be expected to lead to a convergence in prices of commodities and wages in sectors that are involved in trade. A correlation should exist between the liberalization of internal trade and changes in the level of wages (Gremmen, 1985). In the test of this idea a few errors were made, the most important being the expectation of an insignificant coefficient on the capital–labour ratio. Wage differences between the north and the south of Italy or the United States reveal that this expectation is not correct. The results of the re-estimation found that the relation between the level of wages and trade intensity (the sum of countries' marginal propensities to import each others' goods) is not as direct as Gremmen assumed. In addition, it was found that the capital–labour ratio remains an important determinant of factor prices even if international economic integration has advanced as far as it has in the EC. This is not to deny that increasing trade relations lead to decreasing wage differentials, but rather that trade intensity must be considered in conjunction with differences in the capital–labour ratio (van Mourik, 1987).

Free mobility of factors in a common market and an expectation of equalization of factor prices may be an attractive incentive for countries to close the gap in the levels of income and development within the integrated area. How this works in practice is not quite clear. The experience of the EC presents evidence that some corrective measures are necessary – such as social and regional funds.

Economies of scale make specialization more likely. Every technology requires different types of labour, so complete factor-price equalization seems unlikely. Distortions – such as tariffs, subsidies, taxes, costs of transport – make equalization of factor prices real only in a strict model. In the real world there may appear only a tendency towards the equalization of factor prices.

Mobility of labour or labour responsiveness to demand has been a significant facet of economic life for a long period of time. Labour has not only moved among regions, but also among sectors. In the late 1950s, agriculture employed around 20 per cent of the labour force in most industrialized countries. In the 1980s, agriculture employs less than 5 per cent of the labour force in these countries. The theoretical assumption that labour has a greater degree of mobility within a country than among countries may not always be substantiated. Inter-country mobility of labour between Ireland and other developed English speaking countries may be much greater than internal Irish labour mobility.

Outside common markets, international labour migration is characterized by a legal asymmetry. The Universal Declaration of Human Rights (1948), Article 13, denies the right to the country of origin to close its borders to bona fide emigrants. This country may not control the emigration flows according to its interest. The country of destination, however, has an undisputed right to restrict the entry of immigrants, although this is not explicitly mentioned in the Declaration. In these circumstances migration flows are determined by demand. The will to move is therefore a necessary condition for labour migration, but it is not a sufficient condition (Straubhaar, 1988, p. 45).

Country of origin

If political instability and economic troubles (push determinants) overcome the propensity to stay in the homeland (pull determinants), then there are several reasons for international migration of labour. The most significant ones are the possibility of finding a job which may provide better living conditions, as well as better conditions for specialization and advance. A common market may enhance and facilitate movement of labour among the participating countries. In these complex circumstances, migrants act as utility-maximizing units subject to both push and pull determinants.

Migration of labour has its obstacles. They may be found in both receiving and sending countries. Socio-psychological obstacles to migration may include different languages, climate, religion, customs, diet and clothing. This may be one of the reasons why Japan has closed borders for legal immigration. Economic obstacles include the lack of information about job openings, conditions of work, social security, legal systems, systems of dismissal (last in, first out) and the loss of seniority. During recession and unemployment periods there may be nationalistic, racial and religious clashes between the local population and immigrants. Trade unions may lobby against the immigration of foreigners, as well as for driving them away.

The countries of origin have significant losses in manpower. Migrants are usually younger men who want to take the risk of moving. These regions may have the tendency of becoming feminine and senilized. The potential producers are leaving while consumers are remaining behind. The countries of origin lose a part of their national wealth which was invested in raising and educating their population. If the migrants are experienced and educated, then their positions may often be filled by less sophisticated labourers. The result is lower productivity and national wealth.

The brain-drain argument is not convincing in all cases. Many of those who migrate cannot always find adequate jobs in their home countries. The physician who leaves Burkina Faso is one thing, this country needs more medical services. A Mozambiquan astrophysicist is another, since this country has few labs, telescopes and computers, so it cannot use the qualifications of this expert. It makes sense for this skilled worker to go abroad and possibly send money to the country of origin. However, if computer programmers emigrate from Mozambique, there is no point in this country importing computers, and without importing new technology it will remain backward indefinitely. If the migrants return after a period abroad, some of them may be old and/or ill, so they become consumers. All this may reduce the local tax base and increase the cost of social services to the remaining population.

Apart from these costs, countries of origin may obtain benefits from emigration. This movement of labour reduces the pressure which is caused by unemployment, and reduces unemployment benefit payments (if they exist). Possible remittances of hard currency may reduce the balance-of-payment pressure, and if migrants return they may bring along hard-currency savings and new skills which may help them to obtain or create better jobs. This may help the development efforts of the country.

If some countries do not have exportable goods, they have to export labour (if other countries want to accept it) in order to pay for imports. When the rich north wants to send workers abroad, then that counts as trade in services. When the poor south wants to do the same, it is regarded as immigration.

The volume of possible remittances depends on the number of migrants, the length of their stay and incentives. The shorter the stay of migrants abroad, the higher the probability that they will transfer or bring all their savings to their home countries. During short stays abroad, they intend to earn and save as much as possible. If they stay abroad for a longer period of time, then they may wish to enjoy a higher standard of living than during relatively short stays. They reduce the volume of funds which may potentially be remitted to their countries of origin. If the country of origin offers incentives for the transfer of these funds in the way of attractive rates of interest, exchange, allowances for imports and investment, as well as if there is overall stability, then there is a greater probability that funds will be attracted.

One observation ought to be mentioned. Personnel of the TNCs often move internationally. Although this is regarded as international labour mobility, it occurs within the same firm.

Country of destination

The supply of indigenous labour and the level of economic activity decide the demand for foreign labour in the country of destination. A country may permit an inflow of foreign labour, but this country must bear in mind that people come with all their virtues and vices.

Foreign workers may face open and hidden clashes with the local population. The host country population may dislike foreigners because they take jobs from the domestic population, they bring their customs, increase congestion, depress wages and send their savings abroad, to mention just a few reasons.

The country of destination has certain benefits from immigration. The migrants are a very mobile segment of the labour force. Once they enter a country, they are not linked to any particular place. Their mobility within that country has an impact on the equalization of wages throughout the country. Of course, every next wave of immigration depresses the wages offered to earlier immigrants. Foreign labour need not necessarily be cheaper than local. However, foreign labour is more easily controlled by management. The native labour may not have language barriers to move within the home country. So labour in the EC is relatively less mobile than labour in the United States. Indigenous labour in the EC has a relatively lower mobility than the guest workers from countries outside the EC. This is often due to the following reasons: relatives and friends; spouses who have jobs that they do not want to leave; children who go to schools to which they are attached; and ownership of houses which are still under mortgage.

The country of destination may obtain labour which is cheaper and whose training has not been paid for by domestic taxpayers. Migrants increase the demand for housing and other goods, pay taxes (which may exceed what they receive in transfer payments and public services) and take jobs which the domestic labour is uninterested in at the level of pay offered to foreigners. These are the jobs on open spaces, in mines, foundries, construction, assembly, cleaning, hotels, restaurants and other monotonous jobs. The jobs which are most threatened by migrants are the ones which are usually modestly paid. Migrants compete for these vacancies with the local youth and women who may have reduced opportunities for work. Countries of destination reduce the price of inputs (labour) and increase competitiveness, at least in the short run.

Migrant workers may not know the language of the host country, so these people may not be able to take part in the social life. The only place where they may present themselves as creative beings is in production. These workers may work sometimes at a faster pace and better than domestic ones. This may provoke clashes with the local workers. Employers may sometimes prefer to conclude direct agreements with migrant workers than to employ domestic labour. It is not only that the migrant labourers are working for lower wages than domestic labour in the absence of legal protection, but also that foreigners may be dismissed with less consequences for the employer or that the foreign labourer's permission to work may not be renewed.

European Community (EC)

The abolition of barriers to international migration of labour brings an expectation that the international flow of labour will increase in relation to the previous circumstances. This hypothesis can be tested in the case of the EC. The total number of intra-EC migrants of the original six member countries was around half a million before 1960 which increased to a little over 800,000 in 1968. It remained almost constant until the early 1980s and since then it decreased to 650,000 migrants. All other intra-EC migrations were regional, rather than international. The inevitable conclusion is that the creation of the EC has not significantly changed intra-EC migrations of labour. While intra-EC trade increased, the intra-EC migrations decreased. Trade and migration of labour were substitutes (Straubhaar, 1988). The explanation for the decline in labour mobility among the EC countries during 1980s can be found in significant changes (improvements) in the state of their home economies.

The exact data on the flow of migrants are deficient. Therefore, Table 3.1 presents the stock data on migrant workers in the EC in 1988. Migration of labour can be a significant feature even if countries are not formally integrated. More than two-thirds of migrants in the EC up to the mid-1970s came from the non-member, mostly Mediterranean, countries. These foreign agents might have represented one of the integrative tissues of the EC. Despite all enlargements of the EC, in 1988 more than half of all migrants in the EC still came from the non-member countries. The difference between the data presented in Table 3.1 and Straubhaar's data come from the likely underestimation of the stock of migrants by Straubhaar, who relies only on the working permits issued by the country of destination, hence the data provided by countries of origin are neglected. Apart from the non-EC migrants who have legal working permits, one may apprise that there are around 10 per cent extra illegal migrant workers. If one adds family members to the number of the non-EC migrant workers, then the stock of foreign residents in the EC increases about 2.5 times.

An interesting fact, not captured in Table 3.1, is Italy's transition over the last three decades from a net exporter to a net importer of

Table 3.1 Migrant workers in the EC countries in 1988 (in thousands)

Country	Total	From EC countries Total	From non-EC countries			
			Total	Turkey	Yugoslavia	Maghreb†
1 Belgium*	177	130	49	10	2	20
2 Denmark	47	13	34	7	3	1
3 FR Germany*	1,557	483	1,073	511	284	24
4 Greece*	25	7	18	3	—	—
5 Spain	—	—	—	—	—	—
6 France*	1,131	569	561	38	30	334
7 Ireland*	20	16	4	—	—	—
8 Italy	—	—	—	—	—	—
9 Luxembourg	64	60	3	—	1	—
10 The Netherlands	176	85	91	33	5	24
11 Portugal	35	10	25	—	—	—
12 United Kingdom	820	398	423	7	4	5

* 1987
† Morocco, Algeria, Tunisia
Source: Eurostat (1990).

non-European, mainly Mediterranean, illegal labour. Illegal immigrants work in and contribute to growth of the informal economy. Costs of labour are both lower and more flexible in the black economy. This encourages firms to shift resources from the legal economy to the informal one where the available technology is less efficient. Hence, the transfer of capital (and labour) towards the informal economy that immigration makes advantageous for firms is not favourable for the economy as a whole (Dell'Aringa and Neri, 1989, p. 134).

The government is a significant employer in all EC countries. Therefore many jobs may be closed to foreigners even if they are citizens of the EC partner countries. This potential obstacle to employment has been removed by the EC Court of Justice opinion that only those positions which are linked to national security may be reserved for domestic labour. It would be absurd to argue that a person loses skills and knowledge when crossing a border. In order to facilitate labour mobility, in particular of highly educated labour, the EC sets qualitative (content of training) and quantitative (years of study, number of course hours) criteria which diplomas must meet in order to be awarded and mutually recognized.

Unrestricted employment of the EC residents in all EC member countries exists in the manufacturing and agricultural sectors. However, this freedom is limited in the financial and transport services, which stems from insufficient integration of these sectors. This may well change after 1992. Nevertheless, the migrant workers have the right to cumulate and transfer all claims to social security. Also, they and their family members have the right to education. The rights of non-member-country migrant workers depend on the bilateral agreement between their country of origin and the country of destination.

The explanation for the greater migrations of labour from off-shore countries than the inter-EC country flows can be found in the differences in production functions and barriers to trade among countries. The more similar the structure and the level of development between countries and the lower the barriers to trade, the greater will be the substitution effect between trade and labour migration. This also explains migration of labour from Italy just after the creation of the EC, as well as the subsequent reduction in this flow.

Recessions now rarely affect only one country. During the recession the unemployed EC labour stayed in its country of origin. This was because the chances to find employment abroad were smaller than at home. It is the off-shore labour migrants who were closing the gap between the EC demand and supply of labour, rather than the internal EC flows. Reduced inter-EC member countries' migrations of labour are due to the trend which was evening the income and productivity levels among the original six member countries of the EC, as well as the growth in countries which created a new domestic demand for labour. The expectation that a common market significantly increases long-term, intra-group migrations of labour is refuted in the case of the EC.

MOBILITY OF CAPITAL

General considerations

A common market potentially increases the market for a firm. Since foreign direct investment is permitted by definition, firms sometimes find that there is a change in the optimal location for business, in particular as compared with previous locations in countries that are integrated. Also, if permitted, investors from foreign countries may attempt to invest in the common market in order to avoid the common external tariff. This is known as the creation of 'tariff factories'. This will potentially have an effect on increasing investment by TNCs. Entrepreneurs view a common market, just like a customs union, as an economic signal which has a long-term effect – as opposed to changes in prices which may embody only a temporary situation. Entrepreneurs may form expectations with a higher degree of certainty.

This is an important gain for a small country. In a situation without integration, foreign countries can simply threaten a small country that they will introduce protectionist measures against this country. Such a warning can seriously undermine the quality of all economic decision in this country. Integration enhances market access and increases the long-term competitiveness of a small country's economy. A common market eliminates all national incentives to foreign countries' firms to locate in the partner countries (which were previously subject to the countervailing duties). It also excludes non-economic considerations, like political pressures to third countries' investors, to locate in a particular country. If all other things are equal, foreign investors will locate in a country which offers the best cost and market structure.

If there are available factors, investment may increase employment, as well as create new production, consumption, sales, profits and tax revenue. International economic integration has its impact on the business cycle and the rate of growth. All this means change and structural adjustment. In this model, growth may be maximized if only the bare necessities of life are satisfied, while the rest of income is invested. This policy might work only in the short run, with the expectation of more than proportional future consumption gains in relation to the current sacrifice.

A caveat for LDCs is that sometimes they use tariff proceeds for investment purposes. If that is the case, a customs union may dry up a part of domestic investments by lowering tariff revenue. In a situation with many market imperfections, the opportunities for gains and losses are numerous. Long-term gains of international economic integration may offset this loss of revenue.

International economic integration may create increases in investment, rates of growth and welfare, but it may also increase tendencies of increasing regional inequalities. If factor movements are permitted within an integrated area, then some countries and certain regions may offer higher returns to factors than others. The growing regions may attract disproportionate amounts of factors. Other regions may be left with lower quality factors and unattractive opportunities for investment. Economic activity concentrates in already developed regions where there are external savings in the form of previously developed infrastructure, trained labour and all kinds of services which include banks, insurance, legal, maintenance, marketing, education, health and beautification. If one takes account of various possibilities for entertainment and leisure, one finds that both economic and non-economic incentives have their impact on the polarization of economic activities among regions. This contradicts the expectation of the neo-classical theory which anticipates that a free flow of factors will ameliorate differences in average income and growth rates among regions. On the contrary, in the presence of increasing returns to scale and other market imperfections, a free flow of factors can enhance, rather than narrow, disparities in comparative advantage, and potentially leave some worse off. Backward regions and countries may receive some compensation for this process in the form of spread effects. Growth of economic activity in the integrated area as a whole may increase sales and indirectly increase investment in all regions. Another positive impact may come from the spread of new technology from the prosperous regions.

Targeting some key productive activities which have significant linkages with the rest of the economy may require some form of government intervention. Japan's decision to target steel and shipbuilding in the 1950s and 1960s was highly profitable. This choice turned out to be questionable in the 1970s, so Japan turned to autos and machine tools. The Japanese have chosen electronics as their target in the 1980s and 1990s (Tyson, 1987, p. 70). This target may, in turn, become obsolete in future periods. The selected sectors have important spillover effects throughout the economy. Telecommunications affect the dissemination of information, computers have their impact on data processing, while transportation equipment affects the size of the market. These externalities make the private returns from these industries smaller than social returns. The targeting of certain key industries, in a common market or other type of integration, which may have significant linkages with other sectors or partner countries, may have important and long-term beneficial spillover effects on the member countries.

When a firm wants to produce abroad it does not necessarily need to export capital. A firm may rent capital abroad instead of purchasing or building a production unit. Instead of using its own funds, a firm may borrow in its home, host country's or a third country's financial market. In the case of fixed exchange rates, countries may enter into a 'rate of interest war' in order to attract capital into their economies. Integrated capital markets with harmonized rates of interest and mobility of capital may prevent this outcome. While labour markets are regional, capital markets are national or international.

Investment activity is one of the most sensitive indicators of a country's economic climate. What it indicates, however, is not always clear. Increases in investment may indicate the emergence of new business opportunities, interest in the future, reactions to international competition and response to increasing cost pressures. In any case, sluggish investment activity (as during the 1970s) is an indication of rough economic times (Schatz and Wolter, 1987, p. 29).

Both firms and governments do not depend on savings in their home markets. Interest rates and demand for funds in one country are affected by money (short-term) and capital (long-term) markets in other countries due to the linkages among financial markets. Small countries are interest-rate takers, so that even the national housing (non-traded good) market feels the impact from foreign markets by means of interest-rate changes. Free mobility of capital prevents the independent conduct of monetary policy. If a country lowers interest rate in relation to off-shore countries, then capital will flow abroad. This also destabilizes the exchange rate if other things are equal. Also, if a country increases interest rates in relation to foreign countries, if other things are constant, the capital will flow into this country. The supply of money increases, hence inflation is the consequence.

Integration of capital markets fostered by a common market is able to offer various benefits. Member countries may increase the degree of surveillance over borrowing; the need for outside loans may decrease; multilateral movements of surpluses and deficits may be facilitated; existing financial centres may benefit from specialization; and economies of scale, as well as distortions in competition, may be reduced. This lowers costs of financial services and encourages the optimal allocation of available resources. The competitive capacity of the integrated countries increases *vis-à-vis* their major rivals on the international market. This helps small and medium-sized enterprises which can get loans on more favourable terms and improve their access to the international market.

Financial markets may discriminate between big companies and countries on the one hand, and small companies and countries on the other. Large companies and countries provide a greater security that the funds will be returned and interest paid. A large stock of assets provides this confidence. These markets may discriminate against risky investments like sea-bed research, new sources of energy and the like. By integration of capital markets, small countries may mitigate the effect of their disadvantage.

The mere liberalization of capital movements in a common market is not a sufficient condition to create a true financial area. Other supporting measures – such as cooperation and harmonization of monetary and fiscal policies are required. Various financial assistance schemes are necessary for the protection of economic and social cohesion of the group because free mobility of capital may benefit more the already developed regions and countries. In addition, investment decisions are often influenced by differences in company taxation. The risk of tax evasion can be significantly reduced by a generalized withholding tax applied to all common-market residents. These are the issues which will be encountered in the chapter on economic unions.

Foreign direct investment

Capital moves among countries in the form of portfolio and direct investment. Portfolio investment is most often just a short-term movement of claims which is speculative in nature. The main aims are an increase in value and relative safety. It may be induced by differences in rates of interest. The recipient country may not use these funds for investment in fixed assets which may be repaid in the long run, so these movements of capital may be seen by the recipient country as hot, unstable and 'bad'. Volatility of portfolio investment complicates their analysis. The large number of portfolio investments, made in many cases by brokers, obscures who is doing what and why.

Foreign direct investment permits the investor to acquire a lasting, partial or full, control over the investment. The investor does not only employ own funds, but also knowledge and management. These investments are long-term in nature. They may increase the productive capacity of the economy, so they are often used as a lure by host countries as something which is suitable, 'cold' and 'good'. Foreign direct investment may not be found in perfectly competitive markets, hence market imperfections may explain them. They include expected profits, market presence (particularly where markets grow rapidly), avoidance of tariff and non-tariff barriers, integration of operations in different locations, economies of scale and differences in taxation. Foreign direct investment is superior to loans as a way to receive foreign capital. Funds are often invested in longer-term projects and managed by experts. The project debt is serviced only to the extent that profit is made, which is not the feature of foreign loans.

There are three main types of TNC activities. They involve investments which are: import-substituting, resource-based and rationalized (Dunning, 1988, p. 54). *Import-substituting* investments seek new markets, but they replace trade. They are influenced by the relative size and growth of foreign market in which the investment is made, the relative costs of supplying that market through imports or local production, as well as the relative advantage of engaging in direct local production or licensing.

Resource-based investments are based on the availability and cost of both natural resources and labour. As the products of such investments are often exported abroad, the economic climate in foreign markets, transport costs and barriers to trade influence the attractiveness of such investments to TNCs.

Rationalized investments are seeking efficiency. They are, just like resource-based investments, complementary to trade. Their attractiveness lies in cost considerations. They are influenced by the ease with which intermediate or final products linked to economies of scale and specialization can be traded on the international market. This is the case with the United States, which lost competitiveness as a site for labour-intensive production and where enterprises from this part of industry locate abroad.

Transnational corporations

Foreign direct investment is often the result of decisions by TNCs. Therefore, foreign direct investment may be a relatively good proxy for the investment activities of TNCs (keeping in mind that TNCs may control operations abroad by simply giving licences, which is an alternative choice).

Any enterprise which owns or controls production of goods and/or services abroad may be called a TNC. Large companies are in most cases TNCs. They do not have a direct and complete responsibility to any government, but rather to their own spirit. Chauvinism is alien to the international firm, for its business decisions are not likely to be based on either ideological or nationalistic grounds (Rubin, 1970, p. 183). The most crucial determinants of foreign direct investments are the relative difference in returns and profit maximization in the long run, as well as market presence on the one hand, and availability of resources, expectations of growth in demand and political stability on the other. They may be more important than a country's participation in a common market.

Other reasons for foreign direct investment instead of, or together with, exporting, include: taking advantage of the host country's financial incentives (subsidies, taxes); tariff protection; public purchases; market pre-emption; increase in market power; as well as empire-building ambitions. Also, some goods or services must be adjusted in order to meet local needs and this may be done in a cheaper way by locating at least a part of production near the place of consumption.

Most of the TNCs originate in countries with decentralized political systems – such as the United States, Britain and The Netherlands. In these countries, the TNCs and the state foster relations of complementarity. The TNCs do not usually originate in centralized states like France or Italy, for the state does not want to share power with any enterprise.

If producers and government in a big country, A, make a credible threat to close its market to exporters from a small country, B, then one of the options for country B is to establish 'fifth column' production in country A. This would save country B's market share on country A's market. If overheads are covered in country B's home market, then its firm in country A may sell on a marginal-cost basis (Franko, 1977, p. 65). Many European and Japanese TNCs have concentrated on breaking into the United States' market. Earning a profit has taken second place, at least in the short run. A similar observation can be made for a run of the non-EC TNCs to settle in the Community prior to the full implementation of the 1992 Programme.

Trade (export) and development of foreign markets may induce a TNC to embark upon foreign direct investment. There is, however, contrasting evidence. On the one hand, foreign direct investment may forestall trade, if it is necessary for exploitation, production and export of raw materials. On the other hand, relative differences in the costs of labour between alternative locations do not play a prominent role for modern technologies. The share of the costs of labour is minor in relation to capital. The success of Japanese firms in reducing their labour content is one of the factors contributing to the expansion of their direct investment into relatively high-labour-cost areas such as North America and the United Kingdom (UNCTC, 1988, p. 56). Despite the advantage of cheaper labour in Italy, this advantage was met by labour outflow rather than capital inflow in the 1960s.

TNCs primarily tend to follow opportunities for profit. Size and growth of market (instead of mere differences in the cost of labour) seem to be the most prominent drivers of transnationalization of business. That is the reason why roughly 80 per cent of activities of TNCs is in developed market economies. Other reasons include: availability of resources (but this depends on the attitudes of target countries towards TNCs); efficiency in production; diversification; available technology; and exchange of threat (what Exxon does in Europe, Shell will try to do in the United States). A black-and-white expectation with respect to the location of activities due to capital mobility within a common market based on the neo-classical theory does not exist. TNCs that use complex technologies do not worry about tariffs and quotas. They worry about domestic regulations – such as environmental standards. A bit of government intervention may significantly influence the location of TNCs with implications for the future.

Foreign direct investment is part of a firm's function of developing long-term, profit-making opportunities abroad. Before embarking upon foreign direct investment, an enterprise compares alternative locations at home and at various places abroad. If investing abroad seems to be a more promising business decision, then the enterprise has to make sure that it possesses, or can obtain, certain income-generating, firm-specific advantages in production or transaction that can make it operate profitably in foreign environment (Dunning, 1988, p. 42). Those advantages include exclusive or privileged access to specific assets and better organizing capabilities for both production and transactions.

Local firms have several advantages over foreign ones. First, they have a better knowledge of local consumer and supplier markets. Second, they do not have costs of operating at a distance. Third, they often receive favours from the government. Fourth, they do not operate in a different, often hostile, language, tax, legal, exchange rate, social and political environment. Last but not least, TNCs may sometimes have some disadvantages in the eyes of certain local politicans in foreign markets, because they are foreign and, often, large.

A difficulty for foreign firms may be that they have to attract key managers and technicians from the headquarters to a foreign subsidiary. This may ask for both higher wages of such personnel and higher allowances for their families. TNCs which extract and export natural resources are always at risk of becoming a target for nationalization. If a TNC wants to operate in such an environment, it must have or control better advantages (such as superior technology and management, well-known brand name and, especially important for services, access to markets and quality control) than the target country enterprises. Due to these facts, it does not come as a surprise that TNCs are more profitable and successful than the local competitors from the same industry.

While firm-specific, income-generating advantages are a necessary condition for foreign direct investment, they are not a sufficient condition. If trade were free, firms could simply use their advantages by exporting instead of producing abroad (UNCTC, 1988, p. 18). There exist various market imperfections that limit the size of the market for free trade and, hence, justify foreign direct investment. They include tariff and non-tariff barriers to trade, differences in factor prices, sunk costs and after-sales service. Therefore, an enterprise with a specific income-generating advantage considers a number of different possibilities and restraints at various foreign locations prior to settling abroad.

The *eclectic paradigm* (Dunning, 1988, pp. 42–5) explains that the production of goods and services of TNCs outside their national markets is an amalgam of three variables. First, to produce successfully abroad TNCs must have ownership-specific advantages (superior technology, access to markets, etc.) compared to firms in the host country where they are or intend to operate. Second, there should exist internalization opportunities. It must be in the interest of TNCs which possess ownership-specific advantages to transfer them accross national boundaries within their own organization, rather than selling the right to use those advantages to firms located in the country of (intended) production. Third, locational advantages refer to the gains of comparative or location-specific advantages of the target country. If an enterprise possesses only ownership-specific advantages, then it may use licensing in order to penetrate foreign markets. In the case that it has ownership-specific and internalization advantages, such an enterprise will use export as a way of entering foreign markets. Only in the case where an enterprise is able to take simultaneous advantage of ownership, internalization and locational advantages, will it employ foreign direct investment as a means of operating in foreign markets.

Transnational enterprises invest abroad because they foresee gains. Their greatest power stems from their high international mobility to enter and exit from an industry. (The impact of such high capital mobility on a host country's monetary policy will be analysed in the chapter on economic union, section on monetary policy.) TNCs have the possibility of acting as capital arbitrageurs. They may borrow in countries where the rate of interest is lowest and invest in countries where they expect the highest returns. TNCs may spread overheads and risk over their subsidiaries. These enterprises also extend control over international markets. If a subsidiary is producing final goods, then other parts of a TNC may increase export components to this subsidiary. Data for several parent countries show that TNCs account for well over three-quarters of their home countries' trade flows. Intra-firm transactions account for between 30 and 40 per cent of these home countries' trade (UNCTC, 1988, p. 89). This indicates that the TNCs are not only large international producers, but also important marketing channels. They prefer international sourcing of components. This makes them able to organize efficiency of operations on a global scale.

As for the size of the firms which invest abroad, small and medium-sized firms are just as likely to invest abroad as large ones. Size operates as a threshold. A certain minimum size is required for a firm to become a TNC, but once it has jumped the initial barriers to foreign production, size has no effect on the fraction of a firm's output that is produced abroad (UNCTC, 1988, p. 35).

Many TNCs create sophisticated and complicated technologies. They avoid the transfer of this technology through the market in order to prevent competitors from copying it. The longer the technology gap with imitators, the longer the TNC can behave like a monopolist; a TNC therefore usually transfers technology only among its subsidiaries.

The relations between TNCs and host countries may sometimes be quite tense. Mining is an industry which requires a huge amount of investment before commercial exploitation. Various countries often compete and offer incentives for foreign direct investment. At this stage a TNC has the strongest bargaining position. When the TNCs are established in host countries they may react quite differently to changes in, for example, the host country's tax system or interest rates than domestic firms which may not be able to withdraw from the home market. TNCs may therefore become a threat to the host country's national economic policies. To counter this danger, the common market member countries should coordinate and harmonize their policies towards the TNCs. However, a large amount of investment may keep a TNC as a hostage of the host country. These sunk costs may represent a barrier to exit from the host country, and it is at this point that the host country government may show the TNC who is the lord. The host governments may re-negotiate the deals with the TNCs. This kind of danger may induce the TNCs to borrow on the host country financial market only and transfer from elsewhere only the technical and managerial expertise. A possible closure of a subsidiary in the host country would cost some local jobs in both the subsidiary and supplying firms. The affected workers and their families may lobby in favour of the TNC's interest. TNCs may find allies among industries in the host country. As long as TNCs purchase from them, both subsidiaries and local firms may work together in lobbying the government for protection, subsidies, tax breaks and procurement agreements.

Mineral resources, including oil, are as a rule property of the state in many LDCs. It is the government which negotiates terms of entry with TNCs. In the case of manufacturing, the role of the government is somehow less pronounced. In this case, the government usually sets general terms of entry, performance and exit from an industry. While LDCs, as a rule regulate with greater scrutiny conditions for entry of TNCs, industrialised countries control their exit and possible consequences on the loss of jobs.

The greatest leverage on the TNCs may be exercised by resource-rich and prosperous countries like Canada. The experience of this country is one of the most obvious examples of control of TNCs. Before taking a look at the experience of this country, attention will be devoted to the international principles which attempt to govern the treatment of foreign companies.

The basis of the Organization for Economic Cooperation and Development (OECD) Declaration on International Investment and Multinational Enterprises (1976) is the principle of national treatment of foreign companies. This principle means that, provided that national security is not jeopardized, foreign companies have the same rights and obligations as domestic companies in similar situations. It does not equalize foreign suppliers on the importing country market with each other which does most favoured nation clause, but rather, it refers to the treatment of foreign suppliers with domestic ones.

Both Canada and the United States are signatories to the OECD Declaration. A few years before this Declaration was delivered, Canada established in 1973 the Foreign Investment Review Agency (FIRA) to survey inward foreign direct investment. This move was a reaction to a relatively large foreign ownership share of Canadian industry. One may argue that much of the foreign ownership of the host country industry may be attributed to the height of the host country's tariffs, taxes, subsidies and other incentives. TNCs overcome tariff obstacles by setting up in the host country's market. The intention of the FIRA was not to stop foreign investment in Canada, but rather to allow foreign investment only if it resulted in beneficial effects to Canada. The criterion upon which the FIRA evaluated both the takeovers of existing Canadian firms and new businesses included expanded exports, use of Canadian resources, increase in investment, employment and productivity, as well as compatibility with the national industrial and other economic policies. The local content condition may be criticized on the grounds that it distorts investors' input choices, stimulates sub-optimal input mixes and potentially increases prices.

The rejection rate by the FIRA of 20 per cent was an important barrier for possible investors and was high compared to rates of some 1 per cent for other countries which used a similar screening process (Lipsey, 1985, p. 101). This made many firms withdraw their applications to avoid uncertain and costly application procedures while other firms which might be potential investors have not even applied. At the beginning of the 1980s the rejection rate by the FIRA was lowered. The Conservative government transformed the FIRA from a nationalistic authority aimed at increasing Canadian ownership in domestic industry into an organization for the attraction of foreign investment and renamed it Investment Canada in 1984. The fear of too much foreign capital had given way to the fear of too little (Lipsey and Smith, 1986, p. 53).

If the TNCs produce final goods in host countries and if they import raw materials and components from countries which are outside the common market instead of purchasing them from the local suppliers, then they may jeopardize the process of integration within a common market. This area may increase its external dependence, instead of reducing it. When the member countries of a common market compete among themselves for foreign investments in absence of an agreed industrial policy, then one cannot expect that the operation of the TNCs will result in an optimal allocation of resources within a common market or other types of international economic integration (Robson, 1983, p. 32).

One of the host countries' arguments against the TNCs is their internal (transfer) pricing system. TNCs internalize intermediate product markets, and prices in trade among different sister enterprises are arrived at by non-market means. By doing so, TNCs may shift profits out of countries with relatively high taxes to ones with the lowest corporate taxes. In order to shift profits, vertical TNCs may overprice imports of inputs and underprice exports. This pricing system may distort flows of trade. One way to control the operation of the TNCs in the host country may be to request that the internal pricing system between the parent and subsidiary should be as if they were two separate companies. The enforcement of this request may be seriously endangered if there are no substitutes for these internally-traded goods. Another solution may be to harmonize fiscal systems in countries where TNCs operate.

Internalization of intermediate goods or services markets within TNCs is not always done with the primary aim of avoiding taxes on corporate profits. If a TNC wants to keep high quality in the supply of its goods and services, then local or out-of-the-firm suppliers may not necessarily be able to keep the high standards requested by the TNC. Hence, the reason for keeping production (and pricing) internal to the TNC. Still, fiddling with transfer pricing is more widespread in LDCs than in developed countries. The balance-of-payments position often drives LDCs to control flows of foreign exchange. Strict controls may induce TNCs to manipulate with transfer pricing in order to protect and/or increase profits. LDCs are not well equipped to first detect and, second, control manipulations with internal prices of TNCs.

Transnational corporations treat their business in different countries as a single-market operation, and their financial service is therefore always centralized. It represents the backbone of overall efficiency. This is most pronounced in the case where the ownership-specific advantages of a TNC are generating high returns. Other operations – such as employment, wage and labour relations – are always decentralized within the TNCs. Labour markets are local and often highly regulated, so decentralization of these issues is the optimal policy for the TNCs.

Free capital mobility can prevent a small country from pursuing an independent monetary policy; hence the decisions of TNCs to expand or reduce investments may not coincide with the host country's priorities. If the owner of funds has not moved to the host country, then it is likely that the owner will want to transfer profits out of the country of investment. Between half and three-quarters of net investment abroad by Britain is composed of profits by overseas subsidiaries which are not remitted to Britain (Mayes, 1985, p. 140).

It is argued that TNCs invest most often in fast-growing industries like electronics and pharmaceutical industries. In this way these industries fall into foreign hands. Foreigners may thus hit the host country and interfere with sovereignty. An example is when the United States introduced a ban on the export of technology for the gas pipeline from the Soviet Union to western Europe in the early 1980s. Many subsidiaries of United States firms in western Europe were hit by this decision. It is much harder for a host country to hit the parent country of a TNC through a subsidiary.

As noted earlier, modern technologies complicate the employment impact of foreign direct investment. Modern technologies substitute capital for labour. A 'greenfield' entry on a new site adds to employment in the host country if it does not put out of business domestic competitors. A takeover of an existing firm does not necessarily increase employment and it may reduce it if this firm rationalizes the existing activity (Buckley and Artisien, 1988, p. 212). A subsidiary may start as a unit for marketing the final good. If it develops further, it may become a product specialist which may increase employment (direct and indirect) of a certain type of labour.

Takeovers are most attractive to enterprises which have wide international marketing networks, attractive to sellers who are interested to penetrate the widest possible market. This is even enhanced if the acquiring (or merged) enterprise is not linked to any industrial grouping which helps to avoid conflicting interests. That is the reason why the Anglo-Saxon enterprises dominate cross-border mergers and acquisitions in Europe.

A potential case against TNCs is that they rely heavily on the R&D of their parent companies and/or head offices which may charge this in a way which may not be controlled by the host country. This can make both subsidiaries and host countries too dependent on foreign R&D and technology. Is this the case in reality? Some empirical research has shown that subsidiaries had more R&D in Canada than other Canadian firms (Rugman, 1985, p. 486). European elevator companies keep their R&D for elevators for tall buildings in the United States because this country has many tall buildings. A small country often does not have the available resources for basic research in relation to a big country. By imports of technology a small country may have access to the results of a much larger volume of R&D wherever carried out. It can be complementary to R&D already undertaken domestically.

There is a tendency to decentralize R&D within the TNCs. One reason is the reduction in costs of research, while the other is the exploitation of host countries' incentives to research (subsidies, tax brakes). The basic research may remain in the headquarters while subsidiaries do applied development according to the local demand. It is often forgotten that many companies which create knowledge are not always either TNCs or big. The only condition for their creation is that they operate in a competitive environment which is often lacking in small developing countries.

A TNC may introduce a serious threat to the market structure of a host country. It may monopolize the whole domestic market and, by predatory pricing, prevent the entry to the industry of potential host country firms. They may introduce technologies which use relatively more resources in short supply (capital) and relatively less of the factor which is abundant (labour) in the host country. TNCs may offer relatively higher wages to qualified domestic labour in order to attract it. This labour may flow from the host country's firms into TNCs, but this may be due, in part, to the fact that the home firms do not properly value a resource which is in short supply. Vacancies in the domestic firms may be filled by less-trained labour, which may have an adverse effect on the growth of production in the host country. Although technologies used by the TNCs in the host countries may not be the most up-to-date, they may be better than the ones which are currently in use in LDCs.

The policies of the TNCs may have an adverse impact on the allocation of resources in the host country under the condition that the existence and operation of the TNCs have a significant proportion of production, employment, purchases and sales in the host country. LDCs may thus be more influenced in certain segments of industry by the operation of the TNCs than developed countries. This state of affairs asks for a coordinated approach towards the TNCs by common markets and other types of international economic integration of LDCs. It also asks for the establishment and enforcement of a common industrial policy. This may be supported by the regional development banks and/or by joint planning.

This analysis suggests that the TNCs do not pay much attention to the overall needs of the host countries. It is true. However, the fulfilment of the social needs of the host country is not their role. Nobody forces the host countries to accept TNCs. The fulfilment of these social demands is the role of the host country's government that taxes TNCs in order to internalize their externalities. In the situation with unemployed resources, inflation, foreign and budgetary debt, famine and underdevelopment, any coin of hard currency is precious. Any attempt of the host government to restrict the entry and operation of TNCs may dry up this thin trickle of capital inflow. Host countries sometimes behave (or used to do so) as if they want foreign direct investment but do not want the foreign investor. Unfortunately, LDCs are those that need these investments most. Economic adjustment in LDCs is facilitated in the presence of TNCs. Those corporations have know-how, ability to raise funds and widespread marketing channels which help in export growth.

Despite the relative academic hostility, public sensitivity, polemics against foreigners which export home resources and some official ado about the operation of the TNCs, the situation in day-to-day life changes. Many developing and eastern European countries and the USSR welcome TNCs. Apart from some screening, these countries provide the TNCs with various incentives, which include provision of infrastructure, subsidized loans, tax exemptions, subsidies for exports, possibilities for complete ownership and exemptions from duties. But those countries have to keep in mind that they compete with other possible locations. A growing market in the EC (due to the 1992 Programme) and a wide market in the United States are still the most preferred locations for TNCs. If other regions want to attract TNCs, they have to keep in mind that they must have something attractive that TNCs cannot find in Europe, North America and, possibly, Japan.

Apart from these drawbacks, a host country finds significant gains and invites the operation of the TNCs. These corporations may bring in technology which is superior to the existing domestic technology which creates: production capacity in the host country; jobs; tax proceeds; savings in unemployment benefits; and may create exports. TNCs enter into growth industries and provide technological expertise which would otherwise be missing. Some TNCs produce brand-name drinks or cigarettes. These are the goods whose consumption is burdened by excise duties. The governments may need these proceeds and become an ally of the TNCs. If there are some barriers to entry, like huge initial capital investment in an industry, then TNCs may provide this advantage. When the host country's policy is to promote exports or substitute imports, then TNCs may fill part of this role. On the one hand, carrots to TNCs may be tax holidays, subsidies, tariff protection and government purchases. On the other hand, sticks include performance criteria, exports, employment, withholding taxes, as well as repatriation and re-investment rules.

European Community

The provisions of the Treaty of Rome, Article 67, commit the member countries to abolish all restrictions on the movement of capital which belongs to the residents of the EC. Article 68 requires that the national rules governing the capital and money markets must be implemented in a non-discriminatory manner. According to Article 71, any new restrictions should be avoided. A safeguard clause is contained in Article 73. If movements of capital lead to disturbances in the capital market in any member country the Commission shall, after consultation, authorize that state to take protective measures. Article 106 removes the exchange control for the transactions in goods, services and factors which are permitted to move under the Treaty, while Article 109 allows a member country to take the necessary protective measures in the case of a sudden crisis in the balance of payments.

The establishment of the EC, as Mark 1 in the integration process, and its relative dynamism provoked the expansion of the United States' TNCs to invest in this region during the 1960s and 1970s. The implementation of the EC 1992 Programme, as Mark 2 in the integration process, and the completion of the internal market are likely to increase investment of the Japanese TNCs in the EC. However, the actual involvement will depend, in part, on the evolution of the EC's tariff and non-tariff barriers.

Due to the initial fear of foreign TNCs that the EC may create 'Fortress Europe', they rushed to establish themselves in the EC market before discrimination takes place. The EC firms became overvalued to the extent that other locations, most notably in the United States, became more attractive. Still, the EC is an interesting location for investment, so foreign TNCs seek to enter into strategic alliances with the EC firms.

Mark 2 is expected to produce investment-creation effects in the EC and increase competitivenes of the EC firms. While Mark 1 in the integration process eliminated tariffs on internal trade (among other things), Mark 2 aims at eliminating most non-tariff bariers on internal trade, which should increase business efficiency (rationalized investments). This will requre some adjustment in the internal EC production. The rationale for the existence of 'tariff factories' will be removed. Threfore, it may be expected that investment in the business which avoids internal EC barriers will be significantly reduced or eliminated altogether. This will provoke an investment reduction effect. In any case, Mark 2 is expected to increase the operation, cooperative agreements, strategic alliances and investment of the internal EC TNCs. They will more and more look like the ones in the United States which take full advantage of the economies of scale.

The impact of the creation of the EC on the attraction of foreign direct investment from the United States was in the centre of the early studies of the relation between integration (or, as it was called, tariff discrimination introduced by the EC and EFTA) and foreign direct investment. The expectation was that the allocation of foreign direct investment would be influenced by integration. In particular, that the establishment of the EC would increase TNCs to locate in this region. Scaperlanda (1967, p. 26) found, in the examination of the United States investment trend in Europe between 1951 and 1964, that the formation of the EC has not attracted a large share of investment from the United States. Since 1958, the value of the United States' foreign direct investment in the EC was 3.5 billion dollars, while in non-EC Europe, it was 4.0 billion dollars. Factors like familiarity with the country in which the investment is to be located, differences in the application of technology and the financial liquidity to fund foreign investment, outweighed the influence of the creation of the EC on the pattern of investment.

Instead of calculating the trend in foreign direct investment for the whole period 1951–64 and merging both 'before' and 'after' the EC effects (as did Scaperlanda) and masking investment shifts, rather than revealing them, Wallis (1968) broke the period of analysis into two sub-periods. The share of the United States' foreign direct investment to the EC moved along a continuous and increasing path in the period 1951–64 with a kink in 1958. Before 1958, the EC share increased by 0.73 per cent a year, while after 1958, the average annual increase was 2.70 per cent.

D'Arge (1969, 1971a, 1971b) tried to determine the impact of European integration on the United States' direct investment in the EC and EFTA. The effect of the formation of a trading bloc on foreign direct investment may be along the following three lines. It may be a once-and-for-all (intercept) shift in trend, a gradual increase in trend (slope shift), or a combination of the two. The data showed that in the case of EFTA, there was a positive intercept shift (once-and-for-all effect), while in the period following the creation of the EC, there was a combination of shifts in both slope and intercept. Scaperlanda and Reiling (1971) suggested that European integration has not crucially influenced and changed United States' direct investment flows in this region. This was based on a similarity of trends in foreign direct investment between the EC and EFTA after 1959, although there was a presumption that the EC will have a greater effect than EFTA. Still, one thing has to be kept in mind here. At that time, the United Kingdom was the country which received the largest share of the United States' investment. It was also a member of the EFTA (not the EC). Therefore, early studies of the impact of integration on foreign direct investment do not show a clear picture with respect to the relation between the two. A clarification, however, came later on. Evidence was found that in the case of United States' direct investment in the EC, size and growth of market play an important role (Scaperlanda and Balough, 1983, p. 389).

The United Kingdom is a relatively attractive location for TNCs. It has a good industrial infrastructure, labour is skilled and relatively low paid, it belongs to the EC and the language spoken is English. The problem in the past was that the British were unable to combine those factors effectively in relation to most of the EC. The Japanese were inclined to invest in this country. However, they preferred to build new factories in rural areas, rather than to take over the existing factories. They also preferred takeovers to joint ventures. The advantages of the 'greenfield' entry is that previous managerial habits and labour relations are not inherited (Sharp and Shepherd, 1987, p. 60).

Modelling foreign direct investment is a formidable task. The results of various models much depend on the assumptions, so that the conclusions may be only tentative. Nevertheless, there is general support of the hypothesis that tariff discrimination or integration influence foreign direct investment. But this cannot be translated into a statment that an x per cent change in tariffs will induce a y per cent change in foreign direct investment. Therefore, strong policy recommendations on the basis of such models are reckless (Lunn, 1980, p. 99).

Recent studies report that the net effect of international economic integration has been to increase both EC and non-EC investment in the EC member countries. A customs union has stimulated offshore countries to invest in the EC, and the elimination of tariffs on internal EC trade has given an impetus to non-EC owned firms to invest in the EC. The elimination of import duties (save for non-tariff barriers) on internal EC trade has encouraged those firms to distribute their business in the most efficient way (Dunning and Robson, 1987, p. 113).

The net foreign direct investment flow in the period 1979–83, as reported by Sleuwaegen (1987, p. 264), from the EC member countries to other EC partner countries was 16.3 billion ECUs, with France as the most significant single destination. These flows exceeded the United States' direct investment in the EC, which was 11.4 billion ECUs, and the relatively unimportant investment of Japan in the EC which was only 1.4 billion ECUs. The significant point is that the off-shore investors favoured the United Kingdom as their location. This may, however, be a problem of identification. The issue for an endless debate, is how and up to what extent are these investment flows due to integration of countries, rather than other independent factors. Diversity of views expressed in the debate on the effect of European integration on foreign direct investment were surveyed by Yannopoulos (1990).

Table 3.2 summarizes foreign direct investment flows based on the receiving country information in the EC in the 1984–88 period. It is obvious that integration in the EC, during the period of observation, mattered, at least to an extent, for intra-EC foreign direct investment in the case of countries like France, the United Kingdom, Spain, Italy and Benelux. The first choice for offshore countries as the location for foreign direct investment in the EC was the United Kingdom, followed by France and Italy. The overall picture for the EC, however, is different. Integration did not matter for foreign direct investment as much as the neo-classical theory would predict. Due to market imperfections, certain locations in the EC were preferred to others. In many cases, intra-EC investments were so small that they were not measured even in hundreds of millions of ECUs. In fact, the United States (as a non-EC location) was preferred as a place for British, Dutch and German investors. During the period of observation, the British invested 366 per cent more in the United States than in the EC, while the same preference of the Dutch was 172 per cent and of the Germans was 167 per cent. This reveals that integration is only one segment that influences foreign direct investment. Other factors, like rates of exchange, may play an even greater role, at least for some time, as cases for the United Kingdom, The Netherlands and FR Germany *versus* the United States show. Finalizing discussion of Table 3.2, it is interesting to note the importance of Spain as a location for foreign direct investment in the EC. As a new member country of the EC, Spain attracted a noteworthy part of foreign direct investment, in particular in per capita terms, even though the period of observation for this country was two years shorter than for the rest of the EC.

The Single Market Programme of the EC by the end of 1992 will unavoidably prompt TNCs to rationalize their operations in the EC. It is likely that they will try to reduce costs of manufacturing and supporting services in such a way that will force the governments to consider monetary, fiscal, industrial, regional, social and other policy aspects of the single EC market. The absence of any reference to TNCs in the official reports generated by the Single European Act, such as Emerson *et al.* (1988) and the Cecchini Report (1988), comes as a surprising omission. The assumption in those reports seems to be that international specialization and trade is carried out by firms whose operational facilities are confined to a single country. Growth and predominance of TNCs in most areas of economic activity make such kind of analysis inappropriate (Panić, 1991, p. 204).

Control of mergers in the EC is quite strict. Investigation of a monopoly may begin when the market share of the company is above 40 per cent. Enterprises therefore find foreign direct investment the best way to integrate in the EC. A few mergers, like Agfa-Gevaert and Dunlop-Pirelli, were not profitable for reasons which included antitrust, organizational and cultural barriers. Nevertheless, the EC firms developed mutual cooperation in the production of knowledge, while their cooperation with the United States' firms was more geared towards commercialization and production of goods (Mytelka and Delapierre, 1987, pp. 240–1).

The intended transition of the eastern European countries towards a kind of market economy may offer an attraction to TNCs to locate, at least a part, of production in such a large market. This is the only region in the world where international business has not yet expanded on a large scale. Therefore, TNCs may wish to locate there instead of some regions in the EC. Mediterranean member countries of the EC may feel neglected because of market reforms in eastern Europe. However, those fears may be exaggerated, and Mediterranean regions of the EC should not worry, at least not in the medium term. The economies of eastern European countries

Table 3.2 Cumulative foreign direct investment flows among the member countries of the EC, 1984–88 (ECU billion)

From \ To	FRG	Fr.	Ita.	Nl.	B/L	UK	Dk.	Irel.	Sp.*	Por.	Gr.	EC(12)	US	Japan	Total
1 FR Germany	—	1.7	0.8	0.9	1.0	0.1	0.1	n.a.	1.8	0.1	0.0	6.4	10.7	0.3	17.4
2 France	0.8	—	1.9	0.2	2.7	2.4	0.0	n.a.	1.2	0.1	0.0	9.3	6.1	0.0	15.4
3 Italy	0.2	1.8	—	0.0	0.2	0.3	0.0	n.a.	0.5	0.0	0.0	2.1	0.1	n.a.	2.2
4 Neth.	1.4	1.9	1.9	—	0.7	3.7	0.0	n.a.	1.1	0.0	0.0	10.7	18.5	0.4	29.6
5 Bel./Lux.	-0.2	1.4	0.5	1.0	—	1.3	0.0	n.a.	0.4	0.0	0.0	4.4	1.7	n.a.	6.1
6 UK	0.9	3.2	2.0	3.6	1.4	—	0.0	n.a.	3.3	0.7	0.0	15.1	55.3	0.2	70.6
7 Denmark	0.1	0.1	0.0	0.0	0.0	0.2	—	n.a.	0.0	0.0	0.0	0.4	n.a.	n.a.	0.4
8 Ireland	0.0	0.0	0.0	0.1	0.0	0.0	n.a.	—	0.0	0.0	0.0	0.1	n.a.	n.a.	0.1
9 Spain	0.0	0.1	0.0	0.0	0.0	0.0	0.0	n.a.	—	0.1	0.0	0.2	n.a.	n.a.	0.2
10 Portugal	0.0	0.0	0.0	0.0	0.0	n.a.	n.a.	n.a.	0.0	—	0.0	0.0	n.a.	n.a.	0.0
11 Greece	0.0	0.0	0.0	0.0	0.0	n.a.	n.a.	n.a.	0.0	0.0	—	0.0	n.a.	n.a.	0.0
EC(12)	3.3	10.3	7.2	6.0	6.2	8.6	0.0	n.a.	8.5	1.3	n.a.	51.4 (48.7)	93.8	0.9	143.4 (142.0)
US	-2.1	3.1	2.6	-1.0	1.0	4.2	0.0	n.a.	0.9	0.2	n.a.	n.a.			
Japan	0.9	0.7	0.1	0.3	0.4	1.3	0.0	n.a.	0.2	0.0	n.a.	n.a.			
Total	2.1	14.1	9.9	5.3	7.6	14.1	0.0	n.a.	9.6	1.5	n.a.	n.a.			

* 1986–8

Source: Own calculations based on the Eurostat database.

have such distortions that it will take them a long time to restructure. Economic reforms, even if successful, may take many years to increase significantly the purchasing power of their citizens.

The Mediterranean region of the EC still has enormous advantages over eastern Europe. Southern EC countries have direct access to the growing single EC market, with hundreds of millions of consumers whose wealth is growing. Also, Mediterranean members of the EC have hard currencies and liberal laws on the operation of TNCs. Those are the features that eastern Europe will not have in the distant future.

Another advantage of the Mediterranean region of the EC is found in the possible economies of scale. This region of the EC is characterized by a lot of small and medium-sized companies. Those firms have a chance to grow efficiently after the establishment of the single EC market and take advantage of economies of scale. Large European firms have already taken most advantages which accrue from economies of scale, so small and medium-sized firms, and countries in which they prevail in the economic structure, potentially have a greater scope for gain. According to this scenario, the greatest possible gainer may be Spain. Therefore, the situation observed in Table 3.2 may continue to prevail in the future.

The European Community member states from the Mediterranean region may wish to attract non-EC foreign direct investment. As a relatively low-cost gateway to the single EC market, TNCs from third countries may chose southern EC member states as potentially attractive locations. TNCs from newly industrializing countries may wish to invest in the EC in order to be present in a growing and affluent market, as well as to have access to new technology. A similar case can be found in increasing foreign direct investment of the United States' and European TNCs in Japan. They want to be in touch with research-intensive industries and locations of new technology (UNCTC, 1989, p. 16). As for the TNCs from Eastern Europe located in the EC, they can, almost exclusively, be expected in trade-supporting services. TNCs from Eastern Europe will not have in the near future, in most cases, either technological or managerial or financial capacity to enter the EC on a large scale in another way.

CONCLUSION

Factor movements have their costs and benefits. If they are desirable, they should be stimulated. If not, then they should be taxed. Simultaneous inflows and outflows of a factor in countries which form a common market is possible. Firms tend to penetrate each other's markets, so sector-specific factors follow these patterns of firms' decisions. Another reason for this mobility is that firms want to reduce uncertainty. They do not want to keep all their eggs in one basket, hence, if they have opportunities for profitable operation, they go abroad.

If countries in a common market are at a similar level of economic development, then trade can substitute movements of factors. The more similar the level of development and the level of labour productivity, the lower may be the incentives for migration.

The loss of the international competitive position of the EC in relation to the United States, Japan and the newly industrialized countries (in several lines of production) in the 1970s and early 1980s, has increased both interest in and the need for the strengthening of the Community TNCs. These TNCs are the key means for the improvement of the international competitiveness of the EC. Ambitious EC research programmes, like the ESPRIT whose funds well exceed similar programmes in the United States and Japan, can help the EC first to catch up and later to improve its position *vis-à-vis* its major international competitors.

The incomplete internal EC market is the major cause of a sub-optimal production structure in the EC. All economic agents, including the TNCs, behave like welfare-maximizing units in the long-term, subject to the given conditions. These agents should not be criticized for their actions. The completion of the internal EC market, which will include the removal of the non-tariff barriers and harmonization of fiscal and industrial policies, will help the rationalization of production in the EC. This will increase both the size and the growth of the market, which may, in turn, increase investment expenditure.

Given the existing international inequalities and market imperfections, international factor movements are of great importance in international economic integration. The problem is that free capital mobility may increase the cost of international integration, as capital moves from low- to high-income countries, with a few possible exceptions. The efficiency gains from the creation of a common market have to compensate for the costs of polarization of economic activities. Industrial, regional and social policies should be the buffers against all unacceptable costs. The following chapter presents integration of economic policies in an economic union.

4 Economic union

INTRODUCTION

None of the types of international economic integration may exist in their pure form. A customs union does not only deal with the elimination of tariffs and quotas and the introduction of the common external tariff, but also with industrial policy and specialization. It may also deal with the attitude towards foreign direct investment from partner countries, as well as from outsiders. Free mobility of labour in a common market does not only require the elimination of discrimination of labour from partner countries, but also some degree of harmonization of social policy (social security, unemployment benefits, pension funds, vocational training). Without harmonization of these issues, distortions may be created which may induce labour to move in response to other signals than purely to its relative abundance/scarcity and returns. The buffer against unacceptable costs which accrue from the free migration of labour and flow of capital can be found in regional policy, therefore common markets may have some elements of economic unions. The basic argument in favour of an economic union is found in its potential to increase the efficiency in the allocation of resources in relation to a common market.

The creation of an economic union can be defended by the same arguments which are used in favour of the creation, implementation and protection of a single economic policy in a country which has different regions. It can also be attacked by the same arguments that say that one policy for different regions does not make sense (often heard in Canada). This chapter starts with a section on monetary policy because this is where the impact of international economic integration is the quickest and most obvious. It is followed by a section on fiscal policy, which is necessary for the proper operation of an economic union. Industrial, regional and social policies are crucial for the survival of an economic union. While industrial policy is directed towards the creation of new wealth, regional and social policies are turned towards the distribution of already created wealth. In the final section attention is devoted to the experiences of the Council for Mutual Economic Assistance (CMEA) and the Association of South-East Asian Nations (ASEAN).

MONETARY POLICY

Introduction

The integration of monetary policies of countries within a union is necessary not only for the stability of rates of exchange, prices and balances of payments, but also for the protection of already achieved levels of integration, as well as the stimulation of integration in the future. Within a monetary union it should be as easy, for example, for a Frenchman to pay a German within Europe as it is for a Welshman to pay an Englishman within the United Kingdom (Meade, 1973, p.162).

Relatively small countries may have an incentive to integrate in the monetary field in order to avoid the monetary domination of larger countries. The joint money may overcome the disadvantage (vulnerability on external monetary shocks) of atomized monies and may become a rival to the monies of larger countries. A common money of integrated countries may become an outward symbol, but it is not a necessary condition for a successful monetary union.

A monetary system among countries should be distinguished from a monetary union. Countries in a monetary system link their currencies together and act as a single unit in relation to third currencies. A monetary union among countries is an ambitious enterprise. It exists if there is either a single money (*de jure* monetary union) or an irrevocable fixity among the rates of exchange of the participating countries together with factor mobility (*de facto* monetary union). This prevents any change in the rates of exchange as an indirect means of tariff protection or stimulation of exports. It means that the member countries should have recourse to the capital market in order to find funds to cover their budget deficit.

A monetary union requires convertibility (at least internal) of the participating countries' currencies; centralization of monetary policy; a single central bank or a system of central banks which control stabilization policies; unified performance on the international financial markets; capital market integration; identical rates of inflation; harmonization of fiscal systems; replacement of balance-of-payments disequilibria with regional imbalances; similar levels of economic development or a well-endowed fund for transfers to the less developed regions; continuous consultation and coordination of economic policies among the participating countries, as well as the adjustment of wages on the union level.

There may, also, be a pseudo exchange-rate union (Corden, 1972b). In this kind of union, member countries fix exchange rates of their currencies, as well as freely accept each other's monies. But since there is no pooling of foreign resesrves and no central monetary authority, this union is not stable. Since there is no mechanism to coordinate national policies, an individual member country may choose to absorb real resources from the union partners by running a balance-of-payments deficit with them. Also, such a country may change the effective exchange rates of other members by bringing a deficit in the union's balance-of-payments with the rest of the world. A full monetary union is not vulnerable to such instability. Foreign exchange rates are pooled and monetary policy is operated by a single monetary authority. In a pseudo exchange-rate union, there is imperfect coordination of national monetary policies, but in a full monetary union the problem is solved by policy centralization (Cobham, 1989, p. 204).

The presentation starts with the traditional single-criterion theory of monetary integration. A superior (that is, cost–benefit) model further develops consideration of monetary integration. Parallel currencies are presented before the examples from the real world monetary integration in the EC, CMEA and West African Monetary Union. Presentation of the EC monetary integration takes most of the space. It is done deliberately for two reasons. First, monetary integration is most developed in this region and its consideration may reveal various interesting issues and second, it is the most successful example of a monetary union.

Traditional model

Both flexible and fixed rates of exchange have their virtues and vices. The benefits of flexible rates of exchange include their free floating according to demand and supply. This improves the allocation of resources and in free societies removes the need for government interference. There is no need whatsoever for foreign currency reserves because balance-of-payments disequilibria are adjusted automatically. A country is free to pursue independently its national priorities with respect to inflation, employment and interest rate targets. Any possible mistake in economic policy may be straightened out by continuous and smooth changes in rates of exchange.

There are, of course, several cases against the free floating of exchange rates. The most serious case is that this rate of exchange divides the economies of different countries. The floating rates of exchange stimulate speculation, uncertainty and instability. All the alleged possibilities for smooth adjustment without the need for reserve changes were disproved during the 1970s. Any change in the rate of exchange will have an impact on home prices. Its impact will be swifter in the countries which have a relatively greater degree of openness. Overshooting is another problem. Although some changes in economic policy are only announced and not yet implemented, the floating rates of exchange move and overshoot their long-run equilibrium.

The objections to fixed rates of exchange include the following. They do not permit every country to pursue independently their own policy goals with respect to employment and inflation. Countries have to subordinate their monetary policy to the requirements of external balance. When the time comes for adjustment in the rate of exchange, it may be relatively large and disruptive in relation to the smooth and small changes in the exchange rate in the case of the free float. The system of fixed rates of exchange requires reserves of foreign currencies for intervention in the market in order to defend the fixed parity. These funds may be deprived from productive uses.

The arguments in favour of fixed rates of exchange are those which are used for the introduction of a single currency in a country. This system stimulates cooperation among countries as opposed to floating rates which encourage nationalism. The most important feature of fixed rates of exchange is that they bring stability, prices are less inflationary, the allocation of resources is improved because decisions about investment are not delivered exclusively on the basis of short-term market signals, uncertainty is reduced and trade flows are stabilized. All this stimulates economic integration among countries.

There is no general rule about which system of exchange rates is better. If a country has a balance-of-payments deficit, then it has to restore competitiveness. This can be done by a reduction in private and public consumption, so it requires cutting wages directly or devaluation, which cuts wages indirectly. But note that the choice of the system of exchange rate here does not play a role at all. Reductions in real income are necessary under either exchange rate system.

It is a formidable task to offer a definite conclusion about the 'correct' system of exchange rates. The above choices contrast costs against benefits of a particular system. When it comes to practice, the choice may often be between the costs of one system and the costs of the other. In this situation it comes as no surprise that economists cannot be unanimous. In a monetary union small countries may overcome their disadvantage which comes from their relatively small economic size, and create an area of economic stability, as well as reap the fruits of economic cooperation in an area where expectations may be made with a significant degree of accuracy.

Discussion about the exchange-rate regimes (fixed, floating or managed), throws light only on one side of a country's monetary policy in an international context. The other side deals with the domestic monetary policy. Linkages between the national money supply and rates of interest, as well as price levels, must be also considered. Otherwise, the debate may be in vain.

Monetary integration means in its highest form that everybody within a monetary union is free to use own currency for any kind of payments to partners. The minimum meaning of the monetary integration is absence of restrictions, while the maximum meaning requires the use of a single currency (Machlup, 1979, p. 23). Monetary integration may exist even without integration of markets for goods, and the integration of goods markets may exist without monetary integration. The former case is exemplified by countries in the West African Monetary Union which have a single currency and similar monetary policy to France as their former colonial ruler, but there is little real integration of markets for goods, services and factors among them. The latter case may be found in the EFTA where member countries have integrated their markets for manufactured goods, but there is no formal integration of the monetary policy among them.

The traditional, single-criterion model of monetary integration starts with the theory of optimum currency areas which was developed by Mundell (1961). Economic adjustment can be on international and national levels. On the international level, the basic issue of adjustment is whether the countries with trade deficits will accept inflation or deflation in their respective economies. On the national level, in countries which have a single currency but several regions, the pace of inflation is regulated by the desire of the central authorities to permit unemployment in the regions with deficit. If the aim is the achievement of a greater degree of employment and stable prices in a world where there is more than one currency area, then this case asks for floating exchange rates based on regional instead of national currencies. According to Mundell, a region is the optimum currency area. Factor mobility is the criterion which determines a region. Within the currency areas factors are mobile, while among them factors are immobile. Fluctuating rates of exchange are the adjustment mechanisms among various currency areas, while factor mobility is the equilibrating mechanism within them.

Factor mobility as the criterion for an optimum currency area ought to be considered carefully. The difficulty with this approach is that a region may be an economic unit, while the domain of a currency is an expression of national sovereignty which seldom coincides with a region. Also, factor mobility may change over time.

Mobility of capital is sensitive to the degree of economic activity and the outlook for economic prosperity. Labour and capital were flowing towards the Americas and Australia as the areas of development which needed them most in the nineteenth century. During the 'golden' 1960s labour and capital were flowing towards developed and relatively rich regions.

Labour is not a homogeneous factor. Its full mobility may exist only in relatively small geographic areas. The experience of the EC is proof. The flow of labour in the EC in the 1960s up to mid-1970s came mostly from workers from the Mediterranean countries which were not members of the EC (with the exception of Italy). This labour flow may not be taken as labour mobility within the EC.

Regions within a single country grow at different rates. The same holds for countries in a monetary union. These developments cause strain, which is greater the fewer the possibilities for adjustment like factor mobility and fiscal compensations. However, it still does not make a sensible case for southern Italy to have a separate currency, which creates a separate economy from the northern part of the country. The cost of such a monetary disintegration would be unacceptable.

The second major approach focuses attention on the degree of openness of a country (McKinnon, 1963). Commodities in a country may be distributed between tradeables and non-tradeables. The ratio between these goods in a country determines the degree of its openness to trade. As a rule, the smaller the country the greater the relative degree of its trade interaction with the surrounding countries. A high degree of openness embodies relatively high specialization of a country, and it may be taken as the criterion for the optimum currency area. When the tradeable goods represent a significant part of home consumption (unless most of the consumer's goods are imported), then by changing the exchange rates a country may hardly change real wages. Such a country (presumably small) is advised to enter into a monetary union, for it may not be an optimum currency area as a single unit (Corden, 1972b). The greater a country's openness the smaller the chances for the effective use of exchange rate as an instrument for economic stabilization.

Relatively small economies are advised to link their currency with the currency of their main trading partner. This is the case when the former colonies link their currency to that of their former colonial master. The second piece of advice to small economies which conduct a significant part of their trade among themselves is to link their currencies together. In the case of a single currency all financial dealings may be simpler. This is a part of the reason why the fifty federal states in the United States may not be able to separately issue and operate own currencies in an efficient way (although this may hurt the feelings of some Californians).

If small open economies operate near full employment, then internal fiscal measures are advised for the adjustment of the balance of payments. Fixed exchange rates would be more productive in this case than flexible rates for they would have a less damaging effect on prices. A variation in the exchange rate would have a small response in the change in the level of imports because of high dependency on imports. Therefore, a variation in the rate of exchange should be much higher than in the countries which are relatively less open.

An alteration in the exchange rate would have a direct and significant impact on income. Consumers and trade unions would request indexation of wages with the change in prices and exchange rate. If there exists money illusion – the impression that changes in nominal (money) wages are identical to changes in real income – then a change in the exchange rate may be an effective means for the adjustment of the balance of payments. However, money illusion is an unlikely long-term phenomenon. An alteration in the rate of exchange may not be employed for adjustment of the balance of payments independently of other instruments. Flexible rates of exchange may be an efficient means for adjustment of the balance of payments of relatively large economies which are linked by small trade relations.

The assumptions in this approach are that the equilibrium in the balance of payments is caused by microeconomic changes in demand and supply and, also, that prices in the outside world are stable. The argument about the relative stability of prices in the outside world may not be substantiated since the early 1970s. When the prices in the outside world are fluctuating, this is directly transmitted to the home prices through a fixed exchange rate. Openness of an economy may be the criterion for an optimum currency area if the outside world is more stable than the economic situation in a small, open economy. Fixed exchange rates may force small, open economies to pursue a more rigorous economic policy than under the fluctuating-exchange-rates regime which may permit a policy of monetary 'undiscipline'. This is so, because if money illusion does not exist, then the possibility for the alteration of the exchange rate as an adjustment instrument becomes almost useless.

The Benelux countries and Denmark participate in the European Monetary System (EMS). Other small European countries (for example, Switzerland, Austria, Norway, Finland) decided to stay out of the EMS and manage their exchange rates unilaterally, although these countries pay close attention to the developments in the EMS. The argument of openness fails to explain why these countries are still having national control over the exchange rate in spite of strong trade relations with the member countries of the EMS. Also, it fails to explain why relatively large countries like FR Germany and France opted for the EMS.

The third major contribution states that countries whose production is diversified do not have to change their terms of trade with foreign countries as often as the less diversified countries (Kenen, 1969). An external shock in the form of a reduction in foreign demand for a country's major export item may have a relatively smaller impact on the diversified country's employment than on a specialized country's economy and employment. Finally, links between home and foreign demand, as well as export and investment, are weaker in the diversified country than in a specialized one. Big and frequent changes of exchange rate are not necessary for a diversified country because of the overlap in the reduction and the increase in demand for various export goods. This overlap may keep the proceeds from imports on a relatively stable level. In conclusion, Kenen suggests that fixed rates of exchange are suitable for diversified countries. Diversification is the criterion. It helps the stabilization of home investment and adjustment to the external shocks. The United States may be the closest example. Countries with specialized economies and relatively low levels of diversification have a need to take part in currency areas with flexible rates of exchange. Such countries are more vulnerable to external shocks than are diversified countries. Examples may be found in Denmark, Iceland and New Zealand.

While McKinnon deals with internal shocks to an economy, Kenen considers external ones. Kenen's argument may be weakened in the situation where the reduction in foreign demand occurs during a general fall in demand during recession. This reduces total demand so that a country's diversification does not help much in the mitigation of the fall in the demand for exports.

Coordination of economic policies can be a criterion for a monetary union (Werner, 1970). Economic policies which are not coordinated among countries may be the major reason for the disturbance of the equilibrium of the balance of payments. Coordination of economic policies from a supranational centre requires political will on the part of the participating countries.

A criterion for monetary integration may be a similar level of inflation among the potential member countries (Fleming, 1971). Diverging ratios of employment to inflation among these countries would cause hardship. Countries with a balance-of-payments surplus would be driven to accept a higher level of inflation than in the situation when they are free to choose this ratio. Conversely, countries with deficits may be asked to tolerate a higher level of unemployment than they would be willing to accept in the situation when they are free to choose this level.

An optimum currency area may be defined as a region in which no part insists on creating money and having a monetary policy of its own (Machlup, 1979, p. 71). A monetary union which imposes minimum costs on the participating countries may be called an optimum currency area (Robson, 1983, p. 143). An optimum currency area may be defined alternatively as an area in which net benefits of integration (increase in welfare in the form of greater stability in prices, smaller disturbances coming from abroad), outweigh the costs (restraint to individual uses of monetary and fiscal policies) (Grubel, 1984, p. 39). An optimum currency area aims to identify a group of countries within which it is optimal to have fixed exchange rates while, at the same time, keeping a certain flexibility in the exchange rate with the off-shore countries (Thygesen, 1987, p. 163). Very small currency conversion costs and openness is likely to make the EC an optimal currency area, while high levels of government spending will make the EC less likely so (Canzoneri and Rogers, 1990, p. 422).

The notion of an optimum currency area is theoretical rather than practical. A region may be an economic unit which does not necessarily coincide with the domain of a currency. An optimum currency area may be able to sustain itself on its own. Its definition may ask for liberalization of all activities within it and its protection against the outside world. Despite their relevant points, these definitions can hardly be applied to countries in the real world because the states are constituted in a sub-optimal way, so that full economic efficiency can seldom, if ever, be achieved. A single-criterion model has a narrow scope. It is therefore unable to present costs and benefits of a monetary union. The next task is to amend this shortcoming.

Costs and benefits of monetary integration

A more practical and fruitful way to the analysis of monetary unions is to study the optimum economic policy area, rather than the optimum currency area. A single state becomes increasingly ineffective as an independent policy-making unit in modern times of continuous changes in technology, dissemination of information and frequent market changes. This is true for all countries in the world, but it is not true for all of them equally. Therefore, not all of them seek international solutions to their national problems. In the situation where economic problems assume global proportions there is only one optimum policy area: the world (Panić, 1988, pp. 317–30). The most pressing international economic problems cannot be solved by countries acting in isolation. Solutions to these problems can be found in coordinated national economic management. A system of safeguards, which would include assistance in the form of transfer of real resources to the countries which experience difficulties, is an essential feature for the survival of a multilateral system of trade and payments.

The shortcomings of the traditional single-criterion and optimum-currency model may be overcome by a cost–benefit approach. This approach has been widely accepted by Ishiyama (1975), de Grauwe (1975a), Vaubel (1978), Allen and Kenen (1980), Dennis (1981), El-Agraa (1985b), Jovanović (1985), Robson (1987), Devarajan and de Melo (1987), Thygesen (1987), Panić (1988) and Commission of the EC (1990). The costs which may be brought by a country's participation in monetary integration may be traced to the loss of a country's right to alter independently its rate of exchange, the ratio between inflation and unemployment, as well as its regional development policy. Monetary integration brings in a number of benefits which include an increase in influence in monetary affairs and an increase in monetary stability. Both costs and benefits of monetary integration will be analysed next.

Costs

First, the creation of a supranational body to conduct monetary policy (money supply, rate of interest and rate of exchange) in a monetary union may be seen as a significant loss of a participating country's sovereignty. This may be the first cost, which might provoke adverse political, as well as psychological, consequences in the participating countries. The most vulnerable issue may be the loss of the right to alter independently the rate of exchange. The loss is full against the currencies of the partner countries and partial against third countries. A right, often used selfishly, is lost. But the gains here come from the pooling of monetary policies of the participating countries, which can exercise a much greater leverage over their monetary policy in comparison to the situation which preceded integration.

When policy makers want to adjust the balance of payments by means of alterations in a country's rate of exchange, then the most critical issue is the fall in real wages. Labour may accept a fall in real wages under the condition that the other alternative is unemployment. A reduction in the rate of exchange introduces an increase in the price for imported goods, as well as for home goods. The impact of the devaluation depends on the openness of a country. A reduction in real wages introduces an advantage in the cost of labour and a relative decrease in the price of export goods in the short run. This classical scenario may be seriously questioned. Money illusion does not have a significant impact on labour. Every increase in inflation and corresponding fall in real wages under the assumption that there is no change in productivity, stimulates labour and concerned trade unions to increase wages. Short-term cost advantages of devaluation are eroded by such increases.

Devaluation as an instrument of economic policy may not alone eliminate deficits in the balance of payments. The government may state that its policy aim is not to use devaluation in the fight against inflation. Such a policy aim may act as an important incentive to firms to resist higher costs because their goods will become uncompetitive on the foreign and, potentially, home market if trade were free. A recession may be another, although less desirable, cure for inflation. Shrinking markets give firms incentives to keep prices low, while rising unemployment forces trade unions to resist increases in wages.

The exchange rate started to float in the early 1970s and floated for a decade. The experience has provided sufficient evidence that a country's autonomy in the situation with floating exchange rates is hardly great. The reason is that a majority of countries are small and open. This leads us to the conclusion that the sole use of the exchange rate as the adjustment mechanism of the balance of payments is of limited significance. Devaluation of a national currency is a label of failure to manage the economy correctly and carefully according to international standards. The standards of international economic prudence point to the fact that it is the national bureaucracy who is the only loser from the loss of the right to devalue the national currency. Therefore, the loss in autonomy in the management of a country's rate of exchange as a policy instrument is of little consequence.

Second, it was argued that floating rates of exchange permit unconstrained choices between unemployment and inflation in a country. On those grounds, countries may seem to be free to pursue their own stabilization policies. Monetary integration constrains the independent national choice of the rates of growth of inflation, unemployment and rate of interest. This choice, as a second cost of monetary integration, is constrained by the choice of other partner countries. A loss of the right to deal independently may significantly jeopardize national preferences with respect to possible choices. The country with relatively low inflation and balance-of-payments surplus may, in accordance with its economic and political strength, impose its own aims on other partner countries, because this country may have much less pressure for adjustment than the other countries.

This consideration has received a geometric rigour by de Grauwe

(1975a). It is proven that the countries differ with respect to the position of their Phillips' curves, rates of productivity growth and the preferences of governments between unemployment and inflation. These are the differences which explain why, in the absence of a monetary union, rates of inflation among countries will be equal only by accident. For a smooth operation of monetary integration among countries, the condition is not only balanced growth, but also equal unemployment rates, otherwise the monetary union may not survive without inter-country compensatory transfers of resources. The mere integration of economic policy aims may not be effective without agreement on the means for achieving the agreed targets. If countries cope with a common problem and employ different tools, the outcome of harmonization of only economic policy aims may be more harmful than helpful.

The Phillips' curve suggests that there is a measurable, inverse relation between unemployment and inflation. The government could reduce unemployment by means of demand stimulus, such as an increase in budget deficit, while the price for this policy is increased inflation. In Friedman's model, the unemployment rate is independent of the rate of inflation. The followers of this school criticize Phillips for not seeing that continuous inflationary policy provokes changes in the expectations about inflation in the future. They argue that there is only one rate of unemployment which is consistent with a constant rate of inflation (that is, the natural rate of unemployment or the non-accelerating-inflation rate of un-employment). No matter what a government does, the rate of unemployment may not fall below its natural rate. The natural rate of unemployment is determined by the real factors – which include minimum wage legislation, tax policy, dole money, labour mobility, the impetus for vocational training, as well as the choice between work and leisure. Most of these factors are made by economic policy. Every attempt to lower the rate of unemployment below the natural level by means of monetary expansion would only accelerate inflation. Hence, the loss of this economic policy choice is also of limited significance.

The main way to reduce unemployment can be to reduce the natural rate of unemployment. It can be done by reducing the social security benefits below the minimum wage for unskilled labour and by control over the demands of trade unions. Economic policy should be active in combating unemployment. The long-term unemployed have obsolete experience and training which makes them less attractive to potential employers. These unemployed compete less vigorously on the labour market and place less downward pressure on wages. The natural rate of unemployment increases with the expansion of the long-term unemployed. Economic policy should withdraw social benefits from those who refuse vocational training and/or jobs with the exception of those who are beyond the agreed age.

The Canadian experience during 1950–62 with a fluctuating rate of exchange is illustrative. Canada intended to have monetary independence in relation to the United States. Theoretical arguments (illusions) about greater national independence and freedom with respect to employment policy in a flexible-exchange-rate situation seemed attractive. Canadian hopes were high. At the end of this period a mismanaged government intervention succeeded in destabilizing prices in Canada, and growth stagnated. The decision to abandon flexible exchange rates shows that the benefits in the stability of employment and economic independence are smaller than the cost paid in economic instability and efficiency. Given the contemporary capital-market integration among open economies, significant differences among the rates of interest among different countries may not exist. Hence, an open economy may not independently rely on this instrument of economic policy. In the situation, where two or more currencies are close substitutes and where there exists free capital mobility, the central banks of these countries cannot conduct independent monetary policies even under fluctuating rates of exchange. Small open economies may be advised to link their monetary policies to those of their major partners in trade and investment.

Third, a serious problem in a monetary union may be traced to the inflow of capital into the prosperous regions. The regions losing this capital expect compensatory transfers from the prosperous ones. Those countries which feel that their destiny is to be losers from a monetary union would not enter such an arrangement. The system of transfers may be a bribe to these regions/countries to participate. In the situation with budget deficits and expenditure cuts, the funds for transfers may not be found easily. However, the gainers may be quite happy to compensate the losers and protect the net gains from integration.

To sum up, monetary integration introduces significant losses in constitutional autonomy of participating states, but real autonomy to conduct an independent monetary policy for a small country, in the situation of convertibility and openness for trade and investment, remains almost intact.

Benefits

The benefits of monetary integration are numerous and intuitive. They are hardly quantifiable and difficult to apprehend by the non-economist. The most important benefit of monetary integration is that it improves integration of markets for goods, services and factors. Exchange-rate risk for flows among the integrated countries is eliminated, so investors can make their decisions with a high degree of long-term confidence. Intra-union foreign direct investment is not controlled, which improves the allocation of resources. This brings an increase in influence in monetary affairs, as well as connections among major trading partners. Further, by coordination of monetary and fiscal policies, countries are led to fewer distortions while combating macroeconomic disequilibria. This introduces a greater monetary stability. In the situation with stable prices, interest and exchange rates, trade flows are not volatile, for there is no exchange-rate risk and uncertainty. This increases competition, economies of scale and mobility of factors, which improve the allocation of resources and increase economic growth. The central financial institution may finance regional inequalities.

The pooling of national reserves of foreign currencies is also advantageous for the monetary union member countries. By internalizing their foreign trade, these countries reduce their demand for foreign-currency reserves. These reserves may not be necessary for trade within the group, but they may still be needed for trade with third countries. Anyway, there are economies in the use of reserves. Their level is reduced and overhead costs are spread on the participating countries.

The net effect of monetary integration may not be easily and directly quantified. If there does not exist a control group of similar unintegrated countries, then there does not exist a yardstick against which one may compare the relative performance of the countries which practise monetary integration. The costs which may be brought by monetary integration – in the form of an increase in prices or unemployment – are relatively easily identifiable, borne by the few and may just have a short-term nature. If they are not, then an indefinite intra-union system of transfers is a necessary condition for the survival of the union. The benefits which accrue from monetary integration are long-term in nature (hence the need for a relatively short transition period to monetary union where costs prevail), they come in small amounts to everybody and they are hard to quantify with great precision.

Parallel currencies

It may be asked whether an irrevocable fixity of exchange rates is a sufficient condition for monetary integration or whether the introduction of a single currency is necessary. Suppose that there are various currencies in a monetary union which are linked together with a fixed exchange rate. If there is an increase in the supply of any of these currencies, then convertibility may be maintained only by intervention either in the form of the absorption of this currency by the monetary authorities or by reduction in demand (restriction in transactions) for this currency. The first method represents monetary expansion while the other is an act of disintegration.

A common currency may be an outward symbol, but is not the necessary condition for a successful monetary union. Capital mobility and irrevocably fixed rates of exchange of currencies in a monetary union may create a single currency *de facto* in everything except, possibly, in name, while a single currency would make a monetary union *de jure*. A single currency would be ultimately necessary because it would make the irrevocable fixity of participating currencies completely credible.

An evolutionary approach to the introduction of a monetary union may be that a common currency may exist side by side with the currencies of the member countries. Once agents are used to dealing with the common currency, it may gradually replace the currencies of the participating countries. This is the case of parallel currencies. An important issue here is that the new, parallel currency, ought to be linked to the pace of economic activity, otherwise price stability may be in danger. Also, it may bring an extra complication in the monetary affairs of the integrated countries.

In a full monetary union, currencies of the member countries are perfect substitutes. On the one hand, it would be meaningless to speak here about a parallel currency, since any parallel currency would be indistinguishable from national currencies in everything except name. The concept of a parallel currency becomes meaningful only in an intermediate stage of monetary union – when different currencies are not perfect substitutes because of transaction costs and/or exchange rate expectations. Reductions in exchange rate variability would diminish the usefulness of a parallel (basket) currency as an instrument of risk diversification, unless transaction costs in the parallel (common) currency decline by more than the transaction costs in the component currencies. On the other hand, a parallel currency is unlikely to develop in the case when national currencies are only very imperfect substitutes, because of high costs of exchanging currencies. Widespread use of a parallel currency alongside national currencies can therefore be expected only under a high degree of monetary integration (Gros, 1989, p. 224).

A common currency may replace national currencies after some period of adjustment. Stability in the monetary sphere may be a result. But the new and single money in the area will not solve the problem of budget deficits of the participating countries which may be revealed as regional disequilibria.

Gresham's law says that in the case where there are two currencies (in his example, gold and silver coins) circulating side by side in the economy, then 'the bad money will drive out the good', except in the case where there is a fixed exchange rate between the two monies. This result has not materialized in some countries.

In the early 1980s Yugoslav firms were permitted to sell their home-made durable goods to domestic private buyers for hard currency. These buyers received price rebates and priority in delivery. Due to shortages and increasing inflation, domestic private hard-currency holders increased their purchases in order to hedge against inflation. The growth of this home trade relative to the 'normal' trade in the (sinking) domestic currency has been increasing. The discrimination of home firms against the domestic currency was spreading. Firms were happy because they received hard currency without the effort required to export, while people were happy because they were able to get what they wanted. Subsequently, the domestic sales for hard currency were banned because they reduced the effectiveness of domestic monetary policy. This is an example of where a weak domestic currency (prior to the state intervention) was crowded out from domestic trade by a relatively strong foreign currency. Hard currency was not, however, driven out of Yugoslav private savings. Around four-fifths of these savings were in foreign hard-currency savings accounts in Yugoslav banks. This was the way to protect savings from rising home inflation and negative interest rates on savings in the home currency.

Monetary integration in the European Community

Integration in the EC has advanced at a pace faster than that envisaged in the Treaty of Rome. The customs union was fully established among the founding member countries in 1968, which was a year and a half ahead of schedule. This was one of the most significant initial achievements of the EC.

The Treaty of Rome provides the legal base for the EC involvement in the monetary policy. Article 103 requests that EC countries regard their national short-term economic policies as a matter of common concern, as well as to consult each other about those policies. Article 104 allows the member countries to pursue their own economic policies, but must ensure the equilibrium of national balance of payments and confidence in their currencies, together with taking care to ensure a high level of employment and stability of prices. Article 105 requires that the member states coordinate economic policies. Article 106 declares readiness of the member states to remove capital controls. Article 107 asks that each EC country must treat its exchange-rate policy as a matter of common Community interest. Article 108 refers to the balance-of-payments difficulties of the member states. In that case, the Commission shall investigate the situation and make recommendations – including mutual financial assistance of the member countries. According to Article 109, a member country may, as a precaution, take the necessary protective measures in the situation of a sudden crisis in the balance of payments, but the Commission may suspend such measures. The Single European Act requests, in Article 102A, that the EC countries strengthen cooperation in the fields covered by Article 104 and respect the rules of the EMS.

After the initial success in the establishment of a customs union, the EC contemplated the establishment of an economic and monetary union. There were two schools of thought about how to implement this idea. They were the 'monetarists' and the 'economists'.

The 'monetarists' (Belgium, France and Luxembourg) argued that a promising monetary union requires the irrevocable fixity of exchange rates of the participating countries from the outset. The member countries would be driven, then, to coordinate their economic policies in order to mitigate and, eventually, eliminate the discrepancies in their economies which is necessary for a full monetary union. They also argued in favour of a well-endowed fund for the support of the adjustments of the balance of payments. Full freedom of capital movements should be permitted only after the establishment of full monetary union. The last request of this school was that supranationality should be on a relatively low level.

The school of 'economists' (FR Germany and The Netherlands) argued that fixity in the exchange rates for a group of countries which are on relatively different levels of development is a formidable task. They argued that the coordination of economic policies should be the primary task because it would bring economic harmonization among the participating countries. They argued in favour of a free movement of capital from the outset and felt that fixed rates of exchange be introduced only after the fulfilment of the above conditions.

The Werner Report (1970) was offered as the blueprint for the monetary union in the EC. The Report asked for both fixed rates of exchange and free mobility of capital. This therefore represented a compromise between the two schools. Super optimism (monetary union by 1980) was not rewarded because the Report overestimated the will of the member states to abandon their monetary authority in favour of a supranational body. This approach may have failed because it wanted to fix rates of exchange without prior monetary reform among the EC member countries.

The early 1970s were characterized by significant turbulence on the monetary scene. Currencies were fluctuating, so this state of affairs endangered the functioning of trade flows in the EC. The EC Council of Ministers requested from the member governments' monetary authorities not only to follow the ± 2.25 per cent margins of fluctuation in relation to the United States dollar, but also to reduce the level of fluctuation among their respective currencies. This introduced the 'European snake' (common margins of fluctuation). If one plots the daily fluctuations of the currencies of the EC member states, then one will get a snake-like ribbon. The width of the snake depended on the fluctuation of the strongest and the weakest currencies remaining always within the ± 2.25 per cent dollar tunnel fluctuation margins. The creation of the 'snake' was mainly a European reaction to the hectic situation of the United States dollar on the international money market.

The main feature of the 'snake' were interventions. When the sum of the fluctuations in the 'snake' exceeded the margins, intervention was supposed to take place (the strongest currency should purchase the weakest). The dollar tunnel disappeared in 1973, so the 'snake' found itself in the lake. The EC currencies were entering and leaving the system quite often. This introduced uncertainty in trade relations in the EC. Apart from external pressures which the 'snake' was unable to resist, an internal shortcoming (different national monetary policies) also played a role. Something should have been done about this.

The member countries of the EC wanted not just to preserve the

Table 4.1 Composition of the ECU (%)

Currency	Weight in the 'basket' 1979–84	1984–89	1989
1 German mark	33.0	32.0	30.1
2 French franc	19.8	19.0	19.0
3 Pound sterling	13.3	15.0	13.0
4 Italian lira	9.5	10.2	10.15
5 Dutch guilder	10.5	10.1	9.4
6 Belgian franc	9.3	8.2	7.6
7 Spanish peseta	—	—	5.3
8 Danish krone	3.1	2.7	2.45
9 Irish pound	1.1	1.2	1.1
10 Greek drachma	—	1.3	0.8
11 Portuguese escudo	—	—	0.8
12 Luxembourg franc	0.4	0.3	0.3
Total	100.0	100.0	100.0

Source: *Official Journal of the EC* (1989).

already achieved level of economic integration, but also to add to it. A further step was the creation of the European Monetary System (EMS). The approach was completely different from the one which established the 'snake'. Instead of preparing various economic plans for political consideration, the EC member countries first delivered their political decision about the establishment of the system and then agreed about the technical/operational details of the system which was introduced in 1979.

The aims of the EMS are: stabilization of exchange rates through closer monetary cooperation among the member countries of the EC, promotion of further integration in the Community and contribution to the stabilization of international monetary relations.

The key role in the EMS is played by the European Currency Unit (ECU). The ECU is basically a 'cocktail' of fixed proportions of currencies of the EC member countries. The share of every currency in the ECU depends on the economic potential of the member country (aggregate GNP), its share in intra-EC trade and the need for short-term monetary support. The composition of the ECU is represented in Table 4.1. Alterations in the composition of the ECU may occur every 5 years, or when the share of each currency changes by at least 25 per cent in relation to the originally-calculated value. Also, the composition of the ECU can be changed on the occasion when the currency of a new member country enters the 'basket'.

The exchange rate mechanism in the EC has been in the centre of controversy since its inception. Every currency in the EMS has its own central rate of exchange versus other partner currencies and the ECU. In relation to the partner currencies in the system, individual currencies may fluctuate within a ± 2.25 per cent band with the exception of the Spanish peseta and British pound which are permitted to float within a ± 6 per cent limit. In 1990, eleven years after the creation of the EMS, the special (± 6 per cent floating band) treatment for the Italian lira ended, so it has the standard rate of fluctuation. When a currency reaches its limit (upper or lower) of fluctuation in relation to another EMS partner currency, then intervention in national currency of one of the two central banks is compulsory. Intervention within the margins of fluctuation may be either in the national currencies of the members of the EMS or in dollars.

Fluctuation of each EMS currency versus the ECU is slightly stricter. The EC Commission has individualized each currency's margin of fluctuation. It is the strictest for the German mark, ± 1.51 per cent, and widest for the Irish pound, ± 2.22 per cent (the currencies under the 'special treatment' have wider margins of fluctuation).

In order to prevent frequent interventions, the EMS has introduced an early warning system in the form of a divergence indicator. The divergence threshold is ± 75 per cent of a currency's fluctuation in relation to the ECU. The role of this indicator is ambiguous. As soon as the divergence threshold is reached, the countries in question are not formally required to do anything, even to consult. Therefore this innovation has not hitherto played an important role in the EMS. However, consultation and cooperation of the monetary authorities of the EC member countries have compensated, at least in part, for this shortcoming of the EMS.

The EMS funds for exchange market interventions are relatively well endowed. The very short-term financing facility for compulsory interventions provides the participating central banks with an unlimited amount of partner currency loans. The short-term monetary support disposes of 14 billion ECUs for the finance of temporary balance-of-payments deficits, while the medium-term support facility disposes of 11 billion ECUs (but the use of this mechanism is subject to conditions).

The EMS may sometimes slow down the rate of economic adjustment of a member country. When countries borrow on the international financial markets, these markets do not consider exclusively the credit-worthiness (reserves, deficits, experience in adjustments and outlooks) of the borrowing country. These markets consider the the membership of the EMS and its possibilities for financial support. In this indirect way, the financial markets take into account the reserves of other EMS countries. These markets believe that the partner countries will help the borrowing country in financial difficulties. This is a recognition of the relative success of the EMS. However, this situation may prevent a country accepting greater monetary discipline. A government may employ a wicked way to erode the real burden of debt, and use inflation. In any case, a country which follows a policy of relative monetary indiscipline will reduce domestic reserves and lose credit-worthiness in the long run. Foreign creditors may reasonably demand higher interest rates, which usually deters private investment more than consumption and, hence, reduces the future economic potential of the country.

Apart from funds for exchange-market interventions, other EMS adjustment mechanisms include home-price and income alterations, rates of interest, control of capital flows, as well as increased cooperation and exchange of information. Controls of internal trade flows are, of course, prohibited.

The rates of exchange in the EMS are semi-fixed. The EMS did not have as its aim the petrification of rates of exchange among the member countries. The adjustments of the central rates may take place either every five years or according to need. When all other mechanisms for intervention are used up, the country in question may ask for permission to change the central rate of its currency. The Council of Ministers decides about these changes (usually during the weekends when the financial markets are closed). The effects of realignments (devaluations) may be eaten away by inflation. So, the best and, surely, the hardest way for the stability of the system is that the deficit countries increase productivity above the EC average.

A change in the central rate of a currency (devaluation) is still a permitted and used means for the restoration of a loss of competitiveness among the EMS member countries. In the distant situation without national currencies, even *de facto*, the restoration of national competitiveness could be achieved by reduction in wages or by labour migration to the advanced regions or both. The United States is an example where wages are flexible and labour is highly mobile. At the same time, a single currency has smooth internal performance. The United States inter-regional adjustments are eased by a system of implicit federal government transfers of real resources. The federal government spends much and taxes little in the backward regions while it does the reverse in the advanced regions. A similar analogy does not yet exist in the EC. A genuine EC-internal market from 1993 will require EC-wide economic stabilizers which must ease the adjustment troubles of both countries and regions within them. This not only asks for the transfer of real resources, but also for measures to enhance mobility of factors from low- to high-productivity regions.

All member countries of the EC have exchanged for ECUs 20 per cent of their gold reserves (the role of gold is partly reaffirmed) and 20 per cent of their dollar reserves with the European Fund for Monetary Cooperation. These assets are swapped on a revolving quarterly basis for ECUs. Hence the ECU is not a newly-created reserve asset which is an addition to the existing stocks of reserves, like the special drawing rights are. The creation of the ECU transforms a part of the existing reserve assets into another asset. The amount of ECUs issued changes every quarter with respect to the changes in member countries' volume of reserves, the price of gold and the dollar exchange rate. There were around 50 billion ECUs issued in 1990.

The ECU is used as: an accounting unit for intervention; a means of settlement among central banks; part of the international financial reserves; the basis for calculation of the divergence indicator; the unit for the store of value (because of its stability); and the unit for financial transactions and statistics of the EC administration. There are also ECU-denominated bonds. Although the ECU is still remote from the day-to-day use of individuals, many banks open personal accounts in ECUs and offer an interest rate which is a weighted average of interest rates of the participant countries in the ECU. They also offer travellers' cheques denominated in ECUs. Interest-rate differentials reflect mainly differences in the national rates of inflation. Once the exchange rates start to move with inflation differentials, the profitability to hold ECUs may diminish.

The ECU is used by the monetary authorities as the official ECU, while business and population use the private ECU. Nevertheless, the ECU market is not fragmented. All dealings are in a single

ECU, for the definition of both is the same. A central bank can hold ECUs. If the national currency comes under pressure, the bank can sell ECUs and purchase the national currency. This may be a cheaper and less notable way of intervention than a direct borrowing of other currencies to buy domestic when the exchange rate is falling. The major reason for the growth in the use of private ECUs is the demand of business for the simplification of transactions and, possibly, avoiding capital controls where they existed. The ECU is attractive because of its greater stability in relation to its components. Non-European investors prefer to deal in a single, rather than several different, currencies. The market value of the ECU is not directly influenced by the value of the dollar, for it is not incorporated in the ECU basket as is the case with the special drawing rights. Therefore, the dollar holders can buy the ECUs and hedge against the dollar-exchange risk.

There are at least two big problems associated with the EMS. The first one is that, at the time of its inception, it was planned that the adjustment phase would last for two years. After that, the reserves would be held on a permanent, rather than a three-months revolving basis, and that the European Fund for Monetary Cooperation would become the European Monetary Fund. This has not materialized. As long as the member countries are reluctant to transfer their sovereign rights in the monetary sphere to a kind of supranational central bank, the second phase of the EMS will be postponed indefinitely.

The second big problem is that although Britain, Portugal and Greece exchanged both 20 per cent of their gold and 20 per cent of their dollar reserves with the Fund, they chose not to take part in the exchange-rate mechanism of the EMS. Britain is a significant exporter of oil, so the British argue that the pound sterling is a petro-currency. Due to this fact, the pound sterling is much more sensitive to the actual or expected changes in the price of oil than any other EC currency. The reaction of sterling always goes in the opposite direction from other EC currencies. As long as the exchange rate for the dollar and the prices for crude oil remain uncertain, and as long as Britain remains a significant oil exporter, the potential over-reaction of sterling may remain.

Britain does not have capital flow controls (like most of the EC countries), hence the volume of funds for intervention in order to protect a certain rate of exchange should be much larger in Britain than in other EMS member countries. Such interventions may endanger the British home monetary targets. Nevertheless, Britain decided to join the exchange rate mechanism in 1990. Since the aim of this country is monetary stability and the fight against inflation, the choice is smart. Also, the EMS fully included one of the world's major currencies. Greece and Portugal do not participate in the exchange-rate mechanism for, at present, those countries are at a lower level of development relative to the core EC countries, so they want time for gradual adjustment. This makes the EMS incomplete even in its first phase.

The strongest arguments for the non-participating countries to join the exchange-rate mechanism of the EMS seemed to be predominantly political. It is not integration-prone for those countries to stay aloof from one of the most significant achievements of the EC. Also, and more importantly, the creation of a genuine internal market for goods, services and factors will be incomplete without a single market for money.

It must be always kept in mind that, in a single currency area, the national governments would still be free to tax and spend in the way they think is the most appropriate. Budget deficits would still be possible, but subject to only one condition. It is that this excess budget expenditure must be financed by borrowing instead of printing domestic money. Foreign debt has to be serviced by export earnings. The national debt does not present an immediate real burden on the economy because it represents a transfer between present and future generations.

A reduction in the variance of economic variables among the countries may illustrate economic convergence among these countries. The narrowing of the differences in the performance criteria among the countries does not necessarily mean that the standards of living among these countries are becoming more equal. The membership of the EMS can be used by the national government as a convincing argument during the pursuance of the prudent national economic policy in the fight against opposition. The EMS has introduced convergence in domestic monetary policies and inflation rates, but it has not been backed up by corresponding progress in the fiscal sector and external balance. Fiscal deficits widened on the average, which introduces a degree of uncertainty into the EMS and may endanger the stability in the exchange-rate relationship in the future.

Although the EMS has not hitherto brought full convergence of economic performance variables and full coordination of economic policies, it may be heading towards the desired outcome. The best signal is that no member country has left the EMS despite strains.

There is an implicit aim behind the relatively strict margins of fluctuation for currencies in the EMS. It is to drive the member countries to accept similar economic policies and to converge. This convergence does not necessarily aim at averaging out the economic performance criteria.

A country with the best performance in inflation, balance of payments, employment, growth and others has least pressure to adjust and, in relation to its size, it may call the tune in the shaping of other countries' economic variables. Hence, FR Germany was able to dominate within the EMS, which operated asymmetrically in formulating monetary policies of other member countries which had to bear the adjustment burden. Since inflation has been reduced and other monetary variables quite aligned among most member countries, the EMS operates in a more symmetric way.

Mere convergence in inflation and other monetary variables may not be enough for the smooth operation of the single EC market after 1992. The EMS was not able to increase significantly the use of the ECU, the role of the European Fund for Monetary Cooperation was marginalized and the present form of the system was unable to bring spontaneous monetary integration. Those aims might be achieved if there was a European central bank, a system of central banks or a monetary authority. This has not yet happened because of a fear that the monetary issues will be passed on to a remote bureaucracy. The governments are afraid of losing monetary sovereignty (the right to cheat on its citizens without a promise to convert paper money for gold). Another fear is that they may not be able to pursue their own stabilization policy. Those fears are not well founded. In order to carry on with national stabilization, balance-of-payments, regional, industrial and other policies, the governments will still have at their disposal taxes, subsidies, procurement and budget deficits. The only (severe) restrictions to their sovereignty to choose their policies is that they cannot employ exchange-rate changes and have a different rate of inflation from their partner countries.

There may be a temptation for a country in a monetary system to run a budget deficit according to current needs. Altough the governments are often safe borrowers in relation to the private ones, capital markets will increase interest rates to heavy borrowers when their credit-worthiness is jeopardized. If a state in federations like the United States and Canada increases its borrowing, then the value of government bonds falls throughout the country. In such a case, the federal government may step in and correct the distortion.

However, such a corrective mechanism does not yet exist in the EC. Hence, the need for a (kind of) central bank.

The main argument in favour of a central bank is that it reduces uncertainties and conflicts about national monetary policies. It does so by providing a forum in which national views can be represented and resolved, as well as by reducing the discretion that national monetary authorities have in the implementation of (divergent) policies. In the absence of a central bank, national conflicts will be resolved by market forces with adverse externalities for efforts to promote greater stability of exchange rates (Folkerts-Landau and Mathieson, 1989, p. 15).

There are two extreme possibilities for the final shape of the EC Central Bank and a number of mixed ones. One extreme is the model of the FR Germany's Bundesbank. It is independent from the government in the conduct of monetary policy and possibly, therefore, quite successful. The Bundesbank ensures stable prices, high employment, balanced foreign trade, as well as constant and reasonable economic growth. The other extreme is the Bank of France. In this bank the government has a full stake, so France would like to see a kind of accountability (do the central bankers posess a superior knowledge about the country's long-term needs than the governments that represent the opinion of the public?) with the EC Central Bank. FR Germany was the engine of EC monetary stability. Therefore, one may expect that the EC Central Bank, the Eurofed, may look quite like the Bundesbank. It will be tough on inflation.

Many EC member countries would prefer to see a 'German-influenced' Eurofed than the continuation of the current situation where the system is 'German-controlled'. In the system with binding rules or procedures, the smaller EC countries can be represented on the Bank's board where they can, at least to an extent, shape policy. Their sovereignty therefore may be increased in comparison to the present situation.

The decision of 1990 to set up the EC Central Bank in 1994 depends on several conditions. They include the establishment of a single EC internal market, giving independence to the members of the new Central Bank and prohibiting EC member states from the inflationary practice of financing their deficits.

Independent central banks, like the judiciary, are constitutional institutions since they are not accountable to the elected government or parliament. Their autonomy comes from a general consensus about their long-term aims and from the fact that their instruments may be badly abused by the political majority of the day (Vaubel, 1990, p. 941).

The Delors Report (1989) gave a new impetus towards the monetary union. It envisaged the union in three stages. A smart approach was not to state any specific date except mid-1990 for the beginning of the first stage. During the first stage, the EC countries would strengthen the coordination of their economic and monetary policies. The removal of the remaining capital controls would require this in any case. All countries would enter the exchange-rate mechanism of the EMS. Stage two would be marked by the creation of the European Central Bank (system of central banks or a monetary authority). The EC would set the magnitude of the basic economic variables for all member countries including the size and financing of the budget deficit. Also, the margins of fluctuation of the EMS currencies would be narrowed. In the last stage of the monetary union, the EC Central Bank would be the only authority that is responsible for the conduct of the monetary policy throughout the Community. The exchange rates among the EC national currencies would be permanently fixed without any fluctuations. A single EC currency would emerge. It may be a necessary condition for a genuine single EC market. Gradualism and the somewhat unclear division of duties between the EC and its member countries may be a source of confusion in the future development and implementation of this Report.

The British proposed in 1990 an alternative plan that would introduce a 'hard ECU' as the thirteenth currency in the EC. It would be an additional, anti-inflationary control on governments that intend to ease national monetary policy. It would be issued by the EC Central Bank in exchange for deposits of national currencies. The 'hard ECU' would be managed in such a way that each national central bank compensates the EC Central Bank for any losses caused by devaluation of its currency and that any inflating national central bank buys back its national currency with, for example, dollars or yens. Wide acceptability of the 'hard ECUs' would prevent national central banks inflating their currencies. The problem with this plan is that the British see it as an end in itself, not as a vehicle towards a single EC currency. In this case, any nation's relatively stable legal tender may have an advantage over the additional 'foreign' currency.

In spite of its relative rigidity, the EMS makes the rates of exchange quasi-flexible. If a currency is in trouble, which may not be solved by intervention, then the system permits adjustments (revaluations and devaluations) of the central rate of exchange. This kind of adjustment has been happening relatively often in the first years of the existence of the EMS.

Adjustments in the rates of exchange together with capital controls were used by some countries, for example Italy and France, in the EMS to control the domestic monetary system in an easier way than through other, relatively bitter means, like recession. They were able to follow, to an extent and for some time, a different course in the national macroeconomic variables then their foreign partners have.

Capital controls are effective ways to control monetary affairs in the situation when money markets expect adjustments in the exchange rate. Consequently, controls drive holders to keep the currency that is about to be devaluated. Controls can be permanent and temporary (as emergency measures to prevent speculative capital flows). In the absence of capital controls, devaluation of weak curencies cannot be postponed; however, controls make the delay of devaluation possible, but delays increase uncertainty about the rate of exchange. With capital controls, a relatively modest increase in the national rate of interest will achieve the desired monetary-policy effect. Without capital controls, the only instrument that can be used with the same effect is a sudden and, usually, large increase in the rates of interest. The main defence of capital controls is not the fact that they are costless, but rather that they are less costly than the movements of exchange rates and interest rates that would happen without them (Folkerts-Landau and Mathieson, 1989, p. 8).

The removal of the remaining capital controls in the EC in 1990 (with the exception of Spain and Ireland who are allowed to delay the removal until 1992 and Portugal and Greece until 1994) makes residents throughout the EC sensitive to differences in rates of interest. TNCs, including banks, as major beneficiaries of the dismantling of capital controls, are able easily and swiftly to change and diversify the currency composition and maturity of their financial portfolios. By doing so, TNCs and other money holders may jeopardize the aims of monetary policy of individual member countries in the situation with easy and cheap currency substitution. An increase in the national rate of interest in order to reduce the supply of money and cool the economy will have the opposite effect. Increased interest rates will suddenly attract an inflow of foreign capital and increase the national supply of money. (Such swift changes are not very likely in the flow of goods and services.)

Conversely, if the intention of the national government is to stimulate home economic activity by a reduction in the rates of interest, the effect of such a policy will be the opposite from that intended. Capital will fly out of the country to the locations where rates of interest are higher.

Without capital controls, large differences in the rate of interest among the EMS countries cannot be sustained. In the new situation, the EC member countries have no other rational choice but to pool their national monetary policies and cooperate. Any increase in monetary instability among EC currencies will provoke the mobility of funds in the search for a greater security, thus making it impossible to maintain EMS parities without even greater harmonization of national monetary policies (Panić, 1991). Since it was the Bundesbank which was calling the tune in the EMS, pooling of monetary policies among the countries of the EC may increase the sovereignty of smaller countries because they will, in the new situation, have some say in the EC monetary-policy-making process.

Monetary integration is the field where genuine economic integration among countries is tested. The EC countries wanted to supplement the customs union with a monetary union. The politicians and central bankers have until recently succeeded in achieving a more modest aim. The EMS was a voluntary and complicated system of semi-fixed exchange rates which was supported by some cooperation of central banks. A success in the attainment of the original aims of the EMS is obvious. The EMS introduced quite a degree of monetary stability in the EC by a reduction in inflation differentials and a lowering in the volatility of the exchange rates. Fresh blood in the EMS was introduced by a decisive step in the direction of elimination of capital controls. This strengthened the values of coordination of economic and monetary policies in the EC. It is realized that, without a common money, a genuine internal market cannot operate.

The rationale for the common EC economic policies exists in the case where the Community is better placed to do certain things than the member countries. One can hardly think of a better example of this than the case of monetary and trade policies. Economic and monetary union in the EC will further promote and strengthen integration in this region. Economic efficiency will be increased because of improved allocation of savings and investment due to the elimination of exchange-rate risk and reduction in the cost of capital. However, a mere monetary union will not be the end of the story. It will, without any doubt, lead to a full economic and monetary union. A full freedom in the national fiscal policy in the case of monetary unification will not be possible. Therefore, fiscal harmonization is the next step.

Less developed regions/countries in the EC and the ones with deficits in their balance of payments will be deprived if they employ devaluation as a means of adjustment. These countries/regions will have to do better than the others in the EC in the reduction of cost and increase in productivity. Hence the need for regional, industrial and social policies and aid at the EC level. Otherwise, the less developed and deficit countries/regions may threaten to use protectionism and jeopardize the whole 1992 Programme. Once countries are seriously committed to integration, it is harder to stop than go ahead with it.

Monetary integration in the Council for Mutual Economic Assistance (CMEA)

Trade among the CMEA member countries has been characterized by bilateralism during the whole life of the CMEA. This property of the CMEA prevented the development of integration and represented the greatest weakness of this organization. In the planning process, in which there was an over-emphasized role of material balances, a planner looked at foreign trade as a residual sector which had to obtain those things which were in short supply in the country in exchange for domestic goods the planners considered to be in excess supply. Prices in foreign trade were set by bilateral negotiation. Equilibrium in foreign trade was achieved by offering goods which were just valuable enough to cover necessary imports. Trade was in equilibrium on a bilateral level. There were neither surpluses nor deficits in the trade balance, so there was no need for international payments (a small credit could be arranged for temporary disequilibria).

In the case when country A has a surplus in trade with country B and a deficit with country C, country A could not in practice use this surplus to cover its deficit in trade with country C in the CMEA system. Country A did not have an interest in running a surplus with country B, for country A could not be sure that it would be paid by country B in goods or hard currency which it needs and which may be used for the settlement of trade balance with country C. Country B may offer those goods which are available (machines, watches, cameras, etc.) which may be unnecessary to country A. Country A may be interested in hard currency, high technology and raw materials instead. This situation in the CMEA was referred to as inconvertibility of commodities.

Foreigners (apart from tourists) were forbidden to purchase on the home market of each of the CMEA member countries for export purposes. Exports might be conducted exclusively through foreign-trade companies and on the basis of the plan. An important exception was when the CMEA partner countries demanded unplanned quantities of some goods and paid for them in hard currency. This organization of the state trading system was due to the following two reasons. On the one hand, unexpected purchases would disturb the fulfilment of plans, while on the other hand, foreigners would be able to purchase goods at prices which were set below costs of production. Country A did not therefore permit any other CMEA country to legally hold country A's currency for trading purposes and vice versa. Inconvertibility and bilateralism hide the balance-of-payments pressure and embody a lack of integration by market standards.

The rate of exchange in the CMEA countries was set by the state administration. There were three kinds of rates of exchange. One kind was the fixed rate of exchange which was used for trade with the CMEA partner countries. The other was a relatively flexible rate which was used for the settlement of non-trade transactions within the CMEA. This rate of exchange was set on the basis of purchasing-power parity, so, for a certain amount of money, businessmen, diplomats and tourists might purchase a relatively similar quantity of goods and services in other CMEA partner countries. The third kind of exchange rate was used in trade with off-shore countries. These rates were set separately for exports, imports and various geographical regions.

Instead of adjusting prices to a single rate of exchange and having a link with the international market situation, the CMEA countries adjusted rates of exchange to domestic prices. By doing this, production of every commodity became profitable. This distorted the allocation of resources. A national rate of exchange had its meaning only within the national economy. Any alteration of exchange rates had neither a significant nor a direct impact on trade with other countries.

Economic development of the CMEA countries had reached such a level where bilateralism in trade represented a brake on the future economic development and division of labour. Of course, bilateralism has played an important part during the period of the post-war reconstruction, but has exhausted its potential long ago. The CMEA

Table 4.2 Capital in the IBEC

Country	Transferable roubles (millions)	%
1 USSR	116.0	38.1
2 GDR	55.0	18.0
3 Czechoslovakia	45.0	14.7
4 Poland	27.0	8.8
5 Hungary	21.0	6.9
6 Bulgaria	17.0	5.6
7 Romania	16.0	5.2
8 Cuba	4.4	1.4
9 Mongolia	3.0	1.0
10 Vietnam	0.9	0.3
Total	305.3	100.0

Source: van Meerhaeghe (1985).

countries were conscious of these rigidities of the planning system. They endeavoured to multilateralize their trade relations. They founded the International Bank for Economic Cooperation (IBEC) in 1963 for that purpose.

The basic aim of the IBEC was to multilateralize trade in the CMEA. The IBEC should have become a multilateral clearing house. The CMEA asked the member countries to have equilibrium in the total balance of trade, but this was not required in trade with each CMEA partner country. The first international socialist currency, the transferable rouble, was created. The capital of the IBEC is 305.3 million transferable roubles. Each member country's quota is shown in Table 4.2.

Each country's share in the IBEC's capital is proportional to its share of trade within the CMEA. The transferable rouble is in fact an accounting unit which does not perform any other monetary function. Surpluses of one country in transferable roubles could not be automatically converted into unplanned imports from the CMEA partners. These surpluses could not be exchanged for hard currency either, so countries did not have an interest in accumulating them. The IBEC is the first bank in which each depositor (country) has one vote in spite of the difference in deposited capital. Decisions are made unanimously. This is probably the main reason for the passive accounting role of the IBEC. One may apprise that the multilateral trade within the CMEA has never exceeded more than 2 per cent of the total trade of member countries. Multilateralism in trade could not be achieved on these rigid bases.

The establishment of the IBEC has neither promoted trade nor changed the bilateral character of trade within the CMEA. More than a quarter of a century of experimentation with the IBEC has provided enough evidence that it was an illusion to believe that this socialist bank, which offers every depositor equal decision making authority notwithstanding each individual deposit, would be more promising than the traditional banks. This justified a thorough reform of the CMEA monetary system. The banks should be installed in the role in the economy which they have elsewhere occupied since the thirteenth century and before – that is, since the times when it was believed that the Sun revolved around the Earth. By preventing the Bank from playing such a role of easing commerce, the CMEA countries have rendered it useless.

By ignoring market forces, the CMEA countries have lost the yardstick for profitable economic production. The way out of this situation may be found in reforms which introduce freer markets, openness for trade and investment, as well as multilateralism. Experience has shown that all reforms within the framework of central planning system have had little success. The CMEA might only become even more of a hindrance to the economic integration and development of its members. Therefore, the decision of 1990 to start all payments in mutual trade in hard currency from 1991 represents a move away from inefficiency towards the right direction according to the market criteria.

West African Monetary Union (WAMU)

The WAMU consists of seven West African states. They are Benin, Burkina Faso, Ivory Coast, Mali, Niger, Senegal and Togo. Membership of the WAMU has varied over time. Mauritania participated in the WAMU from its inception in 1962 but withdrew in 1972, Togo joined in 1963, while Mali withdrew from the WAMU but rejoined in 1984. The WAMU has provided these countries for almost three decades with a freely circulating common currency, the CFA (*Communauté Financière Africaine*) franc. This currency is linked by a fixed rate of exchange to the French franc without any changes since 1948 at the rate of 1 French franc = 50 CFA francs. The CFA franc is issued by a common central bank which pools the member countries' reserves. France is very involved in this system because of guarantees of an unlimited convertibility of CFA francs into French francs at the fixed exchange rate.

The WAMU's role in the first decade of its life was passive. The WAMU's central bank was charged with the maintenance of liquidity (money supply/GNP) and not with responsibilities for maintaining monetary and price stability and balance-of-payments equilibrium (Robson, 1983, p. 150). Its monetary policy was centralized in the Paris headquarters although the WAMU kept agencies in each member country. The WAMU's monetary policy was not coordinated with the fiscal policies of the member countries. At the beginning of the 1960s these countries were heavily dependent on France for all external economic affairs. The WAMU countries became linked to the EC by the Yaounde and, subsequently, the Lome conventions which provide trade preferences and aid from the EC. They also joined the IMF and the World Bank. The WAMU countries thereby increased the number of external economic partners. France has nevertheless preserved her dominant position in the region. The WAMU countries intended to reduce the strong French influence and increase their autonomy in the monetary sphere. This brought reforms in 1974.

The reform was founded on the grounds that a monetary union among the member countries was necessary for faster economic development but that the monetary arrangements should be organized differently than before. The most important changes occurred with respect to the rediscount facilities. Instead of a 10 per cent annual increase in the money supply as before, the reform allowed a 45 per cent annual increase in the money supply in each country (this amount will be rediscounted by the WAMU central bank). This has increased the power of the national credit committees. Foreign reserves of the member countries may be diversified, but at least 65 per cent of them should be in French francs. The WAMU countries align their exchange-rate policy with France while, in return, France guarantees free convertibility of CFA francs. The site of the central bank was transferred from Paris to Dakar. Prior to the reform, decisions of the central bank were made by the two-thirds majority where France had a half of the bank's board membership. After the reform, the decisions were made by simple majority. France is represented in the Board by two directors like every other country.

In spite of reforms in the WAMU, the monetary and fiscal developments have differed considerably among the member countries. The divergent trends may lead to external imbalances among the WAMU countries. Those countries which restricted the money supply may have experienced balance-of-payment surpluses with other partners, while those which pursued an expansionary monetary policy may have deficits. Intra-group trade in the West African Economic Community (whose membership includes the members of the WAMU less Benin and Togo but plus Mauritania) was only 10 per cent in 1988. Economic trends in a member country which diverge from the trends in other partner countries have their impact on each of the member countries' balance of payments with the outside world (notably France and other EC countries), not with other WAMU partners. The divergent trends in the WAMU countries have their joint impact on the common currency system.

It is difficult to create a counterfactual world in which one may evaluate the degree of success of any monetary union. The relative performance of the CFA-franc-zone countries can be compared to other developing countries. The performance of the CFA-franc countries was relatively poorer than that of all other developing countries in the period 1960–73, while their economic performance in relation to this group of countries was significantly improved during 1974–82 period. A more suitable 'control group' of developing countries can be taken for comparison. This group can be found among other sub-Saharan countries. These countries are much more similar to the CFA-franc countries in climate, endowment of factors and so on. The WAMU countries grew significantly faster than the group of other sub-Saharan countries (Devarajan and de Melo, 1987, p. 491). This result may support the view that the participation in a monetary union and its 'discipline' was much more helpful for the economic adjustment of countries during the period of floating and sharp increases in prices than the free and uncoordinated float of other sub-Saharan countries. Although there was a possibility of changing parity of the CFA franc, the WAMU has kept a fixed parity with the French franc. Such exceptional stability has been the major factor in the creation and maintenance of confidence in the CFA franc (Guillaumont and Guillaumont, 1989, p. 144). Therefore, claims that the WAMU does not operate for the benefit of its member countries may not be well founded. The best proof is that the membership of the WAMU has first stabilized and then increased in number.

The future of the WAMU may be uncertain. Other African countries have devalued their currencies so the the share of WAMU countries in the continent's exports may be in danger.

Smuggling of goods from weak-currency countries into the WAMU, the relative strength of the French franc and the fall in the prices of primary commodities, except oil, ask for the devaluation and possibly loosening of the link with the French franc.

Conclusion

Monetary policy is the sphere where the impact of international economic integration is the quickest and most obvious. In fact, monetary integration is the field where the success of overall integration is tested. A traditional single-criterion model of monetary integration is insufficient for the treatment of this complex part of economic policy. A cost–benefit model introduces the basic rationale for monetary integration. Monetary integration improves integration of markets for goods, services and factors. Exchange-rate risk for flows among the integrated countries does not exist, so the long-term investment decisions can be reached with high quality. Intra-union allocation of resources continuously improves because of the monetary stability. The costs which monetary integration may bring are more a formal than a real concern for small and medium-sized open economies. The greatest problem is that the non-economist cannot easily comprehend the need for and benefits of monetary integration.

FISCAL POLICY

Introduction

The standard theory of customs unions assumes that, by the elimination of tariffs and quotas, trade within a customs union becomes free (but for the existence of the common external tariff). It also assumes that trade is fostered by relative differences in production functions and resource endowments. This is just an illusion. It is not only the tariff and quota system which distorts the free flow of trade, but other fiscal impediments – such as subsidies (discussed in the chapter on customs unions) and taxes – which also create these distortions.

The fiscal policy of a country deals with the influence of the demand, size, revenues and expenditure of the public sector. It affects the allocation of resources, economic stabilization (reduction in the fluctuation of macro-economic variables around desired, planned or possible levels) and equity in the distribution of the national wealth. Harmonization of the fiscal system among countries has two meanings. First, the lower form of fiscal harmonization may be equated with cooperation among countries. These countries exchange information and/or enter into loose agreements about the means and types of taxation. Second, in its higher meaning, fiscal harmonization means the standardization of mutual tax systems with respect to means, types and rates of taxes and tax exemptions (Prest, 1983, p. 61).

A prudent fiscal policy should ensure that the government at all its levels (local, regional and central) should spend only on those activities where it can use resources better than the private sector. Taxes should be high enough to cover that cost, but levied in the way that distorts the economy as little as possible (although there are some valid social cases for the distortion, which include conservation of energy and control of pollution). The budget should be roughly in equilibrium during the economic cycle. The problem which must be avoided is to resist the burdening of a too narrow tax base. In this situation tax rates are high and distorting. The collection of taxes ought to be other than taxes on trade and company profits which are the most distorting kinds of taxes. Unfortunately, they are most common in LDCs. Taxes on trade (both export and import) prevent specialization while loophole-ridden taxes on company profits distort investment decisions. Sales taxes (value added tax) are the most becoming alternative although they are regressive.

Integration of fiscal policies in an economic union refers to the roles of public finance and a union budget. The theory of fiscal integration deals with the issue of optimal fiscal domains in economic unions (Robson, 1987, p. 89). It studies the rationale, structure and impact of fiscal (tax and budgetary systems) of the unionized countries.

Fiscal neutrality among the integrated countries refers to a situation in which the supplier or consumer of a good or service is indifferent to being taxed in any of the integrated countries. This is an important prerequisite for the efficient allocation of resources and for the operation of an economic union. The fiscal authorities should be quite cautious while assessing taxes and spending tax receipts. If they tax a significant part of profit or income, then they may destroy incentives and may stimulate factors to flow to the locations where they may maximize net benefits. However, this can be a powerful tool for the direction of certain business activities towards specific locations which may find some social justification.

The member countries of a union may finance a common budget according to the principles of benefit and ability to pay. First, the principle of benefit is based on the rule of clear balances or *juste retour*. Those which receive the favours of the budget expenditure should contribute to these public funds in proportion to the benefits which they receive. Second, economic benefits of integration do not accrue to the participating countries only through the transfers of public funds. The most important favours come from intra-group free trade, flows of factors, specialization, increase in economic activity and the like. Such a neo-classical expectation may not ask for 'corrective measures', since all countries and regions benefit from integration. However, in the case with imperfect markets and economies of scale, this may not materialize. In this situation, the principle of the ability to pay features highly. Individual contributions and receipts from the union budget do not have to be equal. Net contributions reflect a country's ability to pay. A nominal net contributory position of a country can be more than compensated by various spillovers which stem from the membership of an economic union.

Integration of fiscal policies implies not only harmonization of national systems of taxes and subsidies, but also issues like public expenditure, transfers (redistribution) within and between countries and individuals, combat of cyclical disturbances, stabilization policy and tax evasion. The highest type of fiscal integration among countries represents a unified system of taxes and subsidies, as well as the existence of a single budget which is empowered to cope with all issues of common concern. This has only been achieved in centralized federal states.

Fiscal policy has the property of having a direct (blunt) effect on income of factors and consumption of goods and services. This is in contrast to monetary policy which does this in an indirect (fine tuning) way through financial markets. By a simple change in transfers and rates of taxes and subsidies, the fiscal authority may directly affect expenditure and consumption. Monetary policy may do the same job, but in a discrete manner. Hence comes the need for the coordination of fiscal and monetary policies. If they work one against the other, neither will be effective and the result may be damaging. Stabilization and investment policies for a small country may be more effective in a fiscal and monetary union than in a situation where these policies are pursued in an independent, uncoordinated and often conflicting way with countries which are major economic partners. If intra-union trade is high in proportion to total external trade of the unionized countries, then the stability in the group exchange rates is a necessary condition for the protection of these flows.

This section deals with the structure and harmonization of taxes, as well as the function of a budget of an economic union. The basic classification of taxes is on their base – that is, income (direct taxes) and consumption (indirect taxes). Direct taxes charge incomes of firms and individuals (factor returns), as well as property ownership. These taxes are effective at the end of production and service processes. They have an impact on the movements of factors. A change in these taxes has a direct impact on tax-payers' purchasing power. Indirect taxes are applied to consumption. They affect movements of goods and services. An alteration of these taxes changes the prices of goods and services.

Direct taxes

Corporate tax

Differences in corporate taxes among countries which permit a free flow of capital may endanger the efficient allocation of resources if capital owners tend to maximize their net profits in the short run. Other things being equal, capital will flow to countries with a relatively low level of corporate taxes (although this is only one variable which influences their decision). Investment decisions by TNCs are reached not only on the production efficiency criteria, but also according to the differences in tax rates.

Corporate taxes may be collected according to the classical, integrated, dual or imputation systems. A classical, or separate, system represents one extreme. According to this system, a corporation is taken as a separate entity which is distinct from its shareholders. Corporations are taxed irrespective of whether profits are distributed or not. At the same time, shareholders' income is taxed notwithstanding the fact that the corporation has already paid taxes on its profit.

An integrated system represents another extreme. Here, a corporation is viewed just as a collection of shareholders. Corporate tax is eliminated while shareholders pay tax on their part of corporate profits. Hence, personal income tax and corporate tax are integrated in full.

The dual (two-rate, split-rate) system falls between the two extreme systems. A corporation pays tax at a lower rate if profits are distributed than in the case when they are not. Shareholders pay taxes just as in the classical system.

Imputation is another intermediate system for taxing corporations. In contrast to the dual system, however, relief is provided here at the shareholder level. Corporations pay taxes just as in the classical system while shareholders receive credit, usually in the year they receive dividends, for the tax already paid by the corporation.

The main aim of corporate taxation is not to increase the price of goods and services, but rather to capture part of the corporation's profits. Frequent changes in the corporation tax system should be avoided. They increase uncertainty and administrative burden on corporations. These variations distort the decision-making process about investment and have a long-term effect on the capital which will often avoid or reduce investment in such destinations. A corporation may pass on this tax burden to consumers in the form of higher prices or to its employees in the form of reduced wages. By passing on the tax burden, a corporation may reduce, in part or in full, the impact of the tax on its profit. The possibility for passing on this tax depends on the characteristics of the goods/services in question and the labour market. If a corporation is free to set its prices, then it depends on competition if this passing on is possible. If prices are regulated, then the way of passing on the tax burden is different. Suppose that the prices may not rise. A corporation may reduce the quality of its output in order to save profits. In the reverse case, when prices may not fall, a corporation may improve the quality of its output in order to increase its competitiveness and save or increase its market share.

The authorities of California and several other states in the United States apply a unitary system for the taxation of corporations. A TNC derives its income not only in the place of its residence, but also from the operations of its subsidiaries. The rationale for the unitary approach is that profits of the corporation accrue from its global operations. There may be a continuous multijurisdictional conflict with respect to the taxation of operations of TNCs in an increasingly internationalized world economy (UNCTC, 1988, p. 252). The national tax authorities need to take a semi-arbitrary approach and assess the share of global profits of the corporation which should be taxed in their jurisdiction. This approach contrasts sharply with the traditional, separate accounting rules for tax assessment among distinct fiscal jurisdictions.

The unitary approach has provoked an electrified debate in the United States. The issue at stake is whether the individual states have the right to tax, on the unitary basis, the extra-state operations of corporations. The United Kingdom had an argument against unitary taxation because it conflicts with bilateral tax treaty practice. From 1988 foreign based TNCs are not taxed in California on a unitary basis if they pay a small annual fee (UNCTC, 1988, p. 252).

The importance of the distribution of taxation between individuals and corporations may be analysed in the following example (Varian, 1984, p. 90). Suppose that P_d stands for the price paid by consumers. If one imposes a tax of t dollars per unit of output on the suppliers then the price F_s which they receive is:

$$P_s = P_d - t. \qquad (4.1)$$

The condition for equilibrium is:

$$P_s(q) = P_d(q) - t. \qquad (4.2)$$

Assume that one imposes the same tax of t dollars per unit of purchased good on the buyers. The price paid by consumers is:

$$P_d = P_s + t. \qquad (4.3)$$

The condition for equilibrium in this case is:

$$P_d(q) = P_s(q) + t. \qquad (4.4)$$

Note that the two conditions for equlibrium 4.2 and 4.4 are the same. Thus P_s, P_d and the quantity in equilibrium are independent of whether the tax is levied on demanders (individuals) or suppliers (corporations). This is obviously not understood by many tax authorities. The volume of the government revenue does not change. What changes is its composition, which may provoke hot political debate.

There is a school of integrationists who argue that income has to be taxed as a whole despite its source. It says that all taxes are ultimately borne by the people. This view opposes that of the absolutists, who argue that corporations are separate legal entities which should be taxed in their own capacity (under the assumption that they may not pass on the tax burden either to their employees or consumers). Another reason for the separate treatment of corporations is that they use government services without fully paying for them. This has an impact in the reduction of costs of operation. Tax authorities may use their policy to regulate investment of corporations and to control their monopoly position.

On these grounds, tax instruments may influence the behaviour of corporations.

If capital flows are a significant feature in relations among countries, some of those countries may have an incentive to negotiate tax treaties in order to avoid double taxation and, possibly, achieve neutrality. Tax neutrality between investment in home country A and foreign country B is achieved when corporations are indifferent (other things being equal) between investing in either country. The foreign country's tax equals the corporate tax plus the withholding tax (tax on the transfer of profits). If, under the condition of free mobility of capital, country A's company finds country B's taxes equal to country A's then tax neutrality between these two countries is achieved. If not, investment will flow to the country which has relatively lower taxes. Greater cooperation among the tax authorities in partner countries is indispensable. This is of special importance in the situation with fixed rates of exchange and without capital controls. The measures to reduce risks of tax evasion can take the form of a generalized witholding tax to all union residents and/or a commitment on banks to disclose information about interest received by the union residents. Therefore, the need to create conduit companies, as intermediary subsidiaries which take advantage of tax treaties in order to reduce withholding taxes, will be eliminated.

The Treaty of Rome is short on tax provisions. Article 99 asks for harmonization of indirect taxes, while Article 100 indirectly demands approximation of direct taxes. Table 4.3 illustrates, in a simplified way, differences in corporate tax systems in the EC countries. It does not take into account any of the surtaxes, surcharges, local taxes, credits, exemptions and the like, which apply in nearly all EC countries. Greece does not have an entirely genuine dual system, for distributed profits are not taxed at the company level at all, only at the shareholder level. The differences in systems and rates of company taxes describe the distortions of the tax neutrality for investment in the EC.

Double taxation arises when a single economic activity is taxed twice (by two tax authorities). It is often forgotten that what matters for TNCs is not the fact that profits are taxed twice, but rather the level of total taxation. If income of country A's TNC earned in country B has been taxed by country B, then country A may exempt this corporation from taxes on that part of its income earned in country B. Another method for solving this problem is that country A provides credit to its TNCs on taxes paid in country B. In this

Table 4.3 Systems and rates of corporate taxes in the EC countries in 1990

Country	System	Rate (%)
1 Belgium	Imputation	41
2 Denmark	Imputation	40
3 France	Imputation	37 (retained) 42 (distributed)
4 Ireland	Imputation	40
5 Italy	Imputation	36
6 Portugal	Imputation	36
7 Spain	Imputation	35
8 United Kingdom	Imputation	35
9 FR Germany	Dual	36 (distributed) 50 (retained)
10 Greece	Dual	46
11 Luxembourg	Classical	34
12 The Netherlands	Classical	35

Source: International Bureau of Fiscal Documentation (1990).

case the tax burden on country A's corporation operating in country B is the same as from purely home operations in country A, provided that country B's taxes are lower or equal to those in country A.

Personal income tax

Differences in personal income taxes between countries and different regions of one country may have effects on the mobility of labour. The actual flow of labour depends upon a number of factors – which include possibilities for finding employment, standard of living, social obstacles, social-security benefits and immigration rules. Differences in personal-income taxes may be neither the most decisive nor the only incentive for labour to move. This difference in taxes is highly significant only for the movement of upper middle class.

It is a generally accepted principle that taxes are applied in those countries in which income originates. A person originating from country A who works part of the year in country B and the rest of the year in country A will pay income tax on income earned in country B and ask for tax credit while paying income tax in country

A for the rest of taxable income. This person's tax payment would be the same as if the whole income had been earned in country A, unless country B's income tax is higher than the one in country A.

A tax ratio relates tax revenues to the GNP of a country. This ratio has been increasing over time. There are at least three reasons for this development. First, the welfare state has increased social-care transfers. They are financed mostly by social-security levies. Second, economic development and increase in opportunities had their impact on the growth of taxable income. Tax payers were climbing into higher brackets, so these proceeds increased. Third, inflation has increased tax revenues and devalued their real value. Personal income tax is taken to be one of the most genuine rights of a state. There is little chance that this tax can be harmonized in a union. The EC is fully aware of this issue, so it has few ambitions in this sphere.

A notable exception has often been for the taxable income of frontier and migrant workers. Tax agreements generally avoid double taxation both in the country of destination (where the income is made) and the country of origin (where the income-maker resides). Troublesome issues remain with respect to deductions, allowances and applicable rates. Granting an allowance to a non-resident worker may involve a concession. This would be the case when the same allowance is offered by the country of residence. Generally, full taxation in the country of residence with a credit for tax paid in the source country would be the solution (Cnossen, 1986, p, 558).

Indirect taxes

Indirect taxes are levied on the consumption of goods and services. They influence the final price, hence they affect patterns of trade. Sales and turnover taxes, excise duties and tariffs are the basic indirect taxes. In contrast with direct taxes, these taxes are seldom progressive. The principle for the levying of these taxes will be considered before the analysis of indirect taxes.

Principles of destination and origin

A separate issue in the tax relations among countries which enter into an economic union is represented by the place where the goods are taxed. According to the principle of destination, taxes on goods are applied in the country of their consumption; while according to the principle of origin, taxes apply in the country of their production.

The destination principle states that consumption of all goods in one destination should be subject to the same tax irrespective of its origin. This principle removes tax distortions on competition between goods on the consuming country's market. The goods compete on equal tax conditions. This principle does not interfere with the location of production. The problem is that this principle may give the illusion that it stimulates exports and acts as a quasi-tariff import. This issue will be discussed shortly.

The origin or production principle states that all goods produced in one country should be taxed in that country despite the possibility that those goods may be exported or consumed at home. If the production tax on good X in country A is lower than the same tax on the same good in country B, then if exported at zero transport cost, good X produced in country A will have a tax advantage in country B's market over country B's home-made good X. This introduces a distortion which interferes with the location of production between the member countries. For allocational neutrality, a harmonized rate of tax between the member countries is a necessary condition. If the tax burden differs among the countries, then the origin principle may eliminate any 'trade war' with differences in taxes among countries.

Even within a customs union or a common market, there may exist fiscal frontiers if the member countries accept the principle of destination. The fiscal authorities of each country should know until where and until when they are entitled to tax consumption of goods. The origin principle may have an advantage, for it does not require fiscal frontiers – which saves resources.

Taxes levied according to the destination and origin principles differ with respect to their revenue impact. These two principles determine to which government the proceeds accrue. A full economic optimization cannot be achieved if there are different tax rates levied on various goods. Suppose that country A levies a value added tax (VAT) at the rate of 25 per cent on cars only, while the union partner country B applies a uniform tax at the rate of 10 per cent. Suppose that both countries apply the destination principle for tax collection. In this situation, the production in either country will be maximized because it will not be affected by the tax. Consumption will, however, be distorted. The relative consumer prices will be distorted because cars will be dearer relative to clothes in country A, than they will be in country B. Consequently, country A's consumers buy less cars and more clothes than they would do otherwise. The opposite tendency prevails in country B. In this case, trade between the two countries will not be optimized. Conversely, suppose that the two countries collect taxes according to the origin principle. In this case trade would be optimized, for the relative consumer prices will be the same in either country. Trade will therefore be optimized, but tax will distort the maximization of production because producer prices, net of tax, will be reduced in a disproportionate way. Country A producers will be stimulated to produce clothes rather than cars, while the opposite tendency will prevail in country B. Once the indirect tax is not levied at a uniform rate on all goods, the choice is between the destination principle (which maximizes production but does not optimize trade) and the origin principle (which optimizes trade but does not maximize production) (Robson, 1987, pp. 122–3).

The principle of destination introduces the possibility of tax evasion, which is not possible (if the records are not faked) with the origin principle. If taxes differ, then a consumer may be tempted to purchase a good in the state in which the relative tax burden is lower, and consume it in the state where the tax burden is relatively higher. Consumers may easily purchase goods in one country and send or bring them to another, or order these goods from abroad. This tax evasion depends on the differences in taxation, cost of transport and cooperation of buyers and sellers who do not inform the tax authorities if they know that the aim of certain purchases is tax evasion. The effect of a tax at a rate of 40 per cent in a country where tax evasion is widespread may be much smaller than the impact of the same tax at a rate of 10 per cent in the country where tax evasion is not a common practice.

The tax system in the United States relies on corporate and personal income tax with the origin principle applied. The west European tax authorities rely upon consumption taxes to which the destination principle is applied. If the Europeans export goods to the United States, they may have an advantage embodied in the difference in the tax systems. The United States may contemplate the introduction of a border tax adjustment. This step may involve an addition to, or reduction in, the taxes already paid in Europe. The aim is to keep competition in the United States market on the same tax base.

While the origin principle does not involve visible border tax adjustment, the destination principle includes it to the full extent of the tax. The long-run effect of either principle is the same. In general equilibrium, any short-run advantage by one country will be eliminated in the long run by changes in the rate of exchange and domestic prices (Johnson and Krauss, 1973, p. 241). The United States is a net importer of manufactured goods from Europe and Japan. It is advantageous for the United States to have these countries administer taxes on a destination, rather than origin, basis (Hamilton and Whalley, 1986, p. 377). This is correct in the short run. General equilibrium, the operation of exchange rates and prices (Johnson-Krauss law) will, in the long run, eliminate any short-run (dis)advantage of these countries.

Sales and turnover taxes

Sales and turnover taxes are payments to the government which are applied to all taxable goods and services except the ones which are subject to excise duties. Turnover tax is applied during the process of production, while if the tax is applied during sales to the final consumer it is called a sales tax. There are two methods for the collection of this tax. One is the cumulative multi-stage cascade method, while the other method is called the VAT. Apart from these two multi-phase methods for the collection of the sales tax, there is a one-stage method. This method is applied only once, either at the stage of production or at the wholesale or retail sales level. The following analysis will deal with the multi-phase methods.

Cumulative multi-stage cascade method

According to this method of collection of sales tax, the tax is applied every time goods and services are transferred to somebody else against payment. The tax base includes the aggregate value of goods – which includes previously paid taxes on raw materials and inputs. The levying and collection of this tax is relatively simple, the tax burden may appear to be distributed over a larger number of tax-payers and the rate of sales tax collected by this method is relatively lower than the rate applied by the VAT method.

Companies may be stimulated by this method of collection of sales tax to integrate vertically in order to pay tax only at the last stage of the production process. This may have a favourable impact on the expansion of the activities of corporations and their influence on business life. It may, however, cause a misallocation of resources. This artificial vertical integration may erode the advantages of specialization and the efficiency of numerous relatively small companies if the vertically integrated firm ceases to use their output.

Value Added Tax

This method of collection of sales tax is applied every time a good or service is sold, but it applies only on the value which is added in the respective phase of production, which is the difference between the price paid for inputs and the price received for outputs. This starts at the beginning of the production or distribution process and ends up in the final sale to the consumer. The VAT avoids double or multiple taxation of the previous stages of production. Every tax-payer has to prove to the tax authorities, by an invoice, that the tax has been paid in the previous stages of production. Hence, a kind of self-checking mechanism.

At the early stages of development, countries have relatively simple tax systems which apply to a few goods only. As countries develop, they tend to introduce the tax system which is more sophisticated, has a wider and more neutral tax base and is more efficient. Taxes on international trade (exports and imports) ought to be replaced by sales taxes which are collected by the VAT method. A relatively low rate of tax collected according to this method can raise a lot of proceeds. It does not distort the economy, because it is neutral to the production mix of home and imported factors. Also, it does not discriminate between production for home and off-shore markets and it remains neutral with respect to vertical integration of companies, so specialized firms may remain in business. If sales tax is collected according to the VAT method, then it will be harder to evade it in comparison to the situation when the tax is collected only at the retail stage.

The VAT, on the principle of destination, is accepted in the EC as the method for the collection of sales tax. The method is harmonized, but there is a wide range of differences in the rates of this tax among the EC member countries. If the aim is to have a single rate of this tax there exists much room for improvement.

Once the fiscal frontiers in the EC are removed, an EC system needs to be established in order to ensure that sales and purchases are treated in the same way as similar trade within the member countries. The EC's White Paper proposes the setting up of the EC clearing house system. Its role would be to ensure that the VAT,

Table 4.4 The VAT rates in the EC countries in 1990

Country	VAT rate (%)
1 Belgium	1, *6*, 17, *19*, 25, 33
2 Denmark	*22*
3 France	2.1, *5.5*, 13, *18.6*, 25
4 FR Germany	7, *14*
5 Greece	3, *6*, *16*, 36
6 Ireland	*0*, 2, 5, *10*, *23*
7 Italy	4, *9*, *19*, 38
8 Luxembourg	*3*, *6*, *12*
9 The Netherlands	*6*, *18.5*
10 Portugal	8, *16*, 30
11 Spain	*6*, *12*, 33
12 United Kingdom	*0*, *15*

Source: International Bureau of Fiscal Documentation (1990).

collected in the exporting member country, and deduced in the importing member country was reimbursed to the latter. The crucial role in this system will play computerization of procedures. This system would, in principle, create a situation for taxable persons within the EC identical to that which prevails in the member countries. In practice, however, the existence of widely diverging rates of tax and tax exemptions may expose the system to the risk of fraud and evasion. The EC is aware that some fraud and evasion exist at present, but the scale of such distortions after the removal of fiscal frontiers without harmonization would not be acceptable.

A move towards the origin principle (collection of tax during production) will require a system for redistribution of revenues among countries as if the tax had been levied on consumption. Because of the possibilities for fraud, lack of cooperation among the national tax authorities and the need to find alternative employment for thousands of customs officers, many EC member states do not like such a proposal. If fiscal frontiers among the EC countries stay, the most visible benefit of the 1992 Programme may disappear.

Table 4.4 illustrates differences in VAT systems in the EC countries. The italicized numbers are the standard rates and lower rates for food, clothing and other essential items. Portugal has lower rates in its autonomous regions. Ireland and Britain use the zero rate for food, books and children's clothing. The other countries generally apply an exception with credit (which comes down to the same thing as a zero rate) to exports and supplies assimilated to exports, such as supplies to embassies, to ships leaving the country and the like. In Ireland and Britain these supplies are also covered by the zero rate. A broad-based VAT can be criticized on the grounds that it is regressive. The low-income segment of the population can be helped by transfer payments. This can make VAT directly progressive. Zero rating, exemptions and multiple rates do not always directly assist the low-income group which is meant to be helped.

The EC has conducted a profound survey. About 20,000 businessmen from all twelve member countries were asked to rank the worst barriers to free trade. The most damaging of all were overt obstacles. National technical standards, administrative and customs formalities were on the top of the list. Differences in rates in VAT and excise duties came at the bottom of the list of eight barriers (Emerson *et al.*, 1988, pp. 44–6).

The above result does not mean that the EC Commission is making a mistake while concentrating on the issue of the VAT-rate approximation. A removal of the EC internal fiscal frontiers will not be possible until the VAT rates among the member countries are harmonized. An arrangement that would require minimum changes in the existing tax-rate structure among the member countries would, according to the EC proposal, involve an introduction of the standard VAT rate around 15 per cent and the reduced rate between 0 per cent and 9 per cent for 'socially sensitive' items. In the face of hostility to this proposal, the EC accepted a more flexible approach. The EC may set the bottom rates, while there will be no ceiling for the upper rates. The member governments would be free to decide about the upper limits of tax rate.

This freedom would be subject to the constraint which comes from the operation of market forces. The greater the differences in the relative tax rates among the countries, the greater the danger of intensive inter-country shopping. Even if countries agree on the common system of taxes and their nominal rates, this does not necessarily mean that the system is neutral throughout the union. Distortions may come from the structure of the market in the member countries. Monopolists in one country may pass the tax burden on to the consumers and labour. Consequently, the effective rates of tax may differ, and the tax authorities will have to keep this in mind. The EC bottom rate for basic goods may be set at the 5 per cent level, while the bottom rate for everything else may be at the level of 15 per cent. Britain and Ireland, which apply the zero rate for some basic goods, can be granted an exception. These two countries, as well as Greece, do not have a common land border with other EC countries which makes transportation of goods costlier. Approximation of tax rates among other countries like those between, for example, Belgium, The Netherlands and Luxembourg, on the one hand, and FR Germany, on the other, are highly relevant.

Excise duties

Excise duties are a type of indirect taxes which are levied for the purpose of raising revenue. They are applied in almost every country to tobacco, spirits and liquid fuels. Excise duties are also applied in some countries to coffee, tea, cocoa, salt, bananas, light bulbs and playing cards. These duties are levied only once, usually at the stage of production or import. Another property of excise duties is that they are generally high in relation to other levies.

While VAT is proportional to the value of output, an excise duty may be based either on the *ad valorem* principle (retail or wholesale price) or it may be a specific tax. Within the EC, tobacco products are subject to both. There is a specific tax per cigarette and an *ad valorem* tax based on the retail price of the cigarettes concerned (Kay, 1990, p. 34).

Table 4.5 gives the rates of excise duties in the EC member countries and the harmonized rates proposed by the EC Commission. There is a wide variety in the rates of excise duties among the member countries. This difference is due to the various choices of fiscal and health authorities. If the difference in excise duties among countries exceeds costs of reallocation of resources or transport, it will have a distorting effect on the allocation of resources or pattern of trade. The difference in the excise duty on 1,000 litres of petrol of ECU 348 between Italy and Luxembourg is significant when one keeps in mind that it costs just a few ECUs to transport this amount of fuel by pipeline. The completion of a genuine internal EC market requires harmonization of excise duties.

The VAT is calculated on the price of a good which includes excise duty. Any flexibility in the excise duties will produce differences in the VAT which exceed the accepted margin for the tax. Hence the need for harmonization. A solution to preserve the

Table 4.5 The excise duty rates in the EC countries in 1987

Country	Pure alcohol (ECU per hl)	Wine (ECU per hl)	Beer (ECU per hl)	Cigarettes[1] ECU per 1,000	Cigarettes[1] ad valorem (%)	Petrol (ECU per 1,000 l)
1 Belgium	1,252	33	10	2.5	66.4	261
2 Denmark	3,499	157	56	77.5	39.3	473
3 FR Germany	1,174	20	7	27.3	43.8	256
4 Greece	48	0	10	0.6	60.4	349
5 Spain	309	0	3	0.7	51.9	254
6 France	1,149	3	3	1.3	71.1	369
7 Ireland	2,722	279	82	48.9	33.6	362
8 Italy	230	0	17	1.8	68.6	557
9 Luxembourg	842	13	5	1.7	63.6	209
10 The Netherlands	1,298	33	20	26.0	35.7	340
11 Portugal	248	0	9	2.2	64.8	352
12 United Kingdom	2,483	154	49	42.8	34.0	271
Proposed rate by the EC	1,271	17	17	19.5	52–54	340

[1] The taxes on cigarettes comprise a specific excise duty, the rate of which is given here for 1,000 cigarettes, an ad valorem duty and VAT, the rate being shown here as a percentage of the retail price. The proposals of the Commission, referred to above, also comprise a specific, as well as an ad valorem element (the sum of the ad valorem duty and of the VAT). The latter could be between 52 and 54 per cent of the retail price according to the level retained in each country for the normal rate of VAT taken from the range 14 to 20 per cent.

Source: Emerson et al. (1988).

removal of fiscal frontiers within the EC could be done in a way similar to the one by which the United States preserves the different liquor duties among its states. Liquor and cigarettes should bear the national tax authority stamp. Only the nationally stamped goods could be purchased legally within a state. Import for personal consumption would be unlimited, while bulk transport among the member countries of these goods would be forbidden. The rates proposed by the EC Commission should be viewed just as a yardstick for approximation, for it would be most difficult and highly uncertain to try to unify excise duties in the EC member countries.

The goods which are subject to excise duties are normally stored in bonded warehouses which are controlled by the authorities. Once the goods are taken out for consumption, the excise duty is levied. If the goods are exported, the excise duty is not charged upon the presentation of a proof of export. The importing country of these goods controls the import at the frontier, where it establishes liability for excise duties of these goods. This ensures that excise duty is charged in the country where the goods are consumed.

Once the tax and other frontiers are removed, the wide divergence in excise duties would distort trade because of a real danger of fraud and evasion. As a solution to this issue the White Paper proposes a linkage system of bonded warehouses for products subject to excise duties and approximation of these charges.

The benefits which accrue from the elimination of fiscal frontiers in an economic union include the following gains. Investment decisions of the firms are improved, for the tax system increases the degree of certainty in relation to the situation when every country manages its own tax system. A removal of tax posts at the frontiers saves resources and, more importantly, increases the opportunities for competition. Of course, some facilities for random anti-terrorist, health, veterinary and illegal immigration checks may be necessary. Finally, harmonization of the tax system would enhance the equilization of prices and lower the discrepancies which are due to different systems and rates of taxation.

The budget of an economic union

The budget and its revenue and expenditure is one of the most fundamental instruments, together with the law, which an organization may employ to fulfil its role. This is of great importance for economic organizations. The budget should cover not only the administrative costs, but also dispose of funds for the intervention in the economy. Otherwise, the role of this organization would be mere consultation and research of certain issues. Most international organizations cover just their administrative expenses. A rare exception is the EC, which returns and redistributes around 95 per cent of its receipts. The budgets of the member countries reduce their expenditure for their own intervention in the fields where the EC intervenes.

The theory of fiscal federalism assumes a central fiscal authority and considers its relations with the lower-level authorities. This consideration is complicated by the existence of different currencies in the member countries. If the union is to conduct an effective stabilization policy, it should be endowed with the power to tax and borrow. This implies that its budget may be not only in balance, but more importantly, in deficit or surplus over an economic cycle. The union may not necessarily directly tax corporations and individuals, for it can tax the member governments.

A common approach to the macroeconomic management of the union is subject to a number of pitfalls. The first one is the issue of a union stance on major macroeconomic variables. Even if the member countries agree on the major objectives (rate of exchange, inflation, rate of interest, balance of payments, unemployment and the like) they also have to agree on the economic policy instruments. Even though the countries concur about the major macroeconomic goals, they may use different and often conflicting means to achieve the stated aim. Instead of improving the economic situation, such an economic policy may well worsen it. Therefore, it is not only the main economic aims which the member countries should agree upon, they should also concur with respect to the means which should be employed to achieve the agreed objectives. This implies that common fiscal and monetary policies require each other in an economic union. Integration of fiscal policy in the absence of integration of monetary policy and vice versa in an economic union may be a waste of effort. Of course, the agreed economic policy will not have equal effects on all member countries of a union, just as a single economic policy does not have an equivalent impact on all regions of a single country. A solution to this problem always involves transfer of resources among the member states or among regions within a country.

In spite of former disputes among economists, there is a certain agreement that economic stabilization can be influenced in the short run by a joint action of fiscal and monetary policies. This can

Table 4.6 EC budget expenditure in 1990 (commitments)

Chapter	Million ECU	%
1 Common agricultural policy (incl. fisheries)	28,776	59.0
2 Regional policy	5,408	11.1
3 Social policy	4,310	8.8
4 Research	1,727	3.5
5 Development aid	1,664	3.4
6 Administration	2,362	4.8
7 Other	4,599	9.4
Total	48,846	100.0

Source: XXIIIrd General Report on the Activities of the EC (1990).

control employment and output around their natural levels and avoid excess demand which creates inflation. If the economic ties among countries are highly interlaced, then the optimal solutions to the economic issues can be found in the joint action of the countries concerned.

The major practical obstacle to the integration of fiscal and other macroeconomic policies in an economic union is that the countries concerned may not agree about the objectives. The disagreement may arise with respect to the speed at which inflation will be reduced or about the policy means to be employed. Once they concur about the objectives and policy instruments, the outcome may bring different costs and benefits to the members of a union. The solution to this problem may always involve fiscal transfers among the members – through the budget, which may be quite large (Robson, 1987, p. 99).

Although the EC is not (yet) an economic union, its budget offers the best existing example for analysis. However, its absolute and relative size is rather small in relation to the share and impact on the joint GNP of the member states. As such, it plays no significant role in economic stabilization, nor in redistribution or allocation of resources. In addition, its stabilization role is further jeopardized by the request that it must be in annual balances without the provision to take loans to finance the possible deficits.

Table 4.6 shows the EC budget expenditure accepted for 1990. The Common Agricultural Policy swallows three-fifths of the budget expenditure. If related to 323 million citizens of the EC (not including 17 million citizens of the former GDR) the annual cost of this policy per citizen is ECU 89 or ECU 1.7 per week. In these terms, the cost of the Common Agricultural Policy does not seem too high. In providing security of supplies, this policy is successful. But it is even more so in distorting the agricultural market, international trade and depriving funds to other existing and new activities. Regional policy was introduced after the first enlargement of the EC (1973), and absorbs 11.1 per cent of the budget and is aimed at assisting, usually, the EC-rim regions which are hit by integration and recession. Another redistributional policy – the social policy – helps both the occupational (vocational training, education) and geographical mobility of labour. It absorbs 8.8 per cent of the budget. A notable feature of regional and social policies is that their shares are continuously rising over time. EC research consumes 3.5 per cent of the budget, which reflects the concern about this issue. Development aid – mainly to the African, Caribbean and Pacific countries – consumes 3.4 per cent, while the most important items in other expenditure consist of transport, energy, environment and industry, which absorb 9.4 per cent.

Table 4.7 shows the EC budget revenue in 1990. Customs duties and agricultural levies represent the 'natural' proceeds of a customs union. Although customs duties which are levied on trade with third countries represent 24.3 per cent of revenue, their impact is diminishing over time because tariffs are being continuously reduced, although this may be partly compensated by an increase in the level of trade with off-shore countries. Also, recession can reduce the level of economic activity and, consequently, reduce imports. Agricultural levies are a changeable source of revenue for they depend on the level of imports which depend partly on weather conditions and partly on trade concessions which the EC offers to the off-shore partners. Another element of this fluctuation is that the world-market prices for agricultural goods change often. In addition, the EC is becoming increasingly self-sufficient in a number of agricultural products of the temperate zone, hence there is a reduction in demand for imports. In this situation the only dynamic components of the EC's own resources are the VAT contribution and its GNP-based resources. The EC budget can absorb, via the VAT, at most 1.4 per cent of the common base. The VAT currently mobilizes 60.4 per cent, while GNP-based resources, determined according to a country's ability to pay, contribute 4.2 per cent to the EC budget.

Table 4.7 EC budget revenue in 1990

Source	Million ECU (estimates)	%
1 Agricultural levies	1,037	2.2
2 Sugar and isoglucose levies	1,246	2.7
3 Customs duties	11,350	24.3
4 VAT (own resources)	28,218	60.4
5 GNP-based own resources	1,964	4.2
6 Budget balance (previous year)	2,598	5.6
7 Other revenue	304	0.6
Total	46,717	100.0

Source: xxIIIrd General Report on the Activities of the EC (1990).

The preceding analysis reveals that both the EC budget expenditure and revenue are not related either to the EC's need to influence economic life (save for agriculture), as the national governments can do, or to the economic wealth of the member countries. It should not be forgotten that it is neither the absolute nor the relative size of the budget which matters; rather, what matters is its size in relation to the encouragement which is necessary to change certain behaviour, in the desired direction. In some cases this amount can be rather minuscule, such as the development of small and medium-sized enterprises where simple freedom of establishment, tax incentives and loan guarantees can do the job. In others, like agriculture or adjustment out of sunset sectors, the amounts required to change behaviour can be quite large.

Although required to be in balance by the Treaty of Rome, the EC budget expenditure happened to be in excess of revenue (borrowings to cover deficits are not permitted). The EC policy of 'hiding' deficits by deferring spending or putting deficits for the coming years and other accounting tricks cannot last indefinitely. Instead of singling out economic areas for influence and, then, creating the necessary funds, the EC picks up policies which can fit into the limited funds. Something must be done to change this situation.

When the member countries of the EC agree to pursue a common policy, one can also expect that the means for carrying out this policy may be transferred upward. The problem is that the member countries take the EC as the appropriate plane for the conduct of common policies, but they are quite selfish, for they do not want, in many cases, to transfer the necessary extra funds for these policies and increase the role of the EC budget. Reforms of the EC budget are resisted by the countries which benefit from the present structure (mainly the agricultural regions in the northern EC). An increased expenditure on other policies without extra funds can jeopardize the current distribution of costs and benefits. Without the ability to increase or substantially reorganize spending, the EC should endeavour to coordinate expenditure of the member countries.

The EC budget absorbs only 1 per cent of the EC GNP. It plays only a limited role in redistribution of income and allocation of resources. Its role in economic stabilization has not existed. The influential MacDougall Report (1977) noted that in federal states like the United States and FR Germany, federal spending was in the neighbourhood of 20–25 per cent of GNP. Such an increase in the EC spending cannot reasonably be expected in the near future. In the pre-federal stage of the EC, a budget which absorbs 5–7 per cent of the GNP (without transfers for defence) could have an impact on economic stabilization and evening of the regional disparities. Such a budget may influence social (unemployment, education, health, retirement), regional and external aid policies. Resources may be found in either transfer of funds from the national budgets and/or an increase in the rate for the VAT contributions. The problem is that the member countries are still reluctant to increase the budgetary powers of the EC which is, nevertheless, desirable. The total expenditure on the EC level, as opposed to similar outlays on the national level of the member states, may be reduced because of the economies of scale. A budget with increased resources may represent a built-in stabilizer for macroeconomic management. In addition, transfers among regions may enhance economic convergence and strengthen cohesion of the member countries.

Apart from all stated problems, the EC has a strong means for control of a significant part of public expenditure in all member countries – this is the EC competition policy. State aids absorb a significant part of the national budgets, but control of these outlays does not require extra expenditure from the EC budget. In the foreseeable future it can be anticipated that a crucial reform of the EC budget will, unfortunately, not happen. Such an event would be coupled with considerable political sensitivity. Instead, what may take place is reform, or rather restructuring, within the framework of the existing budget. Increased contributions to the EC budget according to the level of national wealth or the principle of the ability to pay should be encouraged.

Conclusion

A country which often changes its fiscal system may be seen as a potentially risky destination for investments. This may provoke a reduction in the inflow and an increase in the outflow of capital to the relatively more stable destinations. Complete unification of fiscal systems, however, may not be a prerequisite for the smooth functioning of an economic union. The United States with its various states is the best example. The states have differences in their respective tax systems. This system functions relatively satisfactorily without the tax posts between the states for a number of years. One must note, however, that the differences in tax systems among the states are not great. This means that there exists a significant degree of harmonization among tax systems in federal units.

If the EC wants to create a genuine internal market, then it will have to harmonize indirect taxes among its member countries, otherwise the member governments will have to accept substantial diversions in revenues. It is widely believed that a difference in sales tax of up to 5 per cent can introduce distortions which may be accepted and which will not bring unbearable budgetary distortions.

As for the possibility of a significant degree of harmonization (or, in an extreme case, unification) of fiscal systems in an economic union, there are reasons for pessimism. A tax policy is one of the most fundamental, national sovereign rights. It is the means for the achievement of national aims which do not necessarily coincide at all times with those of other partners in a union. Although a union may agree on the basic aims, their achievement may be left to the member countries – which may wish to use different and often clashing instruments. The public is sensitive to changes in tax systems. Full fiscal harmonization in a union may require an increase in taxes in some countries while it may require their decrease in others. Therefore, a partial fiscal harmonization (only the agreed taxes) may be a good initial step. Harmonization of fiscal systems of the countries which are in an economic union requires caution, gradualism and, more than anything else, the political will which economic theory may not predict.

A likely achievement of a single internal market of the EC will enhance the role of the EC institutions. New EC-wide policies (industry, competition, monetary), will ask the EC to play a much more prominent role than it currently has. This will require an increase in resources, as well as coordination of fiscal, monetary, social and regional policies. The EC ought to have the right to tax and spend in its own right, at least up to the agreed extent. How to persuade the national governments to abandon a part of the fiscal sovereignty in favour of the EC in order to reap the benefits of fiscal integration is a question to be dealt with in politics.

INDUSTRIAL POLICY

Background

Explicit industrial policy as a part of overall economic policy had not been in the centre of research interest in the industrialized countries up to the mid-1970s. This is due to underlying economic developments. During the 1960s and early 1970s these countries experienced relatively fast economic growth with low rates of unemployment. Prices of raw materials were stable and relatively low, while labour was flowing without major disturbances from agriculture to the manufacturing and service industries. Excess demand for labour was met by a steady inflow of labour from abroad. This period was also characterized by sporadic government intervention to influence the pattern of national industrial production. Relatively free markets were operating smoothly without significant disruption. During this period, the GATT was active in lowering tariffs, and foreign trade was growing faster than national production.

The 'golden sixties' were followed by a period whose first characteristic was a sharp increase in the price of oil in 1973. This triggered rises in inflation and unemployment, and a reduction in the rate of growth throughout the world. International competition increased sharply because suppliers were fighting on shrinking markets. It seemed that the free market system was not capable of coping satisfactorily with this situation. There appeared an awareness that there was a need for alternative strategies (i.e. interventionist, industrial and trade) to cope with the new situation. Interest in industrial policy as part of the supply-side management has been increasing.

The classical model of a customs union based on free trade and perfect competition predicts that *laissez-faire* is universally beneficial and costless. The new theory of strategic trade and industrial policy demonstrates cases where intervention can play a useful role in reducing the shortcomings of market imperfections. Economic adjustments (reallocation of resources) is not smooth, easy or costless, hence the need for an industrial policy.

The EC and the United States have responded to the circumstances prevailing during the 1970s primarily by protectionism. These and other industrialized countries realized that the solution to lagging productivity, recession and deteriorating export performance may be found in policies which affect the development of national industry. Inadequate economic performance is not a sufficient condition for the justification of industrial policy. The question is not whether the economy is operating (un)satisfactorily, but rather whether an industrial policy might have achieved a better result than a free market system (Adams, 1983, p. 405). Any policy has to be tested according to its gains and losses in a dynamic context.

Once free markets lose credibility as efficient conductors of economic life, the introduction of intervention (economic policies) seems inevitable. Now the question is: how can the government intervene in the most efficient and least harmful way? The choice might be between the risk of leaving the economy to imperfect entrepreneurs and the possibly of an even greater risk of having it run by imperfect governments (Curzon Price, 1981, p. 20). However, there is no a priori reason why an economy run by imperfect governments is possibly at even greater risk than when the economy is run by imperfect businessmen and vice versa.

Risk-taking (entrepreneurship) has been a significant engine of economic growth. The benefits of risk-taking are not without risk, of course. The cost of adjustment to the changed situation is borne by those who are powerless. The governments were quite often following a defensive policy whose aim was to ensure employment in the short run and evade social tensions. The socialization of risk in the form of various economic policies may introduce a safer life, but may prevent both a free operation of entrepreneurial activity of individuals and an even greater increase in the economic pie. This process may be seen as a reconciliation of the public's desire to see a happy marriage between progress and stability (Blais, 1986, p. 41). Those who have full confidence in the operation of a free market system say that the market will take care of itself. Why bother to change those things which will happen anyway? What this school of thought does not consider are a number of market imperfections.

The most influential reasons for intervention may be found in the loss of a competitive position, the management of expansion of new and decline of old industries, the management of industries subject to scale effects and spillovers, as well as attracting footloose industries (Lipsey, 1987a, p. 117). Fostering of strategic industries which have strong links with the rest of the economy can be a very attractive policy goal. These industries supply external or non-priced gains to the rest of the economy. Growing industries like semiconductors and electronics have a much more profound spillover effect than the furniture or apparel industries.

The relative shares of industry and agriculture in GNP and employment have been continuously declining in the industrialized countries over the last three decades. The GNP of the industrialized countries on average consists mostly of services (60 per cent), while the rest is distributed between manufacturing (35 per cent) and agriculture (5 per cent). Hence, the process of deindustrialization leads countries to the post-industrial society. These economies have been called service rather than industrial economies, because industry is a statistically dying sector in relation to services. One has to be cautious with such generalizations. Many services (around half) are directly linked to the manufacture of goods – as in the case of transport, financial and other business services. These services are not directly aimed at individuals for their personal consumption. If they are added directly to the relative share of manufacturing and agriculture, these sectors may significantly increase their relative share.

A relative increase in the demand for services and growth of this sector was made possible by an increase in the productivity of the manufacturing sector. This has made more resources available for the service sector of the economy. Increase in productivity has lowered the price of manufactured goods, hence there appeared an increase in disposable funds for the consumption of services. This makes industrial policy interesting for consideration. First, the meaning of an industrial policy will be explored; then its instruments and the approaches to this policy in different countries will be considered; finally, a certain doubt will be cast on the possibility of implementing an industrial policy, both in single countries and in economic unions.

What is the meaning of an industrial policy?

There are various definitions of industrial policy. Before surveying them, one should keep in mind the difference between competition and industrial policy. The former is directed towards freeing market forces, while the latter is seeking to channel them (Geroski, 1987, p. 57).

Some definitions of industrial policy are specific. Industrial policy can be defined as coordinated targeting. It is the selection of parts of the economy – such as firms, projects or industrial sectors – for special treatment (targeting), which is coupled with a coordinated government plan to influence industrial structure in defined ways (coordination) (Brander, 1987, p. 4). In addition, industrial policies can be those government policies which are intended to have a direct effect on a particular industry or firm (McFetridge, 1985, p. 1).

Other definitions of industrial policy are broad, and include many areas of public policy. It can be any government measure or set of measures to promote or prevent structural change (Curzon Price, 1981, p. 17). Industrial policy may mean all measures which improve the economy's supply potential: anything that will improve growth, productivity and competitiveness (Adams and Klein, 1983, p. 3). Another look at industrial policy can take it as a government policy aimed at or motivated by problems within specific sectors. The 'problems' are presumably in both sunset and sunrise industries. The solutions to these problems need not necessarily be sector-specific although that is a possibility (Tyson and Zysman, 1987a, p. 19). Industrial policy can be defined as the set of selective measures adopted by the state to alter industrial organization (Blais, 1986, p. 4). The term industrial policy describes that group of policies whose explicit objective is to influence the operation of industry (Sharp and Shepherd, 1987, p. 107). An industrial policy implies intervention by a government which seeks to promote particular industries in some way. This may be either to stimulate production and growth of industry's size or to promote export sales (Whalley, 1987, p. 84). This definition does not, however, include government influence on the decline of an industry.

A critical definition of industrial policy states that it is the label used to describe a wide ranging, ill-assorted collection of micro-based, supply-side initiatives which are designed to improve market performance in a variety of mutually inconsistent ways. Intervention is typically demanded in cases with market failures and where major changes need to be effected quickly (Geroski, 1989, p. 21).

Industrial policy may mean different things to various countries at different times. LDCs look at industrial policy as a means of economic development. Once they become developed, industrial policy may be directed towards fostering free competition. In the centrally planned economies, industrial policy means planning and imposing targets for each production sector.

Industrialized countries have had implicit industrial policies for a long period. They were embodied in trade and other policies which have secondary effects on industrial policy. This is due to the interdependence of economic policies within the economic system. Some countries therefore have joint ministries of industry and international trade. This is the case in the British Department of Trade and Industry (DTI) and the Japanese Ministry of International Trade and Industry (MITI), although there are differences in powers and role in the economy between the two ministries.

In most developed countries the whole period after the Second World War was characterized by reductions in tariffs, as well as measures to prevent the demise of sunset industries. Governments' industrial policies may be a simple continuation of old protectionism by more sophisticated means (Pinder *et al.*, 1979, p. 9), and their tax and transfer policies have had an impact on demand, which has affected industrial production. By direct production and supply of public goods, governments influenced, at least in part, the industrial structure of their economies. Other government policies – such as foreign policy – have nothing directly to do with the increase in the economic pie of the country. This is the case when some governments ban the export of high technology abroad.

Various economic policies have their impact on industrial policy, not only trade policy, but also social, regional, energy transport and other policies. Hence, most definitions of industrial policy include, at least implicitly, the need for a stable economic environment and coordination of various economic policies. Only then may specific targeting of industrial policy fully contribute to economic growth and improvement in productivity and competitiveness. On those grounds, broad definitions of industrial policy may embrace all of these facets. Hence, one may take industrial policy to mean such an economic policy as shapes a country's comparative advantage. Its aim is to influence the change in national economic structure in order to enhance the creation and growth of national wealth, rather than to distribute it. The need for industrial change comes from an increase in GNP, changes in technology, foreign competition, as well as changes in demand and the economic environment.

Several types of industrial policy with respect to its scope can be identified (Adams and Bollino, 1983, p. 15):

- General or non-selective industrial policies are available to all industries on equal terms, and they include loans, education of manpower and provision of public services.
- Activity-specific policies are selective with respect to particular activities of the production process like support of R&D.
- Region-specific policies are not targeted to a particular industry or activity, but rather to a selected area of the country.
- Sector-specific policies are directed towards broad sectors of the economy such as agriculture and manufacturing.
- Industry-specific policies deal with specific industries within a broad sector such as computers or sweet production.
- Firm or project-specific policies are designated to affect particular firms, and these policies range from the provision of infrastructure to subsidies and bailouts.

These types of industrial policies do not appear in pure form because any of the mentioned actions may affect several types of policy simultaneously.

Three (non-mutually exclusive) broad types of industrial policy are macroeconomic, sectoral and microeconomic orientation. The macroeconomic orientation is least interventionist because it leaves the functioning of industries and firms to market forces, and simply improves the general economic climate for business. Sector-specific orientation becomes relevant when market failures affect certain industries, and tries to amend the particular market shortcoming. Microeconomic orientation of industrial policy may direct a government to act directly towards specific firms or industrial groups (Jacquemin, 1984, pp. 4–5).

There are another three broad types of industrial policy. They can be market oriented, interventionist or mixed. The first type (market oriented) fosters competition and free markets. The second (interventionist) policy may be directed as in the centrally planned economies. In practice, industrial policy is most often a mixture of the two. The only thing which most often differs between countries is not whether they intervene or not, but rather the degree and form of intervention.

Industrial policy may be adjustment-prone and adjustment-averse. Adjustment-prone industrial policy stimulates adjustment of various industries to enter new production, remain competitive or ease exit from the selected lines of production. Adjustment-averse industrial policy is the policy of protection which impedes changes in an economy by preserving the status quo.

Industrial policy issues

The standard comparative-advantage and factor-proportions theories of international trade may be satisfactory for the explanation of trade in primary goods. They are, however, less so in the explanation of trade in industrial goods. Manufacturing can be seen as a collection of industries with no factor-abundance base. On those grounds it is difficult to explain why France exports perfumes while Japan exports copiers (Harris, 1985a, p. 148).

A country's comparative advantage is not only given by resource endowment, but is shaped over time by the actions of both business and government. The economic policies of a government may, over time, affect comparative advantage by influencing the quantity and quality of: labour, capital and technology. The comparative advantage in manufacturing industries is not an unchangeable fact of nature, but rather the outcome of economic policies which affect incentives to save, invest, innovate, diffuse technology and acquire human capital. Market imperfections were at the margin of orthodox economic analysis, but these imperfections are in the centre of analysis of the new industrial-policy and trade-theory literatures. A country's size; regional disequilibria; skill, mobility and unionization of labour; antitrust and bankruptcy laws are just a few imperfections. To ignore them is to miss the point that their effects can be mitigated by economic policy (Tyson, 1987, pp. 67–71).

Free competition within an economic union brings costs of adjustment to which governments are not indifferent. However, the real reason for this is that the citizens are not indifferent. In the real, second-best and imperfect world, there is enough scope for both market mechanism and selective intervention (economic policy).

A reduction in tariffs may increase a country's market. Free markets are too myopic to make the necessary structural adjustments. These are the shifts of resources from the lagging to the growing industries whose future is not certain in the long run. Adjustment may not necessarily be a swift, cheap and smooth process, so adjustment policies may facilitate these shifts.

One can make predictions about the model of economic adjustment of a country based on the characteristics of a country's financial system. First, if this system relies on capital markets which allocate resources by competitively established prices, the adjustment process is company-led. The allocation decisions are the responsibility of firms, as is the case in the United States. Second, in a credit-based financial system where the government administers prices, the adjustment process is state-led, as in Japan and France. Last, in a credit-based system where price formation is dominated by banks, the adjustment process can be named as negotiated. An example of this can be found in the case of FR Germany (Zysman, 1983, p. 18).

The question still remains: can imperfect governments make this shift any better than imperfect markets? In some cases they can indeed. Here are the reasons, along the lines of the new theory, where intervention may be justified.

First, the time horizon of private markets is relatively short. They may not foresee countries' long-term opportunities with a high degree of accuracy. Japanese manufacturing is financed to a large extent by bank credits while industry in the United States uses this source of finance to a much lower extent. This means that the manager of a Japanese firm who asks for a loan can inform the home bank manager that he expects that profit will come in the ship which is due to arrive within the next few years, while the manager of a US firm in a similar situation must be sure that he can see the smoke of the ship in the distance. Hence, the United States industrial production is much more affected by the short-term interests of shareholders than the Japanese. A government policy may change this short-term outlook towards longer-term economic considerations.

Second, in a different case, risk-averse governments may organize stockpiling in order to cushion the effect of a possible crisis which private markets may neither have the wish nor the funds to do in the long run. The cost of this kind of risk can be quantified in terms of GNP – which would be sacrificed in the case of an unexpected reduction in the availability of certain input.

Third, governments may wish to keep some facilities for the home production as a bargaining chip with foreign suppliers while negotiating prices in long-term contracts. This should deter foreign monopolies from charging monopoly prices.

Fourth, market forces are quite efficient in allocating resources among producers and allocating goods and services among consumers in simple and static settings. Much of the power of markets in these circumstances emerges because prices convey all the information needed by participants in the market which enables them to act independently, without explicit coordination, and still reach a collectively efficient decision. It is possible that markets can, at least in principle, solve simple and static problems in a remarkably efficient way, but it is not surprising to find out that the free-market game fares less well in more demanding circumstances, which include market imperfections (Geroski, 1989, p. 21). Adjustment problems appear because of unsatisfactory operation of the market/price game viewed from the long-term angle. It is the aim, or attempt, of intervention – in particular the forward looking one – to put the economy on the way towards the desired long-term equilibrium.

Fifth, basic research provides significant spillovers throughout the economy. These social gains are difficult for private markets to grasp in most cases, because the private risk and costs may be very high. Also, without intervention, like patent rights, free market forces cannot guarantee sufficient returns to the innovator. The fruits of successful basic research fuel technological progress in a country. This research is funded in full or in part by the government in direct (subsidy) or indirect (tax relief) ways in most countries. Governments and private businesses share risk.

Sixth, industrial policy may facilitate economic adjustment in a more efficient and equitable way than free market forces. This policy may provide support for R&D, education, investment subsidies, protection and other support for the improvement of infrastructure in the early fragile times of a new industry – which free market forces fail to do. As for the adjustment out of sunset industries, government policy may offer unemployment benefits and vocational training. Industrial policy can, to an extent, both anticipate and shape changes. It can be involved either directly in picking the winners/losers or indirectly by creating a business environment where firms can make choices in the potentially successful and desirable way.

Seventh, agriculture is a sector in which every government intervenes. Due to the impact of weather conditions, free market forces cannot achieve stability of supply and stabilize the incomes of the farm population in relation to the labour force in the manufacturing sector. In addition, governments wish to secure the domestic supply of farm goods in the case of war, as well as to protect the landscape for traditional reasons.

The eighth reason for the introduction of an industrial policy is that it may be able to respond, with different internal and external measures, to foreign countries' economic policies. Left alone, the market forces may take the advantage of foreign policies in the short-run, but if the foreign long-term strategy is to undermine the importing country's home production by means of predatory pricing in order to create a monopoly, then the long-term effect may be detrimental for the importing country's economic situation. An industrial policy may be a suitable response because it may change the possible free-market outcome.

Tariffs were historically the most important instrument of industrial policy. Due to a number of rounds of multilateral reduction in tariffs under the GATT, the use of this instrument was restricted and reduced, but other instruments have appeared. Some of them personify protectionist pressures against adjustment, while others are adjustment oriented. They include: subsidies for export, production, R&D and investment; tax and credit policy; public purchases; price and exchange controls; technical standards; direct production by the state; competition and concentration policy.

Many of these instruments may be applied to a single target simultaneously, and may sometimes be in conflict. If the aim is an increase in efficiency, then competition and concentration may be conflicting. It is accepted that many industries may not operate efficiently without a certain degree of concentration, which is dictated by minimum economies of scale. A certain degree of concentration has therefore to be accepted. Small countries usually do not have very restrictive anti-monopoly laws, because efficient production for their home market and possibly foreign markets often allows the existence of only one production unit. Countries like France foster the policy of concentration and efficiency, while others like the United States, due to the huge home market, have a strong anti-monopoly legislation which favours free competition. Sunset, inward-looking industries traditionally lobbied in every country for protection, while new industries which are oriented to the widest international market support free trade. It is interesting that pressure for protection comes more often from management than the workers.

It was a strong belief in Europe in the 1960s that big US-style companies are the key factor for economic growth in a country. These companies may, among other things, spend substantial funds on R&D. Hence, mergers were encouraged. But experience has shown that those countries which spend most on R&D do not necessarily have the highest rates of growth. It was also realized that small and medium-sized enterprises are the important factors for economic revival and employment. Subsequently the policy which strongly encouraged mergers was abandoned. It is recognized that the jobs created by small and medium-sized enterprises are greater in number than those created by large companies per unit of investment. However, jobs created by small and medium-sized firms often have the disadvantage of being relatively less secure than the ones in big companies. Nevertheless, small and medium-sized enterprises are necessary for the balanced growth of an economy, for they provide links among various subsectors. They also create indirect employment throughout the economy.

Subsidies were studied in detail in Chapter 2. It is important to note here that subsidies may be a distortive instrument of industrial policy. They may diminish incentives for the advance of profitable firms if they are taxed constantly in order to provide subsidies to inefficient firms. A subsidy which stimulates the introduction of new capital may distort a firm's choice among technologies which use capital and labour in different proportions. If a firm had to pay the full cost of capital it might have chosen another technology. A one-shot subsidy to investment may help a firm to buy time and adjust to an unexpected change in demand or technology. If the value of subsidies and other favours is smaller than the additional value added in the given industry, reduced by the opportunity cost of subsidies/favours, then subsidization may be justified (but this calculation can be quite difficult). If, for the protection of employment, subsidies are provided on a permanent basis to an industry or firm, its management does not need to perform its role as efficiently as in the firms or industries where market criteria dominate. A permanently subsidized industry or firm is a very likely candidate for nationalization.

A common view of the world holds that firms play Cournot-Nash games against all other players (each firm decides on a course of action, e.g. output, on the assumption that the behaviour of the other firms remains constant), while the governments play a Stackleberg game (this agent knows the reaction functions of all others) against firms and Cournot-Nash against other governments (Brander and Spencer, 1985, p. 84). Unfortunately, these are all games which may produce relatively unstable solutions and price fluctuations. Collusion among the players may lead to a relatively stable Chamberlin solution.

The promotion of the adjustment of some industries does not always go smoothly. Some sunset industries are well established, relatively large employers and possess a strong political lobby. This is often the case with the steel industry. Some steel firms are quite successful in their adjustment. That is the case with the United States Steel Company which closed thirteen steel-making units and diversified out of steel. This company invested funds in a shopping centre in Pittsburgh, Pennsylvania and chemical facilities in Texas. Steel-making accounts for only 11 per cent of the United States Steel Company's operating income (Trebilcock, 1986, p. 141). Other steel companies like a steady life. They are able to mobilize political forces and government instruments (tariffs, quotas, subsidies) in order to resist adjustment (contraction of protection and making labour redundant).

The newly industrialized countries have substantially increased their competitiveness in the traditional industries like steel and shipbuilding. Their position is irreversible in the long-term. These industries cannot be recovered in the developed market economies on the basis of reductions in wages. This policy would involve a waste of resources, for the trade unions would resist cuts in wages to meet the level in the newly industrialized countries which have productivity at the level comparable to the one in developed market economies.

Sufficient subsidies will always keep production at a level which will not survive in free-market conditions, while new and risky industries have to offer higher rewards in order to attract factors. Gains in productivity may be able to cushion these increases in rewards without increasing prices. However, faced with a possibility of higher wages, trade unions may press for increases in wages elsewhere in the economy. Without increases in productivity, the result may be an increase in prices throughout the economy. However, the sunrise industries can be one step ahead of other sectors in this chase.

The policy of shoring up a dying sector is like moving forwards, but looking backwards. The policy of compensation to redundant labour may be superior to the policy of shoring up sunset firms.

Compensation to redundant labour needs to be provided by the whole society because the whole society benefits from the process of industrial change. Shareholders of dying firms should not be compensated for the depreciated value of their shares, because they should channel their funds to the growing sectors which need capital, not to the ones which are declining and which do not need it (Curzon Price, 1981, pp. 27–9).

Interestingly, the British experience has shown that rescuing sunset industries (coal) to protect jobs is not a safe way for re-election. The taxpayers and consumers have increased their awareness of the costs of such a rescue. However, the influence of trade unions in sunset industries may still mobilize a strong lobbying influence in many countries.

In contrast with the sunset industries, the sunrise industries need venture capital: they may be quite small, numerous and unstable. When they are in trouble their voice may not be heard as loudly as the voice of the sunset industries. Investment in these sunrise firms is risky because many of them reach their demise before they reach maturity. However, these firms are the most propelling agents of the modern economy. Although many of them disappear from the market, many of them are created. A high rate of natality of new firms is the best expression of the vitality of the system which creates incentives, so that many new enterprises may be started and risk accepted.

When economic adjustment is spread over a number of years, it may appear easier and less costly. Some 'breathing space' for the structural change (slowing down the attrition or keeping the sunset industries alive) may be obtained, but this argument may not always be valid. First, the damage to the rest of the economy is greater the longer a stricken industry is allowed to prolong the agony and, second, it is not obvious that the prolonged adjustment is really any easier to bear than quick surgery. Even the direct costs may turn out, in practice, to be higher (Curzon Price, 1981, p. 120).

All protectionist measures offered to an industry ought to be conditional, otherwise the problems of an industry may be exacerbated. If the protected industry is a sunset industry, then its adjustment may be postponed or reversed by production or employment subsidies. This increases the costs to society in the long run because the desired change does not take place. The adjustment policies should be of limited duration. They should involve both public funds and private capital, as well as make the cost of action as transparent as possible. Also, the recipients of assistance should be expected to develop comparative advantages prior to the termination of assistance. Market processes should be encouraged and managerial practices improved (Yannopoulos, 1988, pp. 142–3).

Direct R&D subsidies or indirect subsidies in the form of government purchases are powerful instruments for the support of industries which introduce new products. The volume of demand and its structure provides the most important incentive for production. This is also crucial for the strategic industries, the ones whose activities give external and unpriced gains through linkages to the rest of the economy. In the early unstable phase of the introduction of a new product, a secure government demand provides a powerful impetus for the firm to shape the product and open new markets. If this production does not become self-sustaining within a specified period of time, then it may never become profitable, and resources which may be allocated for protection may be used elsewhere in future, with a greater efficiency in improving competitiveness. A long isolation of an industry from market forces may remove incentives for the swift reaction to signals which come from competition in international markets.

Protection may be given to an industry on the condition that the schedule of protection/intervention will be revised downward over time. This strategy may provide a limited adjustment period to the industry by mitigating the full impact of international competition. This programme does not ensure the existence of inefficient industries and firms, but rather their adjustment and exit from the sunset sectors. The self-liquidation of protection is perhaps the only means for maintaining the incentives to adjust. If the adjustment programmes offer funds to firms, then there must be an obligation that these funds must be spent on specified activities. The adjustment programmes should be overseen by technical advisory boards which represent a wide community (Tyson and Zysman, 1987b, p. 425).

State intervention, as observed hitherto, was primarily directed towards the problem industries, which are usually coal, steel, textile, footwear and agriculture. There is a growing interest in intervening in the sunrise industries. Intervention here is in the form of providing or subsidizing innovation, R&D in firms, special tax treatment of new technologies (tax holidays and subsidies), training of labour, education of management, government procurement, as well as more general instruments like planning, policy guide-lines and exchange of information.

The level of industrial policy may be general and specific. The choice is between discrimination and non-discrimination. The level of intervention should be as high as possible and general – that is, available to every firm and branch of industry. Once the policy is installed, the market is the best mechanism for the fine tuning, and agents should take advantage of the policy instruments of this. Market forces then prevent players from inefficient employment of resources. The policy should be tailored to suit local needs (branch- or firm-specific) in the cases when there are no spillovers to other branches or firms. Also, it ought to be used only as the last resort because the government does not have perfect knowledge and may well make the wrong choice, as was the case with the French/British Concorde project.

Picking the winner

The new theory of trade and industrial policy finds, in contrast to the classical theory, that there are certain manufacturing and service industries which are more important to an economy than others. They are the ones with wide forward and backward linkages and unpriced spillover effects on the rest of the economy, as well as economies of scale. Favours to such industries may create a new irreversible competitive advantage for a country's output on the international market. If the level of industrial policy is selective, then it is coupled with the policy of picking the winner (creating a national champion) or bailing out the loser. This has always been difficult, risky and demanded considerable and costly information. If this were not so, then you would probably not read this book but rather look at the stock-market report, and invest and increase the value of your assets by several zeros daily.

Picking the winner can usually be found in countries whose domestic market is small and is unable to support the competition of several firms which operate at the optimum level of efficiency. National demand-pull policies can be fostered by large countries like the United States, which can leave selection of the best suppliers to market competition. Smaller countries have usually to rely on selective policies which are riskier. They have to make the best use out of the limited amount of available resources which have to be focused. There is, nevertheless, contrasting evidence in the cases of France and FR Germany.

While France relied on a highly centralized model of the

economy, FR Germany fostered a decentralized model. However, both of these countries have achieved a relatively comparable level of economic success (de Ghellinck, 1988, p. 140). While picking the winner, the government chooses between supporting sunrise sectors and propping up sunset ones (protection of the existing structure which is adjustment-averse). The balance between the two depends upon both the power of the sectors involved and the intentions of the government.

The policy of singling out industries or firms for special treatment puts the problems of all others aside. The 'neglected' activities may be at a relative disadvantage because they may not count on direct support by the state if they happen to be in need. The neglect of sunrise industries may reduce the risk-incentive attitude of entrepreneurs and jeopardize growth in the future. If a government cannot formulate the basic structural objectives of national economic policy, then it will have to leave it to the politically strongest segment of industry. The policy will be formulated in a hurry in response to political pressures of the moment, with the likely result of protection for troubled industries. Independence, resistance to sectoral pressures and clear economic objectives of the government remove extemporizations in economic policies. Otherwise, the industrial policy of the country will be an instrument for the support of the obsolete sectors and a brake on the expanding ones (Tyson and Zysman, 1987a, p. 22).

Output grows fastest in the sunrise industries. These industries may not necessarily create a significant volume of direct employment, but, due to the linkages, they have a strong potential for the creation of indirect employment. There is, however, a notable technological improvement in sunset industries such as textiles and steel. Therefore, the distinction between the two kinds of sectors is generally for analytical purposes. A smart choice for the risk-averse developing country may be to choose the establishment of a good sunset industry, rather than an uncertain sunrise sector. Of course, the consequence of this choice may be a decline in the standard of living relative to countries which have opted for a different development model.

There are three basic issues with respect to targeting. They are: which industries or firms should receive support, what kind of support should be provided and, finally, for how long? The industries singled out are usually those which are significant employers and those which have important spillover effects on other parts of the economy. If the private markets favour less risky enterprises – such as the development of alternative sources of energy – the government may single them out for special treatment.

If domestic regulations with respect to safety standards are stricter and more costly than abroad, then, other things being equal, this may put home firms at a relative disadvantage in competition with foreigners. This may be a valid case for some support. Political reasons like national defence and pride may influence decisions about the support of certain industries. This assistance should cease: as soon as the beneficiary becomes profitable; or once it becomes obvious that it will never happen; or after the specified period of time for assistance has expired.

Japan is the example of a country which has reaped the fruits of conscious targeting of certain industries. Each time it was one step up the value-added chain. During the 1960s the targets were steel production and shipbuilding because of their significant beneficial effect on the economy. During the 1970s the targets were machine tools and cars. The target for the 1980s was electronics (copiers, computers, audio and video equipment). The target for the 1990s is semiconductors. This may be taken as an example of the shaping of comparative advantage in a dynamic context. Japanese targeting has not been successful in all cases, however, for a variety of reasons. For example, this country targeted production of aluminium and petrochemicals before the first oil shock, after which such choice was not justified.

Elsewhere in the developed market economies, the policy of targeting may not be that smooth. After the Second World War, industrial policy relied partly on unorganized labour which was flowing from agriculture and abroad into the manufacturing industry. This situation has changed. Trade unions now organize labour, which may influence (i.e. postpone) economic adjustment, even though this may be to the long-term detriment of the economy.

Japanese targeting is most notably an information-collecting and interpretation process which helps individual firms in making investment decisions and guides the government in allocating support. The emphasis is on technological areas, rather than on firms (McFetridge, 1985, p. 29).

France is a country whose concern is in the creation of large and efficient firms which may compete in international markets. This country is not very concerned with home competition. France's Interministerial Committee for Development of Strategic Industries targets the key sectors, defines the strategy and picks a firm as a national champion to implement the programme. The means for the implementation of the programme is a contract between the government and the firm. The government does not, however, have perfect foresight. Mistaken judgements have happened in very costly projects like computers and Concorde – which was a success in the high-tech industry, but a commercial failure.

The French strategy for computers was to try to build large mainframes in order to compete directly with IBM, rather than to begin with small computers or peripheral equipment. This was too much for the relatively undeveloped French firms to cope with, and the effort failed. The mistake might have been avoided if the government industrial policy-makers had consulted more with private experts. Private firms also make mistakes, but they are less likely to ignore market forces – in particular when they use loans – than government officials. That is the main reason why Japanese targeting was more successful than French. The early French mistakes were not in vain. During the Airbus project, the government had learned to select the segment of the market for which demand would be high. It also tied customers by early purchasing of aircraft parts in exchange for orders (Carliner, 1988, p. 164).

Targeting of certain industries or firms has not been a striking feature of the United States' industrial system. Their system is established in such a way as to foster individual freedom, not to discriminate among firms or industries. The only exceptions are agriculture and sporadic bailouts of firms like Chrysler. Government consumption, however, gives a big overall demand-pull to the economy due to a huge budget deficit. Hence, the argument that the US government does not intervene in the economy will not hold water.

Human-resource management may be one of the key factors in increasing a country's comparative advantage in the rapidly changing technology and market situation. Macroeconomic policy may just support, in an important way, the creation of comparative advantage, but it is the human factor – properly organized, valued and continuously educated – which should present the major link in the increase of a country's competitiveness.

During the nineteenth and early twentieth centuries, bright pupils in Britain were steered towards the classics at Oxford and Cambridge, while technical subjects were reserved for the less gifted. The situation was reversed in France, Germany and Japan. However, after the Second World War, British industry began to recruit widely from the universities. A career in industry, even if a third choice after the Foreign Office and the BBC, became socially acceptable for the sons (and increasingly the daughters) of the Establishment (Sharp and Shepherd, 1987, pp. 83–4).

Government planners in Japan, France and FR Germany may be more competent and sophisticated than managers in private firms. The best and most ambitious students aspire to government service. In North America, society has a different attitude. Many people look on government jobs as inferior to private ones because, among other things, they are less well paid. It is not surprising to find Japan, France and FR Germany having an industrial policy, while the United States and Canada do not. Nevertheless, shoddy economic policies might be easily amended if civil servants were given a freer hand by the system (Brander, 1987, p. 40).

Implementation of industrial policy

United States

The objective of the United States economic system is to remove impediments to free operation of market forces and to enhance the virtues of private entrepreneurship. Industrial policy has been left predominantly to market forces. The limited power of the federal government executives make them vulnerable to the influence of various pressure groups. The government must win a thousand small battles which are relatively independent of each other before any broad policy can be implemented and secured (Zysman, 1983, p. 268).

The roots of the problem of competitiveness in the United States' industry lies in the old system of production and the accompanying market strategy. The United States' producers have traditionally focused on long production runs of standard goods for mass markets. Designs lasted for years. Large inventories were kept in hand so that no strike or supplier bottleneck could bring production to a halt. Labour was hired and fired as demand rose and fell and suppliers were treated in much the same way. As incomes rise, the mass market increasingly becomes a series of niche markets. Japan, FR Germany and Italy successfully operate in market niches in which they face little competition from producers from low-cost countries. In these niches, design, quality, responsiveness to fashion, just-in-time delivery and fast adjustments are important (Dertouzos *et al.*, 1990, pp. 17–19).

The United States' industrial policy has not been the widespread use of industry-specific policies nor has it been intentional, coordinated or planned. The government is neither organized nor equipped to do so. It has not consciously chosen national champions because of a strong faith in fair play and non-discrimination. This policy has not supported widespread nationalization. The administration has been very hesitant to bail out private firms which are in trouble by loan guarantees. The exception is agriculture, which has been singled out for special treatment by the government in every western country.

The United States' administration has occasionally resorted to bailouts in order to help firms like Lockheed and Chrysler. Concerns behind these moves were national defence and employment. When intervention took place, it was after an open debate. The United States' industrial policy has not relied on nationalization, cartelization or merger promotions, and the government has not provided strong support for exports. The Domestic International Sales Corporation support programme was nowhere near the support programmes of other developed countries (Wescott, 1983, p. 88).

The only important involvement of the United States Government in the adjustment process was the Trade Adjustment Assistance. It was introduced in 1962 as a means of easing the adjustment process which was only due to trade liberalization. It provided free technical consultation and low-interest loans or loan guarantees to the injured firms, offered tax privileges, as well as supplemented income and encouraged vocational training of the displaced labour. The effect of the assistance was to reduce costs and increase efficiency of the declining industries. This was adjustment-retarding in industries which suffer from insuperable, international cost disadvantage (Gray *et al.*, 1986, p. 67), but the assisted industries increased sales. Despite the fact that the Trade Adjusted Assistance was due to expire a decade ago, it is still there and well, although on a smaller scale. The Assistance is planned to terminate in 1992, unless its existence is prolonged again.

The United States' industrial policy has been attempting to maintain a favourable climate for business. Rather than having a single coordinated industrial policy, this policy has been a series of separate policies which affected certain industries. The most notable feature is that these policies stem from various government actions – such as procurement of military hardware, aircraft, space programmes and others – which have substantial spillovers on to the rest of the economy. This influence was strongest in previous decades, when military procurement strongly influenced the development of consumer electronics and civilian aeroplanes.

A permanent United States' policy may only be found in agriculture. However, industrial policy has helped the structural adaptation of textiles and footwear industries, it also gave some support in export financing and it has continuously encouraged technological change and innovation. The most planned and conscious part of the US industrial policy ever undertaken is the policy of accelerated depreciation. Those rules give special advantages to selected types of investment. The adoption of a shorter life of assets and investment-tax credits stimulates investment and promotes technological change. A federal industrial policy which shapes the United States' comparative advantage does not exist. Still, there are many measures which local and state governments can take for the promotion of local business, which creates employment and growth in high-value-added industries.

Firms from the United States have the advantage over firms in many other countries in that they have an unimpeded access to a large domestic market, they capture economies of scale, so they produce standardized products as a rule. Demand for the variety of products has increased the penetration of foreign suppliers who serve specific market segments. The domestic competitive inefficiency on these growing sub-markets has tended to divert attention away from the failure to adjust to home demand, and directed attention towards the unfair trading practices of some foreign suppliers. The government has offered assistance to the affected industries through protection from trade, which is adjustment-retarding policy, instead of propping up the restructuring of the industry.

The Massachusetts Institute of Technology (MIT) Commission on Industrial Productivity found the following six key similarities among the best-practice firms, which are recommended to all US companies (Dertouzos *et al.*, 1990, p. 118). They are the following:

- simultaneous improvement in cost, quality and delivery
- closer links with customers
- closer links with suppliers
- use of new technology for strategic advantage
- less hierarchical organization to promote greater speed in product development and greater responsiveness to changing markets
- human resource policies that promote continuous learning,

participation, flexibility and treating workers as assets to be developed, not as costs to be controlled.

Due to the lack of constitutional influence, the federal government intervention often ends either in protection of an industry or no policy whatsoever. The policy of protection is in stark contrast with the ideology of economic freedom. However, the United States' economic circumstances (trade deficit) disregard the basic philosophy. The adjustment of the protected industry has not taken place in the form of rationalization and innovation in order to meet domestic demand and foreign competition, instead US companies either went out of the industry or abroad to take advantage of cheaper foreign labour. This was the case with the consumer electronics, but not with the clothing and footware industries because the skills of the employed labour and management have a low degree of transferability.

In summary, the United States' approach to industrial policy is founded on the principle of free competition. If intervention is necessary, then it is best achieved within a clearly defined legislative framework. Selective intervention is not always acceptable because it favours certain groups at the expense of the whole society. All these principles may be overridden by considerations of national security (Renshaw, 1986, p. 148).

Although the primary responsibility for the improvement in competitiveness lies with the private sector, the government ought to pursue macroeconomic policies that make new investments attractive, support R&D, reduce barriers to trade and support education of the workers.

The United States has a special responsibility for the proper operation of the market-oriented world economic system. Failure to adjust to international competition may undermine this commitment. An industrial policy in the United States may be suggested as a solution to this problem of industrial restructuring, but there may be a strong case against it if this policy is used to restrict imports and subsidize exports. This may endanger the market-oriented world economic system.

Japan

The Japanese industrial policy has been encountered on several occasions. Here will be noted some other interesting facets of this policy. The Japanese system creates an open and institutionalized communication mechanism between the government and the business community in order to create an atmosphere of confidence. This system permits the planning and shaping of industries before changes in the international market drive the government and business to take reactive measures to deal with the adjustment of sunset industries. The Japanese system permits the key players to anticipate changes and deal with them in advance, rather than to react to changes by the difficult adjustment of obsolete sectors. Such a business climate offers favourable opportunities for investments.

Japanese intervention is used to ensure that resources for expansion come from domestic financial markets, that the domestic market is safeguarded, to foster competition among home producers and to encourage and assist exports. Taken together, these policy objectives represent a powerful development strategy. This means that a single slip by the United States' producers may undermine their long-term competitive position, whereas a Japanese slip may be recovered and overcome later by Japanese firms (Tyson and Zysman, 1987a, pp. 35–7).

Japanese business has a secure (protected) market at home which can reinforce their long-term expectations about the return on investments. Such a domestic market may represent an efficient springboard for a successful competition on the international market. The relative closure of the Japanese market to foreign competition makes the battle for future markets a struggle over the United States', EC and, potentially, east European markets. In spite of limited financial resources in many LDCs, they do represent potential markets in the future.

Industrial policy has to be constructed more broadly than trade policy. Industrial policy in Japan encompasses traditional trade policies which are used in conjunction with control over foreign direct investment, financial and interest rate policy, R&D policy and others. The strength of Japanese policy intervention has been declining since the early 1970s (Tyson, 1987, p. 70). Most Japanese firms and industries are so successful now that they do not need support from the government.

An interesting feature of the Japanese economic system is the role of banks. They are very much involved in the financing of industrial investment, while shares in equity play a much smaller role. The government proposes the areas for financial support which the banks follow closely.

The government speaks with two voices in relative harmony –

through the Economic Planning Agency (short, medium and long-term plans) and the MITI. The major attention of their policies is devoted to the sunrise industries and R&D. The expenditure on declining industries has not been large, the largest share of the state funds for industry has been reserved for the growing ducklings, rather than for the old lame ducks (Dore, 1986, p. 112).

Japan does not have a very strong record in basic research in relation to other industrialized countries. In most cases Japan uses the results of basic research in Europe and the United States. Japan has, however, an excellent record in the carrying out of applied R&D which has support from the Government, but is carried out in private companies which respond to market signals while developing products for commercial use.

The Japanese are very competitive in producing high-tech hardware. But, in spite of the fact that Sony's beta system might be technically superior to the VHS video system, it has never been widely accepted. Sony's strategy for the next generation of video and audio equipment is different. In order to control the production of soft goods, Sony Corporation purchased CBS records in 1987 and Columbia Pictures in 1989. The intention is to control, at least a part, of the best entertainment software which is going to be used as an input in (the best) Sony's hard goods. This may support the thesis that when the Japanese purchase foreign service industries, they are often doing so with the home manufacturing industry in mind.

A fast structural adjustment to changes (or prior to them) in the international trading system has been an exemplary success of Japan. The Japanese willingness to permit the phasing out of production in industries which are growing in the newly industrialized countries allowed Japanese resources to move to higher-income-creating lines of production. This provided a ready market in Japan for the products of these countries, which in turn allowed them to buy 'up-market' goods from Japan. Industrialized countries may take a page from this method of adjustment. The Japanese industrial policy is a collection of more or less independent policies which do not follow a coherent and well developed plan (Lipsey, 1987a).

Comparison of the relative size and growth rates of the GNP of Japan on the one hand, and the EC countries and the United States on the other, may be misleading. The Japanese work more days per year than workers in other industrialized countries where wealth is consumed in the form of increased voluntary leisure. Health problems that accrue from the relatively high level of congestion are not properly accommodated in the GNP. Economic growth may be maximized by allowing only enough consumption for subsistence and by investing everything else. However, not many people would like to live permanently in such a society. The Japanese social system is relatively undeveloped. The primary social concern was fast industrial growth, while it was left to companies to provide health, housing and other benefits to the employees.

Finally, there is the hope that the key to the Japanese advantage lies not in the unique characteristics of the Japanese workers, but rather in the Japanese managerial strategies. It may be simpler to copy managerial technologies than to alter the sociology of the workforce (Tyson and Zysman, 1987a, p. 37). The relative weakness of the United States' industry lies in the way people cooperate, manage, use technology, learn new skills and interact with the government. Although those organizational patterns and attitudes may be at the root of the productivity problem, they are very hard to change, even once the need for change is recognized (Dertouzos *et al.*, 1990, pp. 42–5).

One of the the real reasons, however, for the Japanese success in the development of manufacturing industry may be found in the fact that Japan was relatively late to develop. Both the state of the economy, which was significantly damaged by the Second World War, and a relative lack of well entrenched industrial interests, enabled Japan swiftly to accept and take advantage of new technologies, innovations and management.

France

When contrasted with a rather poor industrial tradition, the French performance in industry was quite significant during the post-war period. Nevertheless, the 'French miracle' has not yet happened. The most propelling sector of the modern economy is electronics, and it is exactly in this sector and chemicals where the French performance is the weakest. Furthermore, the macroeconomic variables, in particular inflation, were unstable.

The French government has the tradition of being profoundly involved in the economic life of the country. The most striking feature is the plan. This feature of the French economic system is often confused with the dirigist planning system which prevailed in the Soviet-style economies. This is not the case in France. The system of planning creates links between the administration and industry. It is a continuous information-gathering, exchange and consensus-building process among state officials, business and banking elites who share a common social and educational background. Most of them have been students at the *École Nationale d'Administration*. Their common aim is to formulate, coordinate and implement actions for the smooth advance of the French economy.

A notable feature of this powerful, continuous and silent dealing among high officials is that consumers' and workers' interests play a minor role in the whole process. This is due to a relatively low level of unionization of labour, their particularization and weak links with the government. The state is thus able to control the growth of selected industries and to direct favours to them without major problems from the damaged segments of the population.

The plan was quite successful in the first two post-war decades. On the one hand, there was economic disorder after the war which asked for a kind of concentration of resources. On the other hand, increasing population growth, flow of labour from agriculture to industry and later to the service sector, as well as immigration, increased the supply of labour for the growth of the manufacturing industry and adjustment to the creation of the EC. The success of the planning was also due, in part, to the recovery of the whole west European region. The crisis of the 1970s revealed that this system is insufficient to cope with the new situation. The change brought industrial policies as the major form of intervention.

The basic characteristics of French industrial policies include state intervention. As a relatively late comer to the club of the industrialized countries, France has a structural weakness which has to be altered by intervention. As a Catholic nation where landowners were the most influential class, France prevented the development of the merchant class which flourished in other Protestant European countries. As a result, entrepreneurial traditions and a class of skilled, dynamic and propelling risk-takers was relatively small. This retarded the development of French industry.

Big firms were created in the twentieth century in order to employ effectively these scarce enterprising resources. It is also the case that the state administration can handle a handful of big firms in an easier way than a number of small ones. The high-level civil servants seldom have any industrial experience. Since they play a key role in the decision-making process about the allocation of resources, the outcome is the predominance of orthodox macroeconomic policies.

Decisions about the allocation of resources is internalized within the state administration, hence little is known about the eligibility criteria and selection procedures. The transparency of this policy has always been weak. Finally, French industrial policies were hesitant to stimulate integration into the international industrial system. This is most obvious in the attitude towards industrial and technological cooperation, protectionism and direct investment, both of foreign firms in France and French firms abroad (de Bandt, 1985, p. 71).

The state is directly involved in a wide range of industries in addition to the plan. These undertakings are required to operate on the principles of efficiency. If they become unprofitable they are seldom bailed out for the reason of maintaining employment. This is in contrast with their British counterparts. The French aim is to foster large and efficient national firms which may compete internationally. Internal competition policy in France has always been weak. However, competition is fostered by participation in the EC. The main strategy of the French administration in the covert process of the conduct of industrial policy is that it uses the financial system as the main tool for intervention. By directing credit, the government elite can, in a hidden way, circumvent the legislative support for an overt industrial policy.

FR Germany

As a country that is relatively poor in natural resources, FR Germany built its comparative advantage on human capital. Manufacturing industry is based on the high-value-added branches like electric and mechanical machinery, vehicle building and precision instruments. Due to the blockade on the world supply of resources during the two world wars, the production of synthetic substitutes for many raw materials and the chemical industry in general greatly contribute to the international competitiveness of the manufacturing sector (Schatz and Wolter, 1987, p. 27).

Deindusrialization of FR Germany and the restructuring of its economy towards agriculture was a matter for discussion among the allied countries after the Second World War. This discussion faded away once the threat from the Soviet Union became obvious. When manufacturing started to be rebuilt, the allies wanted to fragment the business and weaken the authority of the central government. The Federal Republic was created from eleven states. Concentration of production is a facet of all advanced countries. FR Germany is no exception. If a cartel serves a socially useful aim, it is supported even by the federal government.

The property of the economic system of FR Germany is that the government does not play a direct role in economic life. Its aim is to maintain stability in the economic system which will permit the orderly operation of market forces. The federal government is well protected from specific sectoral influences and it intervenes rather indirectly through welfare, vocational training and regional pro-grammes. A market-oriented ideology does not mean that the government does not intervene at all. On the contrary, the government is very active in support of the system of education. It actively promotes R&D through the Ministry of Research and Technology that picks the winners in sunrise industries, small and medium-sized enterprises and improves infrastructure – most notably telecommunications, traffic and health care. This support, however, plays only a complementary role to the efforts of industry. Also, the federal states have a strong leverage over taxation relative to the central government. In order to obtain funds, the federal government taxes at high rates. In this situation the influential policy instrument is tax exemption.

If an industry is in trouble, then it may ask for assistance from the federal government. This body is well shielded from various political influences. Assistance is granted on a regional, rather than a specific-industry basis. To determine the recipients, a three-quarter majority vote is required. The outcome is that no individual state interest may dominate the process (Trebilcock, 1986, p. 278). Furthermore, the law requests that the federal government publishes a report on subsidies twice a year.

The role of banks is vital in the risky business of both economic adjustment and determining the recipients of government aid. FR Germany developed an investment, rather than a commercial, banking system. Instead of working in favour of the short-term interests of shareholders, this system operates in favour of the long-term interests of banks. The system produces a reliable long-term relationship between banks and industry. Banks serve as an early-warning mechanism for the identification of the lame ducks. They are free from the political pressures that may be exerted upon the governments, so they may speak their own mind.

All programmes which ask for the government's assistance must be approved by the banks. The banks must commit their own funds to support the adjustment. Inefficient firms are allowed to close down and the bailing out of AEG Telefunken in 1982 was a rare exception. The government's aim is to keep inflation low. An expansion in the assistance to industry would either increase inflation or shrink welfare programmes. In addition, the banks are allowed to control home companies, even 100 per cent. But the banks seldom keep all their eggs in one basket. Instead of full control over one company, a bank can own control packages of several firms – which makes it able to control the volume of capital which is far greater than the capital invested in the bank. Although the banks are not the only conductors of business, they coordinate the actions of firms with those of the government.

FR Germany's labour organizations have been generally very supportive of the change in the industrial structure. Their cooperation is based on the awareness of the country's exposure to foreign competition. A competitive economic structure is a better guarantee of long-term job security than an obsolete and protected economic structure. Adjustment is supported by general programmes, including regional aid to backward and monostructured areas, that give impetus to professional and geographical mobility of labour.

Despite a different approach to industrial policy from FR Germany, France remained an active and relevant competitor of FR Germany both in the EC and out of it. While France fostered a centralized model of industrial policy, FR Germany was following a market one. The French elite was singling out national champions and supporting their growth as international competitive firms. A similar thing was done by a few large banks and the Ministry of Research and Technology in FR Germany. A common denominator of these industrial policies is intervention. Of course, the degree and type differs. An agreement on the basic aims of the economy between the corporations and government, as well as labour, may be the key for the successful shaping of a country's comparative advantage. This kind of cooperation may be quite difficult in the United States, where these partners see each other as opponents. FR Germany's approach to industrial policy is well protected from interests of individual sectors or firms. An important role in this relatively depoliticized industrial policy is played by the banks.

United Kingdom

The United Kingdom was the first country to industrialize. This process took place during the heydays of the last century when there was very little intervention by the state. The structure of the state was created in such a way that its administration had a limited ability to intervene. Any change towards intervention would initiate a struggle among the government, corporations, banks and unions over the leadership in the intervention process. Without the mandate to intervene in the economy on a large scale in a direct way – which is possible in FR Germany (banks), or Japan and France (consultation and collusion with enterprises) – the British government has no other choice but to rely predominantly on market forces.

Declining international competitiveness and slow economic growth, in relation to other developed countries, are the major problems that faced the British industrial policy in the period after the Second World War. This was due to low productivity and insufficient adjustment to the new technologies. Furthermore, competition from the newly industrializing countries, concern about the short-term returns, emphasis on the basic, rather than applied research and poor industrial policy, had their combined impact.

The decline in the British competitive position provoked the creation of the National Economic Development Council in 1961. The Council sought to establish agreement between the government, the enterprises and the trade unions for improvement in competitiveness. The French model of planning was in mind; but in the British case it is hard to find any significant achievement.

The industrial policy embodied in the Industry Acts of 1972, 1975 and 1982 gave wide powers to the Secretary of State in providing financial assistance to firms. Altough the main purpose of those acts was to promote modernization, efficiency and reorganization of enterprises and industries, in practice a major part of the funds has gone to prop up enterprises on the point of failure (Utton, 1986, p. 66).

Industrial policy in Britain stands in sharp contrast to policies which promote adjustment. It may be taken as an example of policies which prevent change, rather than promote it. The British industrial policy is based on assistance to inefficient industries. In spite of differences in rhetoric, both Labour (interventionists) and Tories (non-interventionists) pursue similar policies from the Cabinet. Although the Tories were reluctant to intervene, many measures of the previous government were continued. This is not solely a property of the British way of life.

British industrial policy has been characterized by scattered attempts by the government to preserve the status quo by preserving jobs in obsolete branches of manufacturing industry. Structural adjustment of the economy does not take place when many inefficient jobs depend on on-going government assistance. Instead of supporting the exit from declining sectors, as was the case in Japan, this policy ensures their survival and increases the costs to society in the long run. The British policy personifies the inability of the government to resist the political pressure from influential groups – with a notable exception during the coal miners' strike in 1984 (although the causes of this strike were more political than economic).

The British industrial policy is geared towards the solution of the regional problem of unemployment, rather than towards the shaping of comparative advantage. The British system was not able to link savings (profits from banking, insurance and shipping services, as well as proceeds from North Sea oil) to the adjustment and development of the continuously competitive, domestic industrial sector.

Change in the economic structure requires shifts in the national spending, from consumption towards wealth-creating investment. The British problem was not to move out of agriculture into industry or to increase the competitiveness of the protected industry. The primary problem was how to generate change within an entrenched industrial economy (Zysman, 1983, p. 206). Instead of having general and transparent rules of intervention for the creation of comparative advantage, Britain intervened on a case-by-case basis.

The problem of unemployment is exacerbated by the policy of subsidized housing. Labour does not necessarily move towards the growing regions where the lists for this kind of housing are long. Reallocated labour may lose this privilege in the troubled regions where these lists may be relatively short.

Policy initiatives – such as the National Enterprise Board – were, among other things, set up to stimulate investment for the development of advanced technologies. The Business Expansion and the Loan Guarantee Schemes help firms enter into new ventures which would not have been otherwise started. The ambitious Alvey Programme on advanced information technology enhances cooperation in research among firms, as well as between universities and industry. The independent National Economic Development Office acts as a mediator between government, labour and industry. Its role is mainly to persuade the actors about the future course of action. The reports along these lines are quite influential. Although British industrial policy has never existed in any coherent form, there is a hope that the decline in British competitiveness may be reversed in the future due to the participation in a large EC market and the 1992 Programme that provides opportunities for unrestricted business on a large market.

However, the adjustment-averse industrial policy may change, at least to some extent. While in the past, the government 'solved' the problem of declining industries in nationalization, the most influential change in industrial policy is the move towards the privatization of public industries. Lacking a free hand in economic policy action, apart from privatization and competition, the government used macroeconomic intervention (money supply) to influence the process of microeconomic adjustment. Any other increase in the powers of the government along the French or Japanese lines would be against the British political system.

The European Community

The Treaty of Rome which established the European Community has not explicitly asked for the introduction of an industrial policy, as was the case with agriculture. The Treaty regulates only the rules of competition in the EC. These rules, together with foreign-trade policy instruments, were the means which were used by the EC in the conducting of its industrial policy. The use of all other policy instruments is severely restricted.

While the Treaty which established the European Economic Community has a general nature, the sector-specific treaties which created the European Coal and Steel Community and Euratom ask for a common policy in their respected fields. These two sectors are characterized by relatively high investment, risk and uncertainty. The two sectoral treaties try to overcome these market failures by a common policy.

One of the principal things which the Treaty of Rome tried to achieve was to increase the competitiveness of European firms in relation to those of the United States at the time of the creation of the EC. The intention was to take advantage of economies of scale which an enlarged EC market provides. It was primarily the development of internal demand which stimulated the development of both the United States and, later, Japan. Competitiveness was created on the basis of the secure, even protected, large domestic market, which did not exist in almost every European state.

In the small European countries, industrial policy was often defensive (subsidies to protect employment), rather than aggressive (risky entry into the new industries). Relatively weak anti-merger laws allowed for the creation of large European corporations in the 1960s – which could, it was thought, successfully compete with their United States and Japanese rivals. However, the problem lay not merely in the size of firms in the EC. A fragmented EC market due to non-tariff barriers introduced inflexibility and shielded national firms from competition and adjustment.

Although the EC firms are rivals on the EC internal market, they are allies in competition against the firms from third countries, both on the off-shore and the internal EC markets. The national economic policies which are used to tackle the same problem may be very different and may have undesirable and unwanted spillover effects on the EC partner countries. Here lies the rationale for a common action of the EC in the field of industrial policy.

Protectionism has been the instrument of EC industrial policy in spite of costs and postponement of adjustment. Resistance to abandoning obsolete technologies and industries permitted others, most notably Japan, to gain the competitive edge and penetrate the EC market with many high-technology goods. If the instruments of protection and cartelization (in the coal and steel sector) are not coupled with other tools of industrial policy, which ensure contraction of obsolete industries or assist for a limited time the introduction of new industries, then such a policy may be ineffective. It may be pursued by those who can afford to be wasteful.

The legal framework for the EC competition policy is covered by the following three articles of the Treaty of Rome. There is a special responsibility of the Commission for the proper operation of competition, because it regulates a much larger number of firms than any member country.

First, Article 85 forbids all agreements among undertakings which have as their object or effect the prevention, restriction or distortion of competition within the common market.

Second, Article 86 outlaws any abuse of a dominant position in the common market. This means that the dominant position is permitted, but its abuse is not. A firm has the dominant position when it enjoys such a strength which enables it to prevent effective competition. This means that the big are provided with power, but they are forbidden to exercise it! The EC cannot control mergers in advance. It may only act upon a charge that a firm abuses its dominant position.

Third, Article 92 regulates state aid. Any aid which distorts competition among the member countries is prohibited. There are a few exceptions like aid to regions affected by calamities, aid to projects which are of interest to the EC and regional development aid which does not endanger competition. However, when and where unemployment prevails, it is quite hard to resist the approval for state aid in various forms.

The EC attempted to change its atrophied industrial policy by the introduction of a more forceful industrial policy. Along these lines the Spinelli Report (1973) offered the Action Programme in the Field of Technological Industrial Policy. Its aim was the removal of non-tariff barriers to trade, liberalization of public procurement, removal of fiscal and legal obstacles to mergers, promotion of modern technology, as well as coordination of industrial with regional, trade and social policies. This broad strategy has not succeeded because of different economic philosophies among the member countries. After the oil crisis, the member countries pursued nationalistic industrial policies and were not very interested in a joint approach. In fact, they passed on to the EC level the adjustment of the problem industries (steel, shipbuilding and textile) via trade, social and regional policies, while keeping the management of sunrise industries. During this period there was only some coordination of technical standards and joint actions in research.

The absence of an EC corporate law presents a serious problem. Big national corporations which tried to merge on the EC level – such as Fiat-Citroën, Agfa-Gevaert, Dunlop-Pirelli, with a notable exception in Airbus Industries – gave these projects up. The Community's TNCs which currently exist are those (e.g. Philips, Shell, Unilever) which existed even before the establishment of the EC.

The abolition of customs duties in the EC benefited only those industries which serve private consumers. Due to the existence of non-tariff barriers, the industries which are exploiting new technologies fail to serve the entire EC market, for they compete for public funds and orders (de Ghellinck, 1988, p. 136). This is why EC firms tended to cooperate more with US or Japanese TNCs, than among themselves. By a joint venture with a Japanese firm, an EC firm makes up for its technological gap without forgoing the protectionist shield and/or privileges in the form of public procurement, major export contracts, tax reliefs and R&D accorded by the state (Defraigne, 1984, p. 369). The outcome of such a policy is the non-existence of EC standards for high-technology goods, as well as the existence of relatively big and protected national corporations which are not very interested in intra-EC cooperation and are unable to respond swiftly to changes in the international market. This was obvious after the oil shocks.

An EC company law would help to realize the objectives of the Treaty of Rome with respect to the harmonious development of economic activities in the Community. Therefore, in 1989, the Commission proposed the European Company Statute. The Statute is needed because the current tax systems create difficulties for firms which operate in several EC countries. Business on the EC market would be made easier if these firms were incorporated under a single code of law.

While the EC creates conditions for competition, its member countries implement their own national industrial policies. The divergence in industrial-policy philosophies among the member countries and the lack of funds prevented the EC from playing a more influential role. The variety of national uncoordinated policies introduced confusion and uncertainty with respect to the future actions of the EC. Until the member countries take advantage of a vast internal market, they may lose the competitive edge in industry in times to come. If it attempts to be durable and successful an EC industrial policy will require agreement between the member states about their aims and policy means.

When a large corporation from a sunset sector of industry closes down in an old industrial city, the first reaction by the state is often to offer subsidies to large new corporations. If a rhinoceros is caught or attracted, it is usually loyal in this area only as long as the carrot lasts. If the corporations are uncertain that the incentives will last up to the end of the investment/production programme, they will not enter into this business. Risk-averse corporations may in this situation request larger incentives, and/or single out projects with high rates of return. Locally-grown jobs can be found in the development of small and medium-sized enterprises. Of course, these companies cannot in the short run create enough jobs to make up for the loss of jobs in an area where a large corporation closes down, but such new firms have lately been responsible for the creation of more than half the net created jobs in the United States. These firms can flourish in the EC, for their production can be efficient because they serve one market segment on the EC-wide market.

In the situation where the strong national elements still dominate, the EC should endeavour to coordinate national policies, promote cooperation and favour the flexibility of the industrial structure.

Coordination of national policies should be in the sunset sectors in a way which avoids a beggar-thy-neighbour policy. In the light of irreversible changes started by the 1992 Programme, actions in the sunrise industries should introduce EC standards which provide room for large-scale production and improvement in competitiveness. The aim is to avoid the creation of incompatible standards – as happened with the PAL and SECAM television receiver systems.

Based on the findings of the FAST (Forecasting and Assessment in Science and Technology) programme, the EC started a score of publicly supported programmes for industrial cooperation among the EC firms in the R&D stage. The aim of the EC is to be involved in the growing industries of the future that have strategic importance for competitiveness, instead of being confined only to the branches that are in crisis. Various technology-push programmes include ESPRIT (information technologies), RACE (telecommunications), BRITE (industrial technologies) and a Europe-wide programme, EUREKA. These EC-wide programmes ought to be propped up by a number of national programmes to spread links among agents that are involved in R&D and the implementation of results.

Competitiveness of a country's goods and services in modern times is created more than inherited. The leader in a technology cannot be sure that this position will be secure in the long run. Therefore, there is scope for cooperation in the EC, both in the pre-commercial and the commercial stages of R&D. In this way, inefficient duplication or multiplication of R&D will be eliminated and resources saved and directed elsewhere.

The adoption of the White Paper (1985) and the Single European Act (1987) provided the EC with the means to implement the 1992 Programme for the achievement of the single internal market by the adoption of 282 proposals. This also represented political determination on the part of the member countries to change their 'atomized' industrial policies. Table 4.8 shows those EC industries which are most affected by the implementation of the 1992 Programme.

There was a fear by outsiders that the 1992 Programme might lead to the creation of 'Fortress Europe' as a mixture of intra-EC liberalization and an increase in the existing level of external protection. But the EC neither has such a plan, nor would it serve its long-term interests. It is expected that the 1992 Programme would lead, among other things, to increased efficiency which would reduce prices in the EC. Therefore, even without a change in the

Table 4.8   Industries most affected by the 1992 Programme

Impact	Industry
1 Reduction in protection Increased competition	a. Financial services b. Pharmaceuticals c. Telecommunication services
2 Shift from fragmented local to integrated EC-wide market	a. Distribution b. Food processing c. Transport (trucking)
3 Gain of technical economies of scale through sale of standardized goods and services	a. Electronics b. Packing c. White and other consumer goods
4 Dependence on public procurement	a. Computer equipment and services b. Defence contractors c. Telecommunication equipment
5 Industries where the single market leads to import substitution (EC goods instead of imports)	a. Chemicals b. Electrical components c. Office equipment
6 Industries where price disparity exists between countries with different indirect taxation (VAT) levels	

Source: Business International (1989): *Gaining a Competitive Edge in the New Europe.*

existing level of nominal protection, the real level may rise. An extra increase in the existing level of protection is neither necessary nor desirable. On the contrary, increased efficiency may prompt the EC to reduce the current level of protection.

The impetus to economic life once offered by a customs union – as Mark 1 in the process of integration has been used up. Something more and new is needed. The genuine EC internal market with an unimpeded flow of goods, services and factors from 1993 – as Mark 2 in the integration process – provides the EC with the new propelling force. The member countries decided to re-introduce the majority voting system (save for fiscal, national border controls, working conditions and environmental issues) in order to ease the procedure for the implementation of the Programme.

The twelve member countries have realized that the costs of non-Europe are too high to be accepted any longer. The EC without frontiers for the EC residents – as envisaged in the White Paper – can increase the EC GNP by up to 7 per cent and employment by 5 million new jobs, if accompanied by matching national policies

(Emerson *et al.*, 1988, p. 165). The sacrifices for these real gains are more freedom and less regulation. The opponents of this plan were not able to create a more attractive and feasible economic strategy and, ultimately, gave these efforts up. Only inefficient producers, who place continuous costs on society, are the ones who will lose. The 1992 Programme has the potential to change the EC and Europe more than most people are able to imagine. However, Mark 2 in the EC integration is only the first step. One has to bear in mind that the 1992 Programme is no more than a medium-term strategy. What will come after is not yet clear. This is a highly political question because it is linked to a transfer of other responsibilities to the EC level.

Services

Introduction

While physical existence determines goods, such a direct relation does not exist for services. There is a large diversity of economic activities, some of which have almost nothing in common with each other, that can be found in service activities. The service sector includes the following services (Nayyar, 1988. p. 280):

- Infrastructural services – transport, communication, electricity and water supply
- Social services – education and health
- Financial services – banking, insurance, accountancy and brokerage
- Technological services – construction, engineering and consultancy
- Marketing services – advertising, wholesaling and retailing
- Commercial services – chartering, leasing and franchising
- Professional services – lawyers, doctors and architects
- Government services – public administration and defence
- Personal services – hotels, restaurants, hairdressers, beauty parlours and domestic help.

Services may be received by various receivers. It can be a person for a haircut, entertainment or transport; a legal entity like a firm or government for banking; an object like an aircraft for repairs or airport services; and merchandise for transport or storage (Snape, 1990, p. 5). Services can be provided to a variety of receivers. For example, banking, insurance, transport, telecommunication, leasing, data processing and legal services can be offered to individuals, business or government.

Issues

In general, services absorb more than half the GNP and employment in the developed countries. However, the service sector is continuously increasing. Deindustrialization tendencies shift emphasis towards the service sector as one of the key solutions to the problem of unemployment and growth.

Notwithstanding its importance and impact on the economy, the service sector has been neglected in economic analysis for a long time. Economists like Adam Smith and Karl Marx neglected services, as being the residual sector of the economy which has no durable properties and no facility for physical accumulation. Production and consumption of services is simultaneous and asks for a degree of mobility of factors. Therefore, these classical economists turned their analysis towards physical goods.

There are also other reasons which make the analysis of services tricky. A wide definition of service states that a service is a change in the condition of a person, or a good belonging to some economic unit, which is brought about as a result of the activity of some other economic unit (Hill, 1977, p. 317). Without a proper definition, the measuring unit is lacking.

Trade statistics list thousands of items for goods on the one hand, but record only just a handful of services on the other. Although many services were previously not tradeable, progress in the development of information technology makes many of them eligible for international trade. Nevertheless, trade in many services is not recorded. The service part, like repair, may be incorporated in the price of traded goods. TNCs do not release data on their internal trade in services, while other service establishments reluctantly make public this information, for it may endanger their competitive position. Also, information can be easily, swiftly and cheaply distributed – which jeopardizes property rights. Such a lack of statistical information makes trade in services difficult to study.

It is easier to sell goods than services in foreign markets. While barriers on trade in goods can be eliminated at the border, problems for the suppliers of services usually start once they pass the frontier control. Trade in services often requires the right of establishment and national treatment. Persons need to be present in order to be able to supply many services.

Experts may enter and settle in foreign countries, but their qualifications and licences may not be recognized. Also, the public authorities regulate services to a much higher degree than they do with the production of goods. They often regulate public share-holding, quality and quantity of supply, rates and conditions of operation. Fiscal incentives are often more easily given to the manufacturing than the service sector. Because of a wide coverage of regulation of service industries, the removal of such control can have a greater impact on trade and investment in services than is the case in trade and production of goods.

Small and open countries which are net importers of goods may choose not to rely solely on their domestic manufacturing industry, which need not operate on an efficient scale. These countries can develop service industries which may create proceeds to pay for imports. The Netherlands developed trade, Austria tourism, Norway and Greece shipping, while Switzerland and Luxembourg specialize in financial services.

The issues linked to trade in services have often been neglected. The rules relating to these problems were not negotiated. As is currently the case, once trade in services absorbs a third of world trade – or around 600 billion dollars annually – negotiations about this part of trade cannot be avoided. The success of the Uruguay Round of the GATT negotiations depends on the issues which relate to agriculture, services, textiles and an efficient dispute-settlement mechanism.

The bilateral free-trade agreement between Canada and the United States shows the international community that some solutions may be found for services. Although these two countries share a number of important common features, the agreement on services was very hard to reach. It excludes large parts of services like transport, medical and child care, cultural industries, lawyers and basic telecommunications. The agreement imposes a stand-still provision on trade in services. New laws which restrict bilateral trade in services are not allowed. This pre-empts all possible protective measures in the future, which may be regarded as the most significant achievement of the agreement. The partners offer each other national treatment, right of establishment and a licensing procedure which should be granted solely according to the competence, not the origin, of the supplier.

The service sector of the economy changes its structure over time. To the traditional services (such as transport, legal, banking and insurance) new and fast-growing ones are added (such as tele-communications, information, data processing, engineering and management consultancy). Services and the jobs which they create may be broadly classified into two groups: (a) those which require high skills and pay (such as business, financial, engineering, consulting and legal); (b) those which are geared to consumer and welfare needs. The suppliers of services in this second group receive poor training, have a high turnover and low pay (such as jobs in shops and restaurants). Economic development in its post-industrial phase should be aimed at the creation of jobs in the former group rather than the latter (Tyson, 1987, p. 79).

European Community

Although Articles 52 to 68 of the Treaty of Rome grant the right of establishment to the residents of the EC and freedom to supply services throughout the EC, this has not materialized on a large scale so far because of various national restrictions. It is in financial services (banking and insurance) where the 1992 Programme is advancing most swiftly. This is also due to the impressive development of telecommunications. The financial services deal with promises to pay. In a world of developed telecommunications these promises can move instantaneously. Customs posts do not matter here, while rights of establishment and freedom to supply services may restrict this freedom. Traditionally, the monetary power was jealously protected and saved for the domestic authorities. This has currently changed. International mobility of capital can hardly be stopped, countries therefore try to make the best use of it. Financial services not only generate employment and earnings themselves but also, and more importantly, the efficient allocation of resources and the competitiveness of the manu-facturing sector depend on wide choice, efficient and low costs of financial services.

The EC resident banks are free to open branches throughout the Community, but the barriers represent different conditions under which this can be done. Foreign banks could not compete successfully with local banks, for the costs of establishment differ widely among countries. In addition, foreign banks may be excluded from certain services (securities) which are reserved for local residents. The Second Banking Directive (1989) introduces the single banking licence. From 1993, member countries of the EC will recognize each other's licensing rules for banks. However, national treatment and local operating rules (liquidity, monetary control) will be applied to branches of banks licensed in other EC countries. Branches of third-country banks located in the EC will not be included in the single banking licence rules. Such branches will operate only where they have been authorized.

The insurance business is very special indeed. If a consumer purchases a bottle of Scotch whisky, he will have the pleasure of consuming this drink even if the producer goes out of business. The same is not true for an insurance policy. Control is exercised by regulation of entry to business. The insurers in the EC are granted the general right to establish, but they are often permitted to solicit business only through local agencies. This is particularly true for compulsory insurance. The rationale for such restrictions may be found in the protection of the consumers' interest, but it may also be employed for the protection of local business. Progress in integration of the insurance business in the EC has not advanced as much as in the field of banking. The EC insurance companies are allowed to compete only under the host-country rules, which significantly reduces the possibilities for real competition. Highly protected national insurance markets will require a lot of harmonization before real competition takes place in this field. This process may take many years.

Uncoordinated national laws can no longer provide the basis for the future development of financial services. This is increasingly important in the light of rising internalization. If the EC wants to preserve, or even increase, the existing amount of business and the employment that goes with it, the crucial thing is that the EC develops an open and efficient market for financial services. Consumers will get a wider choice, better quality and cheaper services, which is essential for the competitiveness of the manufacturing sector.

The operation of commercial transport vehicles and the supply of transport services is restricted throughout the EC. Free competition does not exist. It is understandable that all countries apply qualitative controls (safety standards), but they also use quantitative controls. Cabotage (internal transport service in a country) is generally prohibited, while bilateral permits negotiated between member states regulate haulage between them.

The EC was successful in introducing special transport permits valid for a limited time throughout the EC. However, the number of these permits is relatively small in relation to demand. The shortage of international haulage licences which are acceptable for business throughout the EC has created a black market for those permits. The price of an annual permit for a lorry to carry goods around the EC can be as high as one-fifth of a lorry's operating costs. Liberal rules for EC road haulage, which also refer to cabotage, will significantly increase the efficiency of the transport service and reduce costs of transport to the manufacturing sector, trade and distribution. The United States offers a convincing example of deregulation of the transport service in 1980. The Single Administrative Document for carrying goods across the frontiers within the EC is a significant step in the direction of improving the transport service.

Business services have high rates of growth. They include accountancy, audit, legal, R&D, information, data processing, computing and various engineering and management consultancy services. Technical standards, licensing of professionals and government procurement of services represent barriers to free supply of services throughout the EC. A liberal treatment of these services may reduce their costs and increase business effectiveness and activity. As long as consultants manage to stay at least one step ahead of their clients, their services will survive.

The policy of the EC toward services should be founded on three major freedoms. They are: the freedom to establish activities; the freedom to offer services; and the freedom to transfer capital. Deregulation in the service sector will increase competition – which will reduce costs for consumers, increase opportunities and improve the competitive position of the entire economy. Apart from deregulation, the promotion of the development of EC-wide service sectors needs to be encouraged. The initial steps towards this aim include: recognition of qualification; single banking and insurance licences; removal of restrictions on transport; and the opening up of government procurement for all EC suppliers.

Various restrictions have significantly reduced trade in services in the EC. That is the reason why up to one-third of the EC trade in services was with the United States. Integrated EC network for information (Euronet-Diane) is one of the steps towards reduction of the domination of the United States' supremacy in this sector. Deregulated national and promoted EC service networks will create opportunities for business in this sector EC-wide. It is up to this sector to organize itself and take advantage of these chances.

Conclusion

The survey of various problems which appear during the creation and implementation of an industrial policy within a country has given insights about the magnitude of the problems which face an economic union in this field.

There is a forceful argument which favours the introduction of an industrial policy. The neo-conservative approach – which argues that an unfettered market system can solve economic problems cannot be accepted without reservation. Neither the economic performance of the United States prior to the New Deal nor the contemporary economic performance in the most successful industrialized countries – such as FR Germany, Japan or Sweden – supports this view. Strategic government intervention and comprehensive social welfare programmes, rather than free markets, have been the engines of economic success throughout the advanced industrial world (Tyson and Zysman, 1987b p. 426). In fact, free markets were 'fine tuning' the government choices.

If a country's policy is flexible and adjusts its attitude (policy) towards industry in response to market signals (as in Japan), or if it shapes the market (as in France), it has a greater possibility of adapting than a country which prevents changes (such as Britain). Industrial policy which ignores market signals and supports sunset industries introduces confusion over the future and increases the cost of inevitable change. These costs may be much higher in the future than they were in the past because of social rigidities and rapid changes in technology. The success of industrial policies may be tested by their effectiveness in shifting resources from dying branches, not how effective they are in preventing this adjustment shift and introducing confusion.

The policy of picking the winner (*ex ante*) which – as a strategic industry with important linkages and spillover effects – may propel the economic life of the country in future, may have a favourable outcome: if the choice is correct; if this policy is coordinated with the suppliers of inputs; and if it is limited to a certain period of time in which the national champion is expected to become self-reliant. The other interventionist approach of the rescue (*ex post*) may just postpone the attrition of the assisted industry and increase overall costs to society. The shifts out of obsolete industries into modern ones seem easy in theory, but can be quite difficult in practice. This is, of course, a matter of political choice. The EC opted for the creation of an environment which favours change.

Although both Taiwan and South Korea employed such policy measures as administrative support, preferential tax treatment, subsidies and reduction of import-substitution tendencies, their experiences differ. South Korea experienced strong economic growth together with higher inflation, a worsening distribution of income, increases of foreign debt and concentration of economic power. This contrasts with Taiwan which recorded low inflation, improved distribution of income, current-account surplus and proliferation of small businesses. The same instruments of industrial policy in one country may not produce the same results in another.

The shaping of an industrial policy in each country requires detailed data about available factors, competition, linkages among industries, policies of the major trading partners, as well as data on tax, law and the political environment. Even then, industrial policy prescriptions should be taken with great caution. At the time when Britain was industrializing, it was the textile sector which was the leader in technology, whereas in Germany the needed capital for the start-up of a firm was much higher for a steel mill – which was the leading industry when that country started to industrialize. The problems of development had to be solved by government incentives (intervention) and bank loans. Modern industries not only require capital investment (in many cases this asks for reliance on banks) but also, and more importantly, they require investment in highly qualified personnel. Education policy is always shaped to a large extent by the government.

There are reasons for pessimism about the possibility for the creation and implementation of an effective industrial policy in an economic union or a decentralized country. There are many agents and issues which should be taken into account. Various agents have their impact on industrial policy. They include ministries of trade, finance, social affairs, regional development, defence and foreign affairs. Most of these departments exist at the federal, regional and local levels. There are also labour unions, banks and industrial sectors. They all have various and often conflicting goals. Numerous agents may be, of course, a source of creativity, but in practice they often turn out to be a source of disagreement over the distribution of instruments of industrial policy. The interaction of all these players has an amalgamating effect on a national industrial policy. To reconcile all the diverse strivings of players is very demanding politically.

Luckily, the evidence in the cases of Japan and FR Germany may serve as an example to other countries for shaping their national industrial policies. The crucial property of a promising industrial policy is that if it cannot be organized on the central level, then it ought to coordinate measures taken at lower levels. Without a consensus about the basic aims of an industrial policy among the major players, and their commitment to these goals, then the policy will not be a success.

Central planning and integration may not result in an efficient industrial policy either. The rigid decision-making process circumvents market signals, so the policy choice may well be wrong. Industrial production in some of the developing countries may have a significant part in the GNP. An economic union may provide these countries with some foundation for the coordination of the development of manufacturing and the introduction of a common industrial policy. However, these countries must first agree about the desired pattern of production, which may be quite difficult without a satisfactory distribution of costs and benefits.

Various national experiences in industrial policy reveal seven obvious characteristics of a successful industrial policy (Mayes, 1987, p. 250):

- this policy has to be continuous and stable
- the means employed should be mutually re-inforcing
- the long-term vision of industrial priorities should be realistic
- there should exist an element of choice and selectivity
- investment in human capital should be emphasized
- there should be a consensus and commitment in attitudes towards the basic aims
- industry should be flexible enough to respond to new pressures and opportunities.

In addition, one need not forget that this policy ought to increase the flow of information and bring about means for the ease of adjustment frictions; emphasis ought to be on the growing industries and free from long-term protectionism.

Although industrial policy is wider than trade policy, the frontier between the two is obscure. A promising industrial policy must have the effect neither of prolonged shielding of sunrise industries from competition, nor of preventing the attrition of sunset industries for ever. It ought to facilitate movements of factors from obsolete to modern industries. It has to be well coordinated on different levels of government with other economic policies which affect the industrial sector. This holds both for single countries and for economic unions. The EC has chosen a path which creates the conditions for changes according to the market criteria of efficiency. It is up to economic agents to take advantage of these opportunities.

REGIONAL POLICY

Introduction

While industrial policy is directed towards an increase in production possibilities and GNP through the efficient allocation of resources, the aim of regional policy is to influence the distribution of wealth. Governments attempt to achieve the proper balance between the orderly distribution of national wealth among the regions (equity) and its desire to sustain and increase national economic potential (efficiency).

Modern economies have at least four features. First, the share of labour relative to capital in agriculture is declining: this influences the urbanization of a society. Second, manufacturing industry is less reliant on natural inputs and places an emphasis on the proximity to final markets. Third, the service sector of an economy increases its importance. Finally, free market prices are continuously displaced by administered prices by the state, trade unions and firms. In these circumstances, responses to disequilibria tend to be embodied, at least in the medium-term, in terms of quantity rather than price (Nevin, 1985, pp. 338–9).

Determinants of industrial location include considerations about access to raw materials, power and labour supply, access to markets, government (dis)incentives and cost of transport. An advance in transport and communication technologies has made transport costs rarely the most important determinant of location. While considering feasible spots for its location, a firm may emphasize least-cost location and ignore demand. It may also emphasize demand and neglect everything else. In practice, a firm considers these issues simultaneously.

Industrial development was shaped in the past by various economic and historic factors. One of the most attractive locations was on a crossroads or at the mouth of a river. Colonial powers might obtain resources from, but prevent the development of manufacturing in, their colonies. This was because they wanted to secure markets for their manufactured goods and to prevent competition. If the development of manufacturing took place it was usually in port cities.

Without foreign direct investment, the national rate of growth of capital stock depends on home savings and investment. Suppose that one region/country initially accumulates more capital than the other. In the following period both regions grow, but the one with more capital grows faster than the other. As manufacturing capital grows, the relative prices of manufacturing goods fall. After a certain time, there is a point where the lagging region's industry cannot compete internationally and begins to shrink. Once this starts, the new theory suggests, there is no check. Economies of scale may drive prices down in the capital-abundant region and the lagging region's manufacturing industry disappears. In this model, relatively small beginnings can have large and irreversible final consequences (Krugman, 1990, pp. 99–100).

Once the development of an activity starts in an area and if the system is flexible, then it attracts other activities to the region. Location of a firm was influenced in the past by both endowments of immobile resources and flows of mobile factors. A modern firm is highly mobile in its search for profitable opportunities, not only within its region or country, but also internationally. For a footloose firm, the advantages of one location in relation to other locations are much more man-made than subject to resource endowments. While up until recently it was more efficient to move people to jobs by migration to the location of production, the footloose element of many modern industries supports production in relatively small units. There is an arbitrary element in the location of such industry.

Jobs can be located in the regions where there are people with suitable qualifications and training. Therefore, regions with unskilled labour cannot expect to attract a significant proportion of industries which use modern technologies that ask for trained labour and educated management. Location near large and/or growing markets saves in the cost of transport. If returns to scale were constant, as the neo-classical theory assumes, this may have had equalizing tendencies for factory owners' rewards in different regions. With economies of scale, these tendencies may increase, rather than decrease, regional disequilibria.

The product cycle may make some previously unattractive locations interesting for consideration. Innovation is the process by which new products are created, while technology transfer is the process by which new products are transformed into old products. For example, increasing the number of new goods in the north creates demand and the price of northern goods rises in relation to the price of southern goods. It is profitable to invest in the north, so capital moves there from the south. Similarly, technology transfer shifts demand towards goods produced in the south. This catch-up by the south makes capital move there, and the relative income of southern workers rises. This may 'hurt' the technical leader. Therefore, northern countries have an interest to continuously innovate, not just to grow, but also to maintain their real incomes (Krugman, 1990).

The need, objectives and instruments for intervention

A region may be more easily discerned than defined. The definition of a region depends on the problems which one encounters. A region is a geographical phenomenon with its distinctions from others, it is also a political, governmental and administrative feature, as well as an ethnic concept with its human and cultural characteristics. A region is also an economic concept with its factor endowment and their combinations. Therefore, a region can be defined as a geographic area which consists of adjoining units with similar unit incomes and more interdependence of incomes than between regions (Bird, 1972, p. 272). A region of a country or an economic union may be thought of as an open economy.

Regional policy is intervention by the state in order to influence the orderly distribution of economic activity and to reduce the social and economic differences among regions. It is usually a reactive (*ex post*) policy which primarily reduces the existing regional disparities, rather than a policy which primarily prevents the creation of new ones.

Trade liberalization and/or economic integration can provoke economic adjustment. Regions may be forced by competition to embark upon the painful transfer of resources from unprofitable into profitable activities, and may often blame integration or trade liberalization for this cost. However, this objection may not always be justified. The most basic reason for such adjustment is due to the protection that reduces the pace of reaction of local enterprises on international structural pressures.

Regional policy is aimed at four different theoretical types of regions. First, the regions with a relatively high share of agriculture in production and employment. These are usually underdeveloped rural areas with relatively low levels of income, high levels of unemployment and a poorly developed infrastructure. Second, this policy is aimed at the regions whose former prosperity was founded on industries which are now in decline – such as coal, steel, shipbuilding and textiles. These are the regions which failed to keep pace with changes in technology. In the case of recession, labour in these regions is the first to be made redundant. Third, the regions with a high concentration of industry have congestion and pollution problems. Of course, there exist benefits from a joint use of services that are available in these areas. Regional policy may reduce the existing congestion and pollution or prevent their further increase. Finally, regional policy helps the solution of frontier regions which are far from the strongest areas of a country's or union's economic activity.

The objectives of a regional policy are various, but their common denominator is that they aim at the utilization of regions' unemployed or underemployed resources, as well as increases in output and incomes. In the congested regions, this policy restricts the expansion of activities and stimulates exit from the region. In the developing countries, the primary concern is an enhancement of economic development. This is coupled with regional imbalances, but their solution is not as high on the agenda as increases in economic potential. In areas of economic integration, this problem of regional (in)equalities is of great concern. Countries are reluctant to lag behind their partners for a long time. This is of great concern in monetary unions where there are no balance-of-payments disequilibria, but rather regional disparities.

The first justification for a positive adjustment (regional) policy, as contrasted with free market adjustment, is found in the structural deficiencies of regions. These include: market rigidities, conditions of access to the market and the structure of their production (Yannopoulos, 1988, p. 130). A free market system is unable to achieve satisfactory equilibrium, so intervention is needed in order to increase production in relation to the circumstances where structural distortions prevail.

Regional imports consist of goods and services. In France, most of the country's regions purchase financial, insurance, legal and other services from Paris. All this may not be quantified easily. On the other hand, a reduction in a region's exports may be obvious from the outset. Regional solutions to these disequilibria are inhibited by rules of competition and by the existence of a single currency. Hence the second need for regional intervention in an economic union.

The third reason for intervention may be found in factor employment. The neo-classical theory of international trade assumes free mobility of factors which ensures full employment. Even Adam Smith noted that a man is the most difficult commodity to transport. During recession, the employment situation is difficult everywhere, therefore the potential advantages of some regions that are abundant in labour are removed. Reduced mobility of labour prevents the equalization of discrepancies in economic unions. Hence, growth in one region may create conditions for even higher growth in the same region (polarization effect). This may act as a locomotive for development in other regions (spread effect). In the situation with economies of scale, large sunk costs and other market failures, however, adjustment does not happen according to such a relatively smooth neo-classical expectation. The reallocation of resources induced by the spread effect works at a slower pace than may be politically acceptable, hence the need for intervention.

The fourth reason for intervention may be found in the improved allocation of resources. Free markets usually direct capital towards already-developed regions. Private investors tend to increase the speed of the safe return of their funds and to save as much as possible on investment on infrastructure. It is understandable why they direct their funds towards developed regions. These tendencies of agglomeration (common locations of linked productions), where the developed tend to become more developed while the under-developed remain at best where they are, have significant private benefits on the one hand, and social costs and benefits on the other. A society reaps the benefits of large-scale efficient production. However, if private entrepreneurs are not impeded in their decision-making by government policy, the location of their activity may introduce significant social costs – for example, pollution, conges-tion and traffic jams in some regions with unemployment and increased social assistance in others.

The fifth reason for intervention may be found in the improve-ment in stabilization (macroeconomic) policy. Regional differences in rates of unemployment may reduce the possibilities for the control of inflation and the manoeuvre of stabilization policy. The reduction of inflation in some regions may increase unemployment in others. This may not always be the desired outcome. Diversified regions with a variety of employment opportunities will be able to adjust in a less painful way than the specialized regions with entrenched market rigidities.

The sixth reason for regional policy is that it may reduce public expenditure in the assisted region in the long run. Public support to locate in certain regions might propel economic activity in these regions. Unemployment may drop, so welfare payments may be reduced and tax receipts may increase in the long run.

The seventh rationale points out that regional policy is targeted at regions with some disadvantage (underdevelopment or congestion). Benefits of a regional policy are not confined to the assisted area. Part of the benefit is enjoyed by other regions. The benefit area of a regional policy is larger than the assisted area itself (Armstrong, 1985, pp. 320–2). Integration may be enhanced, factors may be utilized and there may be non-economic benefits.

Finally, apart from the above efficiency arguments for regional policy, there are political arguments which are at least as important as the economic ones. Solidarity and tolerance are the core of any social community. The mitigation of regional disparities may be the necessary reason for the unity of a state or an economic union. Costs and benefits of international economic integration are unequally spread among the participating countries in the situation with market imperfections. Arguments of equality require the solution and/or mitigation of intolerable or growing differences in the distribution of wealth among the population, which lives in different regions. Apart from the market mechanism, the political system does not always take into account backward regions either. The national system of setting wages may on the one hand significantly reduce the wage–cost advantages of many regions, while on the other welfare expenditure can contribute to a greater regional equilibrium (Molle, 1988, p. 71). Complete equalization in the standards of living in different regions is neither possible nor desirable because it may remove incentives. What is needed is a continuous adjustment of regional development within agreed guidelines, and protection of the standard of living which is accepted as desirable.

Whether national or in an economic union, the goals of regional policy – such as balanced growth, equal shares of social and cultural progress of the society, solidarity, regional distinctiveness and stability – are vague and may not be accurately measured. Specific objectives like job creation, reduction in unemployment, housing and development of infrastructure introduce less problems in measurement. What is important is that these goals do not evolve into protection, which prevents structural adjustment and division of labour.

The dilemma of the state may be to administratively control and stimulate regional development via private investment and/or to invest directly in the socially necessary production and infrastructure which private capital avoids as a rule. The available instruments include those which provide incentives and disincentives for firms to move to or from specific regions. Major instruments include capital, investment, output and labour subsidies, vocational training, as well as public purchases. Others include reductions in interest rates, tax concessions, social-security subsidies, reductions in energy and public-transportation costs, free location and trade protection.

Cash grants may be preferred as a regional-policy instrument to reduced tax liabilities. Grants apply directly to all firms while reduced tax liabilities help only those which are profitable. Trade restrictions are not the smartest instruments of a regional policy. They bring costs to the whole economic union while they bring benefits to one or a few regions.

Disincentives for regional expansion in congested areas are a relatively novel feature. In Britain they appear in the form of Industrial Development Certificates which should be obtained prior to expansion or location in the non-assisted regions. However, after the second oil shock, as unemployment increased, the Certificates as an instrument of regional policy were abandoned.

Instruments for intervention are directed towards entrepreneurs and factor owners. They can be employed either directly (support of the existing or shifting towards the new business activities) or indirectly (improvement in infrastructure). Their joint effects may increase employment, investment and output in the assisted regions.

The policy of taking workers to jobs looks at the regional problem exclusively as a problem of unemployment. It neglects that other problems in a region may be worsened further by this shift of labour. The productive part of the population moves while the consuming part remains. The local tax base may not be able to invest in schools and other social services. The overall situation may be worsened by the multiplier effect. In the advanced regions, the new population increases congestion which deteriorates the quality of life.

Unemployment rates may be the most telling indicator of regional variations. When labour has relatively low mobility, then the movement of jobs to workers may reduce regional disparities in unemployment. Against this action is the fact that it may increase costs due to locations which are not optimal for the efficient conduct of business. However, as more industries become footloose, these costs to entrepreneurs may be reduced. Improvement in the infrastructure, including training of labour and education of management together with the spread of timely information, helps the establishment of footloose industries which are at the beginning of their product cycle.

Regional policy in the European Community

International economic integration may aggravate the situation of already backward and peripheral regions in comparison to the previous circumstances. This is recognized in the existence of national regional policies. A union regional policy can be justified at least on the grounds of harmonization of national regional policies and distribution of wealth within the union. It should ensure, at the very least, that the existing regional problems are not made worse by the creation of a union, otherwise the less developed regions/countries would not have incentives to participate.

A coordination of national regional policies in an economic union is required in order to prevent clashes of different policies with common objectives. Alongside the national regional policies of its member countries, the EC has its own role in the fight against regional disparities.

The Treaty of Rome did not explicitly request the introduction of a common regional policy. The Preamble of the Treaty says that the member countries intend to ensure harmonious development by narrowing the differences between regions and promoting the development of the least favoured areas. Article 39 asks for special treatment for different agricultural regions, Article 49 requests balanced employment in order to avoid threats to standards of living in the various regions, Article 75 notes that the policy in the area of transport should not have negative effects in certain areas, Article 92 permits state aid to regions with a low standard of living, Article 125 allows the European Social Fund to grant benefits to unemployed workers, while Article 130 empowers the European Investment Bank to provide guarantees and loans for projects in the less developed regions. The Single European Act recognizes that the Commission may propose appropriate provisions to help the efforts of countries which are at different levels of development during the period of the establishement of the internal EC market (Article 8C).

Differences in economic development among regions exist in every country, but at the EC level they seem much higher. Less developed regions in one country may have different characteristics

Table 4.9 GNP per inhabitant at market prices in ECU

Country	1987	1988	1989*	1990*	1991*
1 Denmark	17,127	17,738	18,504	19,722	20,662
2 FR Germany	15,853	16,566	17,473	18,691	19,854
3 Luxembourg	14,175	14,878	16,009	17,417	18,751
4 France	13,784	14,425	15,343	16,453	17,399
5 The Netherlands	12,598	13,094	13,677	14,659	15,409
6 Belgium	12,206	12,854	13,910	15,149	16,006
7 Italy	11,430	12,215	13,625	14,856	16,059
8 United Kingdom	10,384	12,200	13,131	13,186	14,224
9 Ireland	7,276	7,771	8,639	9,352	10,000
10 Spain	6,468	7,383	8,707	9,529	10,472
11 Greece	4,011	4,447	4,896	5,221	5,513
12 Portugal	3,273	3,616	4,197	4,646	5,157
EC	11,540	12,439	13,459	14,354	15,362

* Projection

Source: Eurostat (1990).

from less developed regions in others, including large differences in income. In addition, congestion in southern Italy is greater than that in the south-west of France. Table 4.9 presents GNP per inhabitant at market prices between 1987 and 1991. The comparison of the relative difference in GNP per inhabitant among regions and countries at the current exchange rate may well overestimate the real difference between the advanced and backward regions or countries. The difference between Denmark as the richest country according to this measure and Portugal as the least developed country was 5.23:1 in 1987.

A useful device which may overcome part of the problem associated with the measurement of GNP at market prices can be found in the use of a current purchasing-power standard. This statistical device may more adequately represent the real level of local purchasing power. Table 4.10 provides data on the differences in GNP per inhabitant in the EC at purchasing-power standard between 1987 and projections till 1991. This kind of presentation changes, to an extent, the picture of the relative wealth of countries in comparison to Table 4.9 and the gap in the relative wealth. The difference in average real income between the richest (Luxembourg)

Table 4.10 GNP per inhabitant, purchasing power standard in ECU

Country	1987	1988	1989*	1990*	1991*
1 Luxembourg	17,642	19,130	29,767	22,528	24,387
2 FR Germany	16,611	17,907	19,286	20,670	22,142
3 Denmark	16,524	17,184	18,224	19,519	20,813
4 France	15,973	17,168	18,567	20,060	21,555
5 United Kingdom	15,668	16,994	18,182	19,359	20,661
6 The Netherlands	15,229	16,244	17,615	19,048	20,428
7 Italy	15,151	16,422	17,761	19,189	20,580
8 Belgium	14,677	15,971	17,508	18,955	20,311
9 Spain	10,826	11,821	12,969	14,108	15,233
10 Ireland	9,514	10,304	11,467	12,607	13,614
11 Greece	7,943	8,619	9,303	9,895	10,479
12 Portugal	7,907	8,553	9,438	10,297	11,151
EC	14,651	15,828	17,106	18,417	19,751

* Projection

Source: Eurostat (1990).

and the poorest (Portugal) was 2.23:1 in 1987 according to this measure.

If one considers the nominal difference between the richest regions of FR Germany and The Netherlands on the one hand, and relate them to the poorest regions in Portugal on the other, this difference becomes much higher, even alarming. These discrepancies may be capable of dividing the EC. Therefore, the EC has, since its creation, intervened in regional matters through the European Investment Bank. A real regional policy of the EC was created after the British entry in 1973. The EC objective is to mitigate the existing, and prevent the creation of the new, regional problems.

It is obvious from tables 4.9 and 4.10 that the southern EC countries and Ireland are less developed than the northern part of the EC. The reasons for this situation can be found in differences in resources, level of education of the labour, access to markets, as well as social and economic infrastructure. These are more national than regional characteristics. It is, therefore, necessary to take national factors into consideration, rather than to study merely the regional factors which cause problems (Molle, 1988, pp. 78–80).

Local (i.e. member states') regional policies have an advantage over common policies because the local authorities may be better informed about local needs and problems. However, the EC is better placed to coordinate national regional, as well as other national, policies. In addition, the EC may contribute own resources, introduce common priorities and take into account regional interests when it delivers decisions. Also, the rules of competition ensure that the member governments do not distort competition by a 'subsidy war'. Normally, the EC puts a ceiling on the permitted subsidy per establishment and/or job created in various regions.

Up to the 1970s there hardly existed an EC regional policy. The idea of an economic and monetary union, together with the British entry, shaped the EC's regional policy. This policy offered benefits to the EC rim countries (Britain, Greece, Ireland, Italy, Portugal and Spain), just as the Common Agricultural Policy brings the largest benefits to Denmark, France and The Netherlands, and just as the customs union favours Belgium, FR Germany, Luxembourg and The Netherlands.

The European Regional Development Fund (ERDF) was established in 1975. It controlled the expenditure of resources which were allocated to the member states in fixed quotas. Member countries with an average GNP per capita below the EC average received the greatest share of the funds. Member governments had simply to submit projects to the EC to meet the quota, as well as to commit certain funds themselves to these projects to obtain the EC funds. The EC did not have any leverage in the selection process. It was simply reacting to national initiatives. There was also a minuscule non-quota part of the ERDF which absorbed only 5 per cent of resources. The EC was able to use these funds freely. Such a situation was criticized and the ERDF was reformed in 1985.

The new ERDF divides its funds among the EC member states by indicative ranges instead of fixed quotas as before. These indicative ranges only guarantee that the government will receive the minimum range over the period of three years if it submits sufficient projects. The projects submitted will be evaluated according to criteria which are consistent with the EC priorities and objectives. The intention of the EC is to receive a greater number of applications in order to increase competition. The ERDF support may be up to 55 per cent of the public expenditure for regional projects. It is allowed to co-finance programmes and it may prop up the development of the indigenous development potential of regions. The ERDF attempts to mobilize local resources because it is increasingly difficult to attract investment from wealthy to poor regions. Additional attention is devoted to coordination of both member countries' regional policies and the EC policies which have an impact on regions.

The EC has envisaged the adjustment problems of its Mediterranean regions which may result from the entry of Spain and Portugal in 1986. The EC therefore introduced the Integrated Mediterranean Programme in 1985. The aim of this coordinated programme is to help the Mediterranean regions of the EC (Greece and selected regions in Italy and France with a population of around 50 million) to adjust to competition from the two new member countries of the EC. The Programme disposes of ECU 4.1 billion in grants and ECU 2.5 billion in loans over seven years. It integrates all available sources of finance on the EC, national, regional and local level, as well as coordinates other activities of the Community. It is not aimed only at adjustment of agricultural production (olive oil, wine, fruit, vegetables), but also at adjustment of existing and creation of new small and medium-sized enterprises. Alternative employment for jobs lost in agriculture is to be found in services (tourism) and small and medium-sized enterprises.

The EC regional policy is just a supranational addition to, instead of being, to an extent, a replacement for various national regional policies. Its first shortcoming is that the ERDF funds are modest in relation to regional needs. It should not be forgotten that this policy is a relatively novel facet of the EC. It is improving continuously. The ERDF's share, as well as other regional expenditure in the EC Budget was 11.1 per cent in 1990. This share has an increasing tendency. The effort to reduce disparities between rich and poor countries in the EC is great in circumstances of relatively slow growth and cuts in expenditure. Another brake comes from national governments, which prevent greater involvement of the EC in their own regional affairs. A greater degree of coordination of national economic policies may avoid prodigalities of scarce EC funds and may not result in help to the rich in the relatively less developed countries, to the detriment of the poor in the developed countries.

Conclusion

If a country or an economic union has differences in the level of living standards of the population in different regions and differences in economic development of its regions which do not have at least a tendency towards equalization, such a country may not have a well-integrated economy. Therefore, all countries and economic unions have some commitment to reduce regional disequilibria for various economic and, more importantly, non-economic reasons. If a regional policy is to be effective, then the authorities at all levels of the government have to coordinate their activities in order to influence decisions about the allocation of resources. In spite of these coercive powers, regional policies of countries have limited achievements. It, should come as no surprise, therefore, that the achievements of a union's regional policy, which often relies more on persuasion and influence than on coercion, is scanty indeed.

Demand, technology and supplies of factors often change. Regions which fail to adjust continuously to the new developments remain depressed. A broad objective of regional policy is to help the redistribution of economic activity among different regions. Its impact may not be measured easily for it is not an easy task to construct a counterfactual world which would specify what would have happened without this policy. The difference between the actual and the counterfactual situation may be attributed to regional policy.

Raw materials are traded without major restrictions, while it is manufacturing industry which is protected. On these grounds, the resource-exporting regions (countries) may be supporters of free trade in a country or an economic union, because they will be able to obtain manufactured goods at favourable terms of trade. The question, however, arises as to whether regional policy increases or decreases market imperfections. In the second-best world, all answers are possible. If the costs of such a policy are less than the benefits which it brings, then the policy is justified. The rationale for a regional policy, which basically redistributes income (equity), must be found in solidarity among regions which constitute countries and/or economic unions.

There are at least three arguments in favour of an EC regional policy. First, without policy instruments like tariffs, non-tariff barriers, devaluation or rate of interest, regions that are not able to adjust as fast as the rest of the EC face an increase in unemployment and a decrease in living standards. In this situation, there is a case for the demand for fiscal transfers on the EC level that ease the adjustment process. The possibility for such transfers ought to be permanent. Otherwise, when in need, the region that is in trouble may not be sure that other partner countries will give real resources on a case-by-case basis. Second, coordination of national regional policies at the EC level can avoid self-defeating, divergent, regional programmes taken at the national level. Third, footloose industries and economies of scale do not guarantee that integration will bring an equitable dispersion of economic activities. Some direction for the development of economic activities in the form of regional policy may be needed.

SOCIAL POLICY

Introduction

The aim of social policy in a country is, at least, to assure the socially acceptable minimum standard of living for all its population. In any country or economic union, social policy deals with problems which include wages, unemployment insurance, the welfare system, pensions, health, education and mobility of labour. The short-run redistributive (security) aim of this policy does not necessarily clash with economic adjustment. In the long run these two objectives supplement each other. There will be no security without adjustment and vice versa in the long run. Social policy should not prevent the economic system from its adjustment. On the contrary, it ought to stimulate shifts from low productivity economic structure to the one that demands a qualified and highly productive labour force and management.

The foundations of a social policy may be traced to the nineteenth century, when the social security system was introduced. Between the wars, there was an increased concern that economic and social risks should be shared by the whole society. After the Second World War and up to the 1970s a sustained and relatively high rate of economic growth made possible a big increase in social-policy expenditure in most developed countries. This has not involved great political costs, because the governments' budgets were usually not in the red. Since the recession in the early 1970s, it became obvious that social expenditure had become so dear as to become a danger to the adjustment of the whole economic system. This situation begs for reform. Social policy has been transformed from a safety net designed to ease economic adjustment to the conception whose role is to provide citizens with something approaching property rights or entitlements to the status quo (Courchene, 1987, pp. 8–9). In the situation with continuous budgetary deficits, this system cannot be afforded any more. Otherwise, it will establish the present situation and prevent economic adjustment. The social cost of preserving everybody's entitlement without conditions would be endless. The following section tackles the possible reform of a national or an economic union's social policy and outlines the EC social policy.

A new social policy

A national or economic union's administration often becomes a resort for the rescue of the unsuccessful. As soon as a firm, industry, region or a social group perceives or encounters a difficulty, they ask first for government intervention instead of adjusting. The budgetary situation drives all countries to think more of how to reform social policy and its expenditure and less whether to reform this policy or not.

A society should create the conditions for the attainment of a minimum standard of living for the whole population, which would include income guarantees, but to such an extent that it does not downgrade the values and incentives to work, move and acquire new knowledge, nor to such an extent that it impedes economic adjustment and growth. Expenditure should be coupled with the social ability to pay and should not overtax the most enterprising and propelling agents which push the economic and social life of the society ahead. Social policy should be coordinated with other economic policies in order to increase its effectiveness. There are no disputes about these issues whatsoever, but they arise with respect to the ways of achieving these goals in an equitable balance.

The overviews of the British welfare system stress that it should be changed because it is incomprehensible, uncoordinated, unnecessarily expensive to administer, a chief cause of unemployment, discriminatory, arbitrary, unfair, deteriorating instead of improving, penalizes marriage, subsidizes family break-up and de-stabilizes and divides society (Courchene, 1987, p. xv). At least some of these characteristics of the social system are, unfortunately, not only a British feature. Everybody agrees that the social system ought to be improved. Disagreement arises about how to do that.

The system of unemployment insurance is one of the first on the agenda. This system often downgrades the value of work in some societies. Short-term employment and reliance on longer unemployment insurance eligibility periods is a tolerable way of life for some segments of the population. If wages are relatively low for some groups of workers while unemployment benefits are close to their wages, then some from this group of wage-earners may shift to the welfare-recipient segment of the population. Incentives to work, retraining and education may be weakened. This social policy method was created to cushion the short-run trouble when labour was passing between jobs. It is not a suitable method for correcting structural or long-term unemployment. A reform should introduce a link between the duration and height of the unemployment benefits for relatively younger and middle-aged groups of the unemployed to their vocational retraining and length of previous work, as well as introduce incentives to reallocation.

Structural unemployment, in particular among the young, is an indicator of poor vocational training. Also, unemployment should not be taken in the traditional way, i.e. labour is either in or out of full-time work. There is a potentially large scope for part-time employment. These kind of jobs need to be stimulated and helped to evolve into permanent ones. Stimulative fiscal instruments can be important incentives along these lines.

Education is another major field for reform. This is important because human-knowledge services become increasingly relevant in economic life. Knowledge is the cornerstone of modern manu-facturing and service industries. It is the key factor in a country's ability to remain competitive in modern industries and some services. Hence, education should be coordinated with the needs of industries and services which require highly educated labour.

Higher training of students is very expensive and is becoming increasingly so. On the one hand, top experts may be attracted to private industry, so universities should keep their offers relatively high. On the other hand, it is becoming increasingly expensive for them to maintain up-to-date libraries, computers and their software, laboratories, equipment and various consumables. During the periods of budgetary cuts which hit universities and public research institutes, these schools may not rely on random donations. The only way to solve this financial problem may be to increase tuition fees. Everyone who wants post-secondary education should have free access to try in the first year. Those who want and are eligible to go further, may face higher tuition fees. It would be appropriate that students bear larger costs of their education. The students are, of course, one of the most needy groups of the population. They should be assisted by a well-endowed system of loans under favourable conditions (Courchene, 1987, p. 153).

Health care is a social sub-system which will be most difficult to reform. Every society pays a great deal of attention to the health system. It has a great social value. Free access to the minimum of health care personifies one of the most fundamental values of equality in modern society. On these grounds, the expenditure for health care, particularly in ageing societies, may not be reduced. The only window for reform may be found in the partial charging of medical care by those in the relatively high income groups.

Social policy in the European Community

The Treaty of Rome does not exclude social issues, but they are not mentioned often in the text. The Preamble mentions the continuous increase in the standard of living as the basic aim of the EC. Articles 48 to 51 introduce free movement of labour among EC countries and also guarantee eligibility for social insurance. As for education, Article 41 suggests coordination of efforts in the sphere of vocational training, while Article 57 asks for the mutual recognition of diplomas and other certificates of formal education. Articles 117 and 118 introduce cooperation among the member countries with respect to standards of living, vocational training, employment, social security and protection of health in the work-place. Article 119 introduces the principle of equal pay for equal work between men and women, while Article 123 creates the European Social Fund with the aim of improving employment opportunities, raising the standard of living and increasing both the geographical and the occupational mobility of workers.

Following the coming into force of the Single European Act, the idea of economic and social progress is strengthened. Article 130A sees economic and social cohesion as both a prerequisite and an instrument of harmonious development. Article 130B asks the governments of the participating countries to conduct and coor-dinate economic policies in such a way as to attain the objectives set out in Article 130A.

These aims deal with a few social policy issues. One can hardly resist the conclusion that the EC is as strong on the social policy side as its member countries permitted. They want to keep their sovereign rights in most of the social policy issues. The relatively little space devoted to social policy in the Treaty of Rome reflects the belief that the impact of social policy on the operation of the EC was not regarded as of primary importance.

One of the first legal documents which the EC delivered in 1958 was the social insurance system for migrant workers who originate from within the EC. The basic principles are that these workers have the same social insurance rights as workers from the host country, social insurance contributions may be transferred among EC countries and that the social insurance contributions will be taken in their aggregate amount.

The only exceptions to freedom of employment for foreign workers originating from other EC countries were the following. They were denied the right to work in jobs which deal with public order, health, safety and public administration. It would be absurd to argue that people lose knowledge, skills and experience after crossing a frontier. Notable progress has recently been achieved for general practitioners, specialists, nurses, midwives, architects, chemists and veterinary surgeons. They may now practise their trade throughout the EC. The only exception to freedom of employment is in the public service, which is directly connected with the exercise of sovereignty.

The European system for exchanging job information (Sedoc) was set up in order to increase mobility of labour among the member countries. Many employers do not list their openings with Sedoc and other labour exchanges because they consider these applicants as having poor work histories. In spite of differences in wages, labour in the EC moved from the Mediterranean countries into the EC during the 1960s and early 1970s. The exception was Italy which has been in the EC since its establishment. There was the Social Action Programme in 1974 which called for full and better employment, improvement in living and working conditions, as well as participation of workers and employers in the EC decision-making process through the Standing Committee on Employment. Due to the economic crisis, it did not have a notable success.

There are around 3 million non-EC migrant workers employed in the EC. Since this number does not include Spaniards and Portuguese (they will receive full mobility in the EC after 1992), this has been a relatively stable number for a decade. The group of non-EC migrant workers in the EC consists of around 8 million people if families are included. On top of these, one may surmise that there are around 10 per cent as many illegal migrant workers. Some of them came illegally, while others have work permits which have expired and who decided to stay and work illegally instead of going home and waiting for an uncertain renewal of their permits. Some employers may have a certain preference for illegal workers. They pay them lower wages than the legal workers, they do not pay social security benefits, they may be easily fired and the employers reduce the cost of labour, so they may gain a competitive edge in the short-term.

The first generation of migrants is now ageing. The migration issue is not a question of labour movements, but rather one of integrating these people in the host countries. Almost half of the migrant population is born in the host countries. This generation is confronted with different cultures and they are often in search of their identity. Their future depends on training and legal security with respect to residence and employment rights.

Social-security benefits may have a significant impact on the level of wages. If employers are required to pay relatively high social-security benefits, then they may offer lower wages and vice versa. different levels of expenditure on social-security benefits among countries may have an influence on competition among countries in the short run.

The aim of the European Social Fund, as the main instrument of the Community's social policy, is to improve employment oppor-tunities, to contribute to raising the standard of living and to increase the mobility of labour between occupations and between regions. At the beginning of its operation, the Fund was merely reimbursing half the costs of vocational training and relocation of workers in the member countries. Two problems were obvious. Interventions were retroactive and they were concentrated in the country which had the greatest expenditure for these activities (FR Germany).

The Fund was reformed in 1971 when it was allowed to intervene in the field of vocational training with an emphasis on the young, under 25 years of age, and to intervene with respect to structural unemployment in regions with sunset industries. After reform, around 90 per cent of expenditure went to the occupational mobility of workers while the remainder was spent on geographic mobility. A new reform in 1984 reserved 75 per cent of its resources for the training and employment of young people under 25 years of age. In the EC of twelve countries, the most disadvantaged regions are guaranteed 45 per cent of all appropriations. The Fund covers up to half the eligible costs, but never more than the total public expenditure, in the country concerned. In support of adults, the Fund gives priority to women, the long-term unemployed, the handicapped and migrants from within the EC. With allocations of ECU 4.3 billion in 1990, the Social Fund is not by itself capable of solving the problem of unemployment which affects 16 million workers in the EC, excluding those from the eastern part of FR Germany.

A pessimistic expectation is that there may be in the neighbourhood of 10 million unemployed young Europeans in the 1990s. They will be at the bottom of the EC pool of labour and, due to their poor training, they will be unemployable. This problem may be somehow easy to overlook while they are still young. Once they create their own families, however, they will constitute an unusual underclass (Merrit, 1988, p. 93). Incentives to vocational training and geographical mobility may represent a long-term solution to this problem. Nevertheless, the employment policy remains the responsibility of member states. A coordination of national policies in this field started in the form of exchanges of information, experience and resolutions.

The European Social Fund has had a minor, but growing, role in the EC. It has never had enough funds to satisfy all the needs which exist in the EC. This fund spent 8.8 per cent of the total EC budget in 1990. The greatest portion of the expenditure from this fund has gone to Britain and Italy so far. Social policy in the EC has been much less of a well-organized policy and much more a mix of various social issues which the EC member countries were willing to transfer to the EC.

The EC has not done much about education. There was an EC programme in 1976 which intended to promote cooperation in higher education in the Community, standardize teaching courses, increase access to education throughout the EC and improve and widen teaching of EC languages spoken in the member countries. The EC required the member countries to create classes for the children of migrant workers in order to give them the opportunity to receive, at least a part of, education about the culture and in the language of their country of origin. Since 1984, the Social Fund was more concerned with the problem of youth unemployment than with anything else. This may have a negative impact on competitiveness in the long run. Nevertheless, the ERASMUS programme, approved in 1987, encourages a fraction, however small, of the EC student population to spend a part of their studies in another Community member country.

Changes in technology have divided labour into two broad groups: those who work in modern and those who are employed in obsolete industries. When labour is fragmented, then business has an excessive power to influence economic policy. The social dimension of the single EC market after 1992 creates opportunity for some, but concern for others. The EC does not intend to make its labour market less flexible and to increase the cost of employment. What it does intend is to help the poorer regions to adapt to the new conditions of a single market and to meet the workers' worries about this change. Those that fear that the Programme 1992 will bring detrimental competition within the EC, ask for safety measures in the form of the European Social Charter.

The European Social Charter (1989) is adopted as a declaration by all EC member states with the exception of Britain. Although without legal force, the Charter presents political obligation. Britain was not in favour of the Charter, because of fears that the Commission would use it as a foundation for various proposals in the social sphere. The Commission is using the Charter in order to shape a number of EC-wide labour laws. For example, Britain thinks that it would be better for employers and employees to negotiate the length of working time, than to have uniform EC-wide rules.

The Commission proposes binding regulations on health and safety, as well as on free movement of labour (recognition of qualifications, social security rights). Those are areas whithout disputes among the member countries. Problems, however, arise with part-time employment. The Commission intends to propose that part-time employees receive the same benefits as full-time workers. Britain is the strongest opponent of such a policy, since excessive regulation may discourage creation of part-time jobs.

The EC intends to do the following four things in the future. First, to use structural funds to fight against structural unemployment and help an even development of the EC. These funds will dispose of ECU 50 billion in the period 1988–92. Second, to harmonize work safety standards. This harmonization will probably go up to the strict rules of FR Germany, rather than down to those which prevail in the Mediterranean member countries. Of course, the latter states may need both time and funds to catch up with the new standards. Third, a European Social Charter would declare the workers' rights to social security, to join trade unions and to have information and dialogue on the employers' major plans. The aim of this declaration is to calm the workers' fear of the single EC market. But critics ask whether these declarations will be it, or whether they will present an introduction to something more costly. Fourth, the introduction of an optional European Company Statute which may make it easier for companies to set up or merge throughout the EC.

A stumbling block is the possibility and form of workers' participation.

Conclusion

The effects of social policy may not be measured directly. Indirectly, social policy has its impact on the length of life expectancy, reduction of illiteracy, increase in training and safety of labour. All this increases the production potential of a country.

The demand for social expenditure is almost insatiable. Expenditure for these services may be increased during periods of prosperity – at least political cost, as was the case in the 1960s. During economic slow-down and budgetary deficits, the mushroomed social services have to be reformed. Unemployment insurance turned out to be more of an income-support instrument than oriented towards labour adjustment. This should be changed in favour of the mobility of labour, particularly younger people, both among occupations and regions. Sometimes it is better to give a pension to sixty-year-old workers than to provide dole money to those in their teens and twenties.

The real danger stems from the fact that without reform of social policy, individual countries and the EC as a whole may encounter problems in the present and future with methods which were designed in and for past times. In an economic union, a coordination and reform of social policy is required. The problem is that the participating countries may not wish to abandon their own rights in this policy and transfer them to the union level. The creation of a single EC market will create enough opportunities and incentives to change such an attitude.

Integration of economic policies in an economic union can be defended by the same arguments which defend an economic policy in a country which has different regions or in a federal state. Once the common policies are accepted, the member states find that it may be easier to keep moving than to stop the process of integration. Common economic policies which both create new and redistribute the existing wealth are necessary in an economic union if it is to survive in the situation with market imperfections.

The experience in integration among the developed market economies is supplemented by the observation of the activity in integration among the former centrally planned economies and LDCs. The following two sections of this chapter will consider the CMEA and ASEAN.

COUNCIL FOR MUTUAL ECONOMIC ASSISTANCE (CMEA)

Introduction

The CMEA (or Comecon) has existed for four decades. Regretfully it does not appear to have lived up to its potential or to the expectations of its members. This situation is due to the following two reasons. First, the USSR is territorially the largest country in the world. As such it has a vast domestic market which permits diversification in production, so that international trade is not the key factor in its economic prosperity. Economic autonomy of the USSR is a serious obstacle to planned integration in the case when some 30 or 40 per cent of international trade among market-economy countries consists of intra-firm trade. Second, this situation in the CMEA was also due to central planning which worked out detailed tasks with respect to production, investments, prices and trade. Foreign trade flows were not due to differences in absolute and comparative costs among countries, but rather were only an extension of the plan. Many of the impediments to trade which are studied in the theory of international economic integration (tariffs, quotas, taxes) did not appear in the CMEA system.

A communiqué announced the establishment of the CMEA in 1949. The Statute of this institution was, however, delivered a decade after the communiqué. The main aim of this institution is a continuous increase in the welfare of the people in all CMEA member countries coupled with gradual equalization of the level of economic development among the member countries. Other aims – which include: development and improvement of economic cooperation, development of socialist economic integration, acceleration of economic and technical progress – seem more like means towards achieving the main aim. The principles upon which the CMEA is founded are the sovereign equality of all member countries, voluntary membership, socialist internationalism, mutual benefit and fraternal assistance.

Basic features

Majority voting within the CMEA is prohibited. This was the real reason why the CMEA did not have real power, as well as the reason why the USSR had not succeeded in completely controlling all CMEA member countries. (The Luxembourg Agreement effactually prohibited majority vote in the EC. But the Single

European Act, a medicine to cure Euro-sclerosis in the medium-term, is re-introducing this way of voting for certain issues in the EC.) The CMEA's institutional set-up was complicated. There were very many CMEA bodies. The CMEA intended to compensate for the lack of real power by means of a formidable institutional structure. Decision-making in this bureaucratic labyrinth was very slow because every country could block any proposals by dissenting.

It was just after the promulgation of the CMEA Statute when 'The Basic Principles of International Socialist Division of Labour' were accepted in 1962. 'The Basic Principles' gave guidelines for future cooperation among the CMEA countries. During the 1950s there were great disequilibria in the economies of the CMEA countries. On the one hand, there were shortages of consumer goods, while on the other, there was a glut of producers' goods. This situation contributed to open dissatisfaction in Hungary in 1956 which was quelled by Soviet intervention. Little attention had been paid to specialization until then. On the basis of the 'Basic Principles', the socialist division of labour was implemented through the coordination of economic plans and specialization in production on the basis of employment of disposable factors in each country. As a relatively less developed country in the CMEA, Romania did not want to accept such a kind of specialization, for, under this pattern, the development of industry in Romania would be impeded.

Romanian opposition to the introduction of supranational planning within the CMEA was supported by Hungary and Czechoslovakia. The latter two countries were implementing reforms which were directed towards a socialist system in which the market played an important role. A relative dilution of the CMEA was prevented by the intervention of the Warsaw Pact in Czechoslovakia in 1968. After that event the USSR had to find a way to close ranks within the CMEA.

'The Comprehensive Programme of Socialist Economic Integration' was offered and accepted in 1971. The 'Comprehensive Programme' was basically a list of proposals which referred to a number of issues in economics and science and which dealt with a long period of time (15–20 years). The pivotal clause within the 'Comprehensive Programme' concerned joint planning and joint investment projects in the priority sectors (raw materials and energy, machine industry, food, consumer-goods industries and transport). If a CMEA country was not interested in decision-making with respect to an issue, then the decision or recommendation would not refer to the country in question. This principle of 'interested party' was implemented in the CMEA structure as protection against the introduction of supranationality.

Competition takes place among firms in market economies. In centrally planned economies, competition exists among different plans which are offered to the central decision-making body. The adjustment of national plans meant at an earlier stage only an exchange of information for bilateral trade negotiations. This was changed so that this procedure began three years before the end of the five-year period which was covered by the plan. This gave the planners time to change and supplement their investment plans. Adjustment of plans among the CMEA countries was done on the basis of mutual prognoses, consultations, planning of the interested countries in certain fields, exchange of experience and planning principles. The intention was to consciously link bilateral and multilateral measures for the development of cooperation in economics, science and technology.

Planning, as a process in which the future of a certain field is consciously shaped, has a theoretical advantage because mistakes and costs which bring blind market forces are deliberately avoided. The politicization of integration, however, reduced the advantages of planning and, with respect to the speed of integration, was much slower than in the market approach (Robson, 1987, p. 219). Endless bilateral negotiations made progress in integration very slow. It might be a sign that countries did not want it enthusiastically (on such terms).

During the negotiation process about common projects, negotiators from the member countries apprised costs and benefits of the project in question, compare projects with alternatives, estimate concessions given to and received from partners and, finally, compare possible projects with national priorities in development. This was a complicated and difficult task (Robson, 1987, p. 218).

There have been around twenty common projects, most of them in energy and raw materials. Common investments were made in the country which is endowed with a substantial amount of mineral resources. This attitude of the CMEA had as its consequence the fact that the largest number of common projects were located in the USSR. The most important projects in the common infrastructure are found in energy. These are the greatest pride in the CMEA, for they represent genuine integration. The *Druzhba* oil pipeline is 5,500 km long and links oil wells in the USSR with consumers in the former German Democratic Republic, Poland, Czechoslovakia and Hungary. The *Soyuz* gas pipeline is 2,750 km long and supplies

European countries with Soviet natural gas. The *Mir* is a huge electric grid which links CMEA countries from Mongolia to eastern Europe. Other important common projects include the production of cellulose and asbestos in the USSR, the production of cobalt and nickel in Cuba and cotton spinning in Poland.

The greatest part of the above-mentioned projects were directed towards the production and transport of primary products from the USSR. This was the way in which the European CMEA member countries compensated the USSR for the supply of resources which could be easily sold on the international market for hard currency. Investments of the European member countries in the USSR were done in the form of exports of goods, labour and know-how. European member countries of the CMEA protested because of the low interest rates which they received, payments in kind and high costs of projects. But the security of supplies from the USSR in the future compensated these causes for worries.

Factor mobility

Mobility of capital within the CMEA framework was of little importance. If the funds moved, then it was due to the interest of the countries to which the funds belonged. From the point of view of normative economics, the funds should move from the countries which have a surplus of capital (in which profit and interest rates are relatively lower) to those countries which have a shortage of capital (in which profit and interest rates are relatively higher) and in which there exists confidence that the invested funds will be recovered. Capital mobility within and without the CMEA, however, had a political dimension in spite of its economic rationality. The CMEA countries, just like countries in the west, exported capital everywhere they wanted to win friends and export political influence.

The International Investment Bank (IIB) was established in 1970 in order to finance the common investments necessitated by the socialist division of labour. The IIB gave medium- and long-term loans which were in most cases of benefit to all CMEA member countries. The capital of the IIB was 1 billion transferable roubles. The IIB was also entitled to take funds from the international capital market. At first Romania did not want to participate in the IIB, for decisions were made in this bank according to majority vote (each country has one vote), but subsequently joined. This decision-making process was in contrast to the operation of all other CMEA bodies. However, there was a lack of interest in the active operation of the IIB. It can be explained by the need for relatively advanced countries of the CMEA to invest in their own economies. In this situation, the relatively advanced countries did not want to help, to a large extent, the development of relatively less advanced CMEA countries. Also, rate of interest on the one hand, and profitability, supply and demand of funds on the other, were not connected.

According to CMEA opinion, labour movements were inherent to capitalism. These flows were of very little significance in the CMEA, although there exist differences among member countries in the relative height of wages, which are due partly to the relative abundance or shortage of labour. Labour flows from the relatively backward countries of the CMEA towards the relatively advanced ones (from Bulgaria to the USSR, from Poland to the former German Democratic Republic) have been observed in the past. In 1989–90 (the fall of the Berlin Wall) there was a massive flow of population out of the CMEA, in particular from the German Democratic Republic to the Federal Republic of Germany before reunification in 1990.

The exchange of scientific and technical information between the CMEA member countries was formally very developed. It was based on the critique of capitalism in which private owners control achievements of science and prevent wide application of new ideas in order to make super-normal profit. There was a problem of the financing of research in the CMEA. Relatively advanced countries did not have much impetus to share the fruits of their achievements with other users because of high costs and the uncertainty of research, which they bore alone. Recipients of the scientific information had neither the interest nor the funds to take part in research when they could get the results of such research free from others. The CMEA countries try to compensate for their relative backwardness in technology by purchasing western equipment and licences.

Prices in trade

The eastern European theorists maintained that capitalism was in crisis and had destabilizing cyclical and speculative movements of prices. On these grounds, the CMEA endeavoured to find their own socialist prices (which embodied equality in economic relations) in contrast to capitalist prices (which personify inequality). In the centrally planned system of economic autarky, a concern with quantities rather than values is dominant.

Fluctuations in prices could endanger the planned nature of the CMEA economies. The economic results in this system are measured in metres, litres and tons, not in money – which is only an accounting unit. Prices in this system respond neither to costs of production nor to the relation of supply and demand. They also do not reflect the relative abundance or shortage of goods and services. They are set arbitrarily and are used for accounting purposes only. Hence, they do not play any role in the allocation of resources. The gap between prices and costs of production is caused by relatively low prices for producer's goods, low rates of interest, as well as taxes which burden consumer's goods. The system of prices in the CMEA member countries gives neither a satisfactory nor a rational denominator for production of goods and services. It is much more suited to a big and closed country than to a small, developed and specialized country which pursues a policy of openness in trade and investment.

Domestic rationality in production can be tested by comparison with prices on the world market. It is not a simple self-comparison, but rather a comparison with the most efficient world producers. Trade and comparison with the most advanced world economies could give a positive impetus to the advance of socialism. The CMEA member countries negotiated about the volume and structure of trade, as well as bargained about prices (terms of trade). Every country's administration decided own prices, so that prices among the states could not be compared. In their internal trade, the CMEA countries intended to clean the world market (capitalist) prices of cyclical and speculative movements and used five-year weighted averages. Since the explosion of world market price for oil, on the basis of a Soviet request, the prices for intra-CMEA trade have, from 1976, been delivered every year (instead of every five years) on the basis of the world market prices from the preceding five years.

This system of prices does not cause problems for standardized goods (raw materials), but problems arose with respect to manufactured goods. The question can be asked: can and should a Bulgarian computer be worth as much as a Japanese? Such a system of just and equivalent socialist prices in trade within the CMEA was very slow to bring the beneficial effects which come from the world market. At the same time, it isolated the CMEA from abrupt and disadvantageous effects which came in the form of sharp increases in prices which distort planning. It could also bring odd situations.

Prices for oil in the CMEA were rising between 1982 and 1986 while they were decreasing on the world market.

The CMEA member countries use current world-market prices in trade with third countries, while in their internal trade they use prices which were reached after bilateral negotiations on the basis of historic world prices, as explained above. These bilateral negotiations were quite tough, for it is formidable to get the world market price for each particular good. Commodity exchanges deal with only a limited number of goods. Also, the bulk of world trade is covered by long-term contracts which do not necessarily have a close relation to current world market prices. Prices play no role in the allocation of resources in the centrally planned system. Therefore, it can hardly be comprehended why the CMEA countries spend so much time fighting over prices or why there was a world market price formula.

The CMEA price system enabled the USSR in the 1955–59 period to charge 15 per cent higher prices during exports to the CMEA partner countries, while on the import side the USSR paid to the same partners 15 per cent lower prices for the same or similar import goods than to the western countries (Mendershausen, 1959, 1960). On these grounds the USSR could take advantage of the CMEA member countries by means of its monopolistic position. Such a result may be questioned on several grounds. Econometric problems arise with respect to the comparison of data, price, quantity and quality of goods. Also, the USSR had to accept higher prices from the western partners in order to attract them for trade. At the same time, the USSR had to offer relatively lower prices in export in order to penetrate the western markets and earn the necessary hard currency to pay for imports.

If the terms of trade were favourable for the USSR until the 1960s, after that period the situation altered. The USSR exports mainly primary goods and energy to its CMEA partners while the partners export industrial goods to the USSR. Relative prices of manufactured goods have risen in relation to prices for primary goods, so that the terms of trade are working against the USSR within the CMEA. This tendency was manifested in 1975 when the Soviets insisted on a change in the pricing system. These potential losses from trade, or subsidies to the CMEA partners, took place when the USSR exported energy and raw materials below the world market price and when it imported manufactured goods at prices higher than those which prevail on the world market for goods of similar quality. The USSR may have consciously directed such subsidies to the CMEA partner countries in order to prevent or stimulate policy changes in these countries. One of the crucial factors which induced Britain and France to decolonize was the need of their colonies to become subsidized. However, it appears that in the past the Soviets compensated for possible losses in trade within the CMEA by their political influence.

Various studies have found the existence of Soviet subsidies to the CMEA partners. Where they disagreed was on the magnitude of these subsidies. The accumulated Soviet subsidies over the period 1973–84, due to divergent price developments on the CMEA and world markets, amounted to 18.8 billion transferable roubles (Dietz, 1986) – which is three times less than in another estimate, even for 1980 (Marrese and Vanous, 1983). Yet another study reports the Soviet aid in all forms to eastern Europe as being around 134 billion dollars between 1971 and 1980 (Bunce, 1985). The major cause of these subsidies was the price (and its change) of energy.

The USSR leaders did not want its population to be aware that the CMEA partners were being subsidized. The socialist cooperation was supposed to be founded on equality, therefore it was unnecessary to compensate partners for their friendship. In addition, Soviet citizens would not be happy to find out that their country subsidized other partner countries which have higher living standards. At the same time, east European political leaders did not want their population to know that national sovereignty was being 'sold' in return for Soviet subsidies to help the running of their economies (Marrese, 1986, p. 311).

Prices were relatively stable in the CMEA countries and direct inflation did not exist. Nevertheless, producer prices differed from consumer prices by bonuses, subsidies and taxes. These additives might have created quite a significant gap between the two kinds of prices, although the planners attempted to keep consumer prices fixed. Inflation of a kind, however, existed. It appeared in the form of shortages, cutting of the supplies of electricity, restrictions to foreign travel, long queues in front of shops, low quality of goods and the like. The solution of the price problem in the CMEA countries could be found in domestic reforms which would introduce and use the advantages of the market system in the sense of initiatives end efficiency of production according to market needs. By doing this, one could avoid the absurd situation in which the Soviet sewing machine producers received bonuses for fulfilling their plan, although there were piles of sewing machines in the shops which nobody wanted to buy.

Trade

Trade and specialization (division of labour) represent the core of international economic integration. Because of the non-market formation of prices within the CMEA, the trade data which were released by the CMEA were most usually useless for international comparisons, as well as calculations of trade creation and trade diversion. Of course, this did not hold for data which referred to litres, metres and tons.

The CMEA could not be taken as a customs union. Indirectly, customs protection was replaced by a complicated system of direct control of foreign trade quotas which were set by the plan. State ownership of the means of production, state foreign-trade monopoly and a high degree of self-sufficiency removed the need for the existence of customs duties.

Customs duties might have some justification in the case when they protect an infant industry for a limited period of time, reduce consumption of imported goods in order to decrease and/or redirect home consumption and when the proceeds are needed for the budget in the short term. Since the state could get funds from enterprises without obstacles and directly protect/promote firms and industries, there was no need for customs duties in the centrally planned system. Since the 1970s the CMEA countries started introducing tariffs. The main reason for this move was the creation of a base for negotiation and concessions in trade from the west.

Intra-CMEA trade has been characterized by bilateralism, as the most protectionist economic system, during the whole life of this organization. Bilateralism is a kind of exchange control. It is usually introduced when countries face severe payment problems for which the more subtle kinds of intervention are not adequate to achieve the desired policy objectives (van Brabant, 1980, p. 128). If the bilaterally negotiated price for a good was too high for a country, then this country tried to produce the good at home. If this was an expensive good, then the country purchased it in the western countries. Either action is integration averse. The aim of bilateral balancing was economic independence. In the case of deficit, the currencies of the CMEA countries were not accepted internationally; they had little reserves while the opportunities to arrange *ex post* credits were limited. These countries did not want to become too dependent on unplanned capital import which might have jeopardized their major policy objective – which was independence (van Brabant, 1980, p. 114). Therefore, the level of trade of the

CMEA countries was lower than was the case for market economies at a comparable level of development.

Bilateral balancing in trade among the CMEA member countries was a usual thing. Since the mid-1970s and the energy crisis, this has not been the case in trade between the USSR and all other CMEA member countries. The USSR has become a creditor of these countries. These disequilibria in trade enabled the USSR to favour (large surplus) some countries or 'punish' (small surplus) others.

A specific CMEA trade took place with hard and soft goods. Hard goods in the CMEA were either deficient goods (food) or those that could be sold easily for hard currency (raw materials). These goods became an accepted means of payment because of their scarcity. Countries which are abundant in raw materials (the USSR and to an extent Poland and Romania) were under pressure from the other CMEA countries. Countries which have 'soft' (manufactured) goods tried to swap them for as many 'hard' goods as possible. Sellers of 'hard' goods requested in return better quality 'soft' goods. As a rule, however, hard goods were traded for hard goods and soft goods were traded for soft goods. Note that money did not fit into this barter. Holders of money were not even sure that their national money was fully convertible into the home goods they wanted.

Reforms

A permanent increase in welfare (consumption by kind and volume) of the citizens of the CMEA member countries was the rationale for the existence of the CMEA. With an increase in economic development, consumers (public and private) request improvements in the quality and an increase in choice of goods and services. This requires an improvement in the operation of the economy. The rate of growth has continuously fallen in the CMEA countries since the 1960s. One reason is found in a relatively low starting base of the CMEA countries in the post-war period, with the exception of Czechoslovakia and the former German Democratic Republic. The other reason is the exhaustion of the effects of extensive economic development. This development model relies on increases in employment, investment and the plentiful use of raw materials. Such a model had its full justification in the CMEA at the time, but its achievements were limited to one-time-positive effects. Such a development model offers little opportunities for development in the long term.

An increase in the rate of growth, prevention of its fall or, at least, maintaining this rate at the current level, together with the introduction of intensive economic development (based on increases in productivity and efficiency in production – i.e. better use of inputs per unit of output), were the reasons for reforms of the centrally planned system in the CMEA countries. In order to turn unfavourable domestic economic flows, the CMEA countries looked westwards for loans and modern technology. In the situation of forced full employment, additional loans increase the quantity of money, so that the existing economic disproportions become more expressed.

The central plan has neither been able nor will be able to satisfactorily harmonize the infrastructure, production and trade of each good out of the millions that circulate within every economy. Nor has it been able to take account of changing consumer preferences, world market prices, new mineral discoveries and weather conditions. The consequences of central planning systems include shortages of goods, services and spare parts, poor quality, delays in delivery, separation of producers from consumers and lack of interest in their interrelationship, lack of direct competition which stimulates innovation, as well as protection from impacts (both positive and negative) from the world market. These shortcomings could be removed to a large extent by a kind of self-regulating market system. Of course, the immediate and, possibly, short-term reaction would be a change in prices, inflation, economic cycles and unemployment.

The interlace of trade ties between the integrated partners is a measure of the degree of integration. Bilateralism in trade and inconvertibility of currencies in the CMEA expresses a disconnection among the CMEA partners, which within four decades have developed neither competition nor large scale cooperation. The CMEA has not lived up to its potential in a great many areas. It lags behind the west in modern technology (apart from military, air and space). Therefore, the CMEA lagged behind the place in the world which it wanted and could have reached. Hence, the controversial thesis by Sobell (1984) that the CMEA was a highly integrated scheme cannot be accepted.

Production for the foreign market is harder than for the domestic market. A firm's production in the CMEA was not subordinated to consumer demand, but rather to the plan. Firms produced not in order to make profit, but rather to fulfil the plan targets. Their existence was not imperilled by import competition. When the plan was fulfilled, the firm received bonuses. These favours were much more easily obtained through negotiations with the central planning administration about the production targets, than through efforts in exports.

A more flexible economic system will enable the CMEA countries to reap significant gains from integration. The condition is, of course, the introduction of a kind of market-type system of economic cooperation. Ideological aversion to such reforms was significant for a number of decades. The costs of preserving the status quo become increasingly high in the light of forgone gains (rate of growth, competition, introduction of new technologies, alternative use of subsidies to inefficient firms and to costly trade, etc). In any case, reforms towards a market-type system are gaining momentum.

Attitude towards reforms differed among the countries. It is not only due to the shape of the economy, but also to the country's objectives and the capability of their leaders to carry them out. Hungary tried to soften the rigid central planning system in 1968. However, the hangover from the old way of conducting the economy was such that, even after the reform, the state controlled over 80 per cent of the GNP. The dominant role of the state sector and control of the economy prevented the operation of market forces and may be the major factor for the economic crisis. The Hungarian model of reform was interesting to study, but not to follow.

Poland tried to reform the economy during the 1970s by a heavy investment programme, taking loans from the west. The technical capacity of the economy was changed, but the economic system remained the same. This led to investments in a number of projects that turned out to be unprofitable. Protectionism and a lack of competition, owing to the system of central planning, was to blame for wrong choices. A profound economic crisis in Poland in the late 1980s was due to an increase in the rates of interest and the inability of projects to service foreign hard-currency debt. The result was hyperinflation. The cancellation of foreign debt in Poland and elsewhere in eastern Europe might give a big push towards reform. But cancellation prior to profound changes in the economic system would do no good at all. Bureaucrats would just wait for such a move in order to carry on with the mismanagement of the economy without any control from the market (stock exchange). Nevertheless, profound reforms towards a kind of a market-type economy are taking place in Poland.

The leaders of the CMEA countries considered ways for improving the operation of the CMEA on a number of occasions during the 1980s. They identified priority sectors for cooperation and development. These sectors included food, energy, transport, consumer goods and science and technology. The problem was that these sectors also had priority in the previous two decades. The centrally planned economic system was unable to solve these issues and presented a hindrance to the economic development and prosperity of the CMEA member countries.

Perestroika in the USSR is a step in the right direction. However, the citizens start to be nervous about its achievements when what they see are longer queues, soaring inflation, decline in real income and rationing of meat and dairy products. They feel that they are worse off than before and disregard doubtful statistics which sometimes offer different conclusions. *Perestroika* in the USSR has produced changes, but hitherto without visible positive results for the population. The worst thing which may happen is that the opponents of reform use these events to try and stop the introduction of further phases of the reform. In this case, any reform in the USSR may be prevented for a long period of time.

Market-type reforms, which started in eastern Europe and the USSR in the late 1980s, ought to discover sources of competitive advantage which are found in developed market economies. They should start with innovative small private firms. In many developed countries, the average size of firm is becoming smaller, not bigger. Small and medium-sized enterprises create the necessary web among different parts of the economy. The lack of small firms comes from the basic weakness of the east European and Soviet economic system. In the situation where shortages prevail and without the confidence that the planned and agreed quantities of inputs will be delivered in time, the only way to obtain, in a reliable way, the necessary inputs is to make them oneself (and to stockpile). Firms did not have the choice between make and buy. Such a situation increases prices per unit of output, reduces competitiveness and weakens links among firms.

Market systems cannot operate satisfactorily without a greater degree of freedom to set prices which ought to reflect demand and supply (relative scarcities). The politicians are afraid of even higher inflation which will be the consequence of the evening of the gap in prices among goods and services, as well as among factors. Such changes are needed not only within each state, but also in their trade relations. Instead of such changes in the past, the politicians have chosen a reform of the system which sets prices in a central way. The proclaimed self-financing of companies along the market-type reforms will not mean much as long as the government sets prices which are unrelated to supply and demand. The need to change behaviour of both firms in production and buyers in consumption will be reduced.

The enterprises in eastern Europe and the USSR had very soft budget constraints. They were taking loans without any fear of going broke. If the projects were profitable, enterprises and management would receive bonuses and medals. If they were unprofitable, the government was always there to bail them out. Proprietors of firms in a market economy, the shareholders, are not only interested in the income-generating capacity of their assets, but also, and equally important, in the market value of their assets. A mistaken judgement about investment would be instantaneously reflected in the market value of the shares. Such a market-control gauge of business in eastern Europe and the USSR ought to be developed and made reliable. Since workers in the centrally planned economies did not have shares in their firms, they were afraid of investment in new technology that would make them redundant. Hence, driven by their short-term, income-maximizing aims, they requested from the management and the state increases in wages, rather than investment in the new technology that would respond to a change in the demand. Even if they had shares, there is no reliable stock market to trade them. Therefore, private holding companies that would manage many firms may be an attractive start for market control of the efficient operation of enterprises.

Conclusion

Various piecemeal reforms within the framework of the central planning system in eastern Europe and the USSR had very limited success. Central planning is quite tough and it successfully resists profound reforms. It became obvious at the end of 1989 that what is needed is change of the whole economic system and a replacement of planning with a kind of a market-type economic system. A market system promises attractive rewards, but its immediate cost is a lack of job security. With reforms, the CMEA member countries may alter unfavourable economic trends; without them, the economies would be led to chaos.

The CMEA decided in 1990 to abolish coordination of national plans and multilateral cooperation. These were the most important functions of the whole organization. Since 1991 all CMEA trade is conducted at world prices in convertible currencies. Not much, then, is left of the CMEA. This organization is quite likely to evolve into an advisory body like the OECD. Many of its member states expressed interest in joining the EC, although they are aware that preparations for entry may take them even a couple of decades. In the meantime, the developed market economies may help eastern Europe and the USSR in their reforms. The way to do this is to liberalize trade, as well as to make eastern Europe and the USSR compete on the western market with the goods and services of many advanced developing countries.

There will still be scope for significant economic transactions among the eastern European countries and the USSR for a while, with or without the CMEA. This is due to technology linkages, as well as to reforms that lead to a market-type economy. Reforms will ask for a large adjustment in prices, including a significant devaluation in national currencies. In this situation, the level of relative prices between eastern European countries, including the USSR, and western countries will be significantly more obvious than the relative price levels within the east. Imports from the west would be much dearer for eastern countries than imports from other east European countries and the USSR.

ASSOCIATION OF SOUTHEAST ASIAN NATIONS

There exist a large number of schemes which integrate LDCs throughout the world. The achievements of these arrangements are, unfortunately, at the best modest. In some cases, like the creation of the East African Community (1967–77) formed by Kenya, Tanzania and Uganda, economic integration was a step towards disintegration of these countries! During the colonial era, these countries were closely integrated. They had a common currency, common fiscal authorities, common communication infrastructure and the like. Once these countries achieved independence, trade flows among them started to face barriers and the common currency was abandoned. Economic integration was a means in the new situation to re-integrate these countries. Differences in the perceptions and dissatisfaction with the distribution of costs and benefits of integration were major factors which contributed to the demise of this scheme.

Luckily, this experience has not discouraged other LDCs to

integrate. On the contrary, schemes were mushrooming on all continents. One of the major reasons for a limited degree of their success is that these countries try to do many things all at one time. If one keeps in mind that these ambitions are subject to severe financial limitations, then the lack of success in comparison to the initial expectations does not come as a great surprise.

One of the most promising schemes which integrates LDCs is the Association of Southeast Asian Nations (ASEAN). The experience of this organization encourages LDCs. It is becoming a kind of example scheme for countries at the initial stages of industrialization. Europe should not remain the only area of a relatively profound and successful integration.

Indonesia, Malaysia, the Philippines, Singapore and Thailand established the ASEAN in 1967. After obtaining independence, the oil-rich state of Brunei joined the organization in 1984. The main property of the six countries which make up the ASEAN is a stark diversity of their levels of development measured by income per capita, population, area, religion, language and culture. Of course, this diversity may increase the creative potentials, but it may also enhance disputes. The Bangkok Declaration, as the founding document of the ASEAN, was short. It asked the member countries to cooperate in the issues of the regional interest without the supranational institutional set-up. This simple institutional framework of the ASEAN stands in sharp contrast with other LDCs' integration schemes, which have many ambitious objectives and a cumbersome bureaucratic apparatus (Wong, 1988, p. 315).

The ASEAN countries were adjusting slowly to the new situation. The humble start of this scheme – that is, without exaggerated plans for internal cooperation – was working in favour of integration. During the first years of its life, the ASEAN existed only symbolically. In fact, one of the basic reasons for its creation was political: a reduction of tensions between Indonesia and Malaysia in the 1960s. The increase in regional activity came after the unification of Vietnam in 1975. The member countries wanted to cooperate in the control of export of revolution.

The ASEAN Secretariat for the coordination of activities was established in Jakarta nine years after the creation of the ASEAN. The main decision-making body is the Ministerial Meeting. Apart from these two bodies, a few other committees on agriculture, industry, finance, transport, trade, science and technology are added to this simple institutional framework.

The ASEAN has two elementary rules. First, unanimity is the

rule for decision-making. This may also represent a basic shortcoming of this organization. Decisions are reached after an endless process of consultations and negotiations. The outcome is that only a few common projects are implemented. Also, the member countries have different economic policies. As a large country in the region, Indonesia favours protectionism, while many other countries stand for free trade. Second, the ASEAN countries treat foreign direct investment in a liberal way. This distinguishes ASEAN from most other integration schemes among the LDCs. The economic strategy of most countries is open to the world, rather than introverted. Foreign direct investment may stimulate such a liberal economic strategy. These basic characteristics of the ASEAN, together with a simple institutional set-up, are thought to be the key to the survival of the scheme.

The structure of trade of this grouping is similar to trade of other LDCs. Primary products comprise the bulk of exports. The developed market economies embraced 60 per cent of the ASEAN trade while intra-ASEAN trade took 17 per cent of the whole throughout the 1980s. This is in stark contrast to other integration schemes of the LDCs where the intra-group trade seldom embraces more than 10 per cent of the total trade. The ASEAN does not have either the stated aim in the creation of a customs union or a free trade area, or a specific timetable for the liberalization of trade among the member countries. Nevertheless, tariffs were sharply reduced for internal trade for all traded goods, save for the sensitive ones, in 1984. Of course, to qualify for this preferential treatment, the local value added should be at least 50 per cent.

Regional cooperation took place in the form of common industrial projects. The most important are the projects for urea production (Malaysia and Indonesia). Other industrial projects were also attempted, for example, the production of diesel engines, soda-ash and superphosphates, but without success because of different national interests. Industrial policy did not feature very highly in ASEAN during the 1980s. The result was that they were competing on foreign markets with similar goods without any intra-ASEAN coordination.

In spite of the limited achievements in cooperation among the ASEAN member countries, the experience of this grouping is different in relation to other integration schemes of the LDCs. First, the ASEAN countries always try to find new ways for cooperation in spite of the limited achievements which have been achieved hitherto. Second, these countries have a united perception of numerous international economic problems which affect the ASEAN – such as the multifibre agreements. Third, a relatively slow progress is possibly the only real way for integration of a group of countries with heterogeneous characteristics. International economic crises have slowed down the progress in integration among the ASEAN countries which, unfortunately, tried to find introverted solutions to this problem in the 1980s. Nevertheless, these solutions cannot last in modern times unless the countries involved accept a continuous reduction in their standard of living relative to others. Faced with a threat of possible loss of competitiveness on the international market, the ASEAN countries may again increase the momentum of their integration.

5 Measurement of the effects of international economic integration

INTRODUCTION

It is not a strange thing in economics to find out that the development of the theory on a particular topic and the development of empirical research have pursued rather different courses. It is difficult to imagine a better example of this divergence than the study of the effects of international economic integration (Mayes, 1988, p. 42). Various studies have attempted to measure the effects of international economic integration. Some of them intended to show the advance in international economic integration as the interlace of economic ties among countries. Others wanted to measure the increase in welfare. Yet another group of studies attempted to measure the distribution of costs and benefits of international economic integration. The theory of international economic integration encountered in this book is so complex that it may not be represented mathematically with great precision.

QUANTITATIVE MODELS

Econometric models which attempt to measure the effects of international economic integration can be divided into *ex ante* and *ex post*. The former models are often founded in a simple extrapolation of trends. These models cannot be based on reliable data, but rather on their guesses. The problem represents the fact that one has no reliable data on future developments. It is assumed that the future flow of foreign trade is a function of income, production, relative prices, change in the level of trade barriers, substitutability among import sources, as well as between imports and domestic production.

The *ex post* models attempt to measure a hypothetical situation (counterfactual world or anti-monde) which may represent what could have happened to trade in the case without integration. The difference between the actual and expected imports of each of the participating countries represents trade creation, while the same difference in imports from outside countries shows trade diversion. These differences may be attributed to autonomous changes in prices, changes in income and competition, reductions in barriers to trade, as well as to mistakes.

The models may single out a reduction or removal in barriers to trade as the most important reason for the changed pattern of trade. This may not be the most reliable way for the assessment of effects of integration. Trade may have been diverted from third countries because of foreign direct investment which has substituted imports, and not only because of changes in tariff structure. Instead of comparing the actual behaviour with what would have happened without integration and attributing all the difference to integration, one could better compare what a model predicts with integration against what it predicts without integration (Mayes, 1988, p. 45). By doing this, the possible biases may be reduced. However, one will neither be fully certain about what would have happened without integration, nor about the influence of integration on the economic policies of the member countries.

Most of the quantitative studies measure trade creation and trade diversion in the context of the EC. An early and influential study found that trade among the member countries of the EC was 50 per cent higher in 1969 than would be the case without integration (Williamson and Bottrill, 1973, p. 139). Another study found that there was a 25 per cent increase in both exports and imports in EFTA in the 1959–65 period (EFTA Secretariat, 1969, p. 10).

There exists a fair degree of agreement among various studies that trade creation outweighs trade diversion. The disagreement exists with respect to the magnitude of this difference. The net effect of the trade-flow effect is usually positive (trade creating), but it is relatively small. This is obvious from a profound survey by El-Agraa (1989). In spite of their relative magnitude (smallness) the perceived static gains always give support to some economists' and some politicians' arguments in favour of integration.

The reason for the relative smallness is that some countries which take part in international economic integration may trade a relatively small part of their goods. Alternative explanations should also be found. Mere trade creation/diversion effects do not properly represent changes in welfare. The total effect of international

Table 5.1   Unilateral and multilateral free trade simulations for Canada

Variable	Unilateral free trade change (%)	Multilateral free trade change (%)
1 Wage	9.98	25.21
2 Real GNP	3.49	7.02
3 Welfare gain	4.13	8.59
4 Length of production runs	41.40	66.84
5 Average fixed costs	− 18.93	29.94
6 Labour productivity	19.57	32.62
7 Total factor productivity	8.58	9.50
8 Trade volume	53.14	88.61

Source: Harris (1985b).

economic integration is a blend of various effects of integration in the long run. Countries may not embark upon international economic integration because of clear balances in trade with partners, but rather to reap the dynamic benefits of integration. Hence, the net trade creation/diversion effect is just a part of the explanation of the question why countries integrate.

While traditional general-equilibrium models report small welfare gains from integration – i.e. less than 1 per cent of GNP in the EC (Lipsey, 1960, p. 511) – this is not the case with modern analysis, which considers imperfect competition and economies of scale. In the generation of recent econometric studies which attempt to measure the effects of international economic integration, the study by Harris (1984) has a prominent place. It assesses the impact of the unilateral and multilateral reduction in tariffs on the change of the GNP in Canada. The model considers twenty-nine Canadian industries. Increasing returns to scale exist in twenty industries, while constant returns to scale prevail in the rest. Canada, as a small country in economic terms, is a price taker for the import goods, but it may influence to an extent the price of home export goods. In every industry there are two goods (one is imported and the other is exported). Labour is mobile within the country while this freedom is not allowed for internationally.

Table 5.1 is an outline from a huge and complex study. This general-equilibrium model explicitly considers increasing returns to scale, imperfect competition and capital mobility. It concludes that the unilateral lifting of tariffs and non-tariff barriers in Canada would once-and-for-all (i.e., Canada's long-term growth rate would not be affected) increase this country's GNP by 3.5 per cent and welfare by 4.1 per cent. Multilateral elimination of tariffs and non-tariff barriers would once-and-for-all increase Canadian GNP by 7 per cent and welfare by 8.6 per cent. These beneficial effects would be most obvious in the increase in wages in Canada and the reallocation of resources towards sectors where comparative advantages exist. This would encourage economies of scale, and the existing resources would be used in a better way than in the previous situation. Given resources would produce a larger quantity of output. This would mean reduced prices per unit of output and, consequently, increased living standard on average.

This model was subject to serious criticism, just as any other model is. Harris used data about trade barriers which impeded trade in 1976. The Tokyo round of tariff reductions under the auspices of the GATT was finalized in 1979. Since then, tariffs were reduced on average by one-third until 1987. Therefore, Harris's estimation of gains for Canada which accrue from unilateral or multilateral elimination of trade barriers must be modified. (The higher the initial tariffs the higher the welfare gains from their elimination.) The magnitude of some of the parameters is known only in a semi-perfect way. Consequently, only the best estimates can be used. All criticisms may improve similar models in the future.

A recent study, chaired by Cecchini (1988), analysed the effects of completing the EC internal market by the end of 1992. A part of it was published as the 'Cost of non-Europe' (Emerson *et al.*, 1988). This project estimated the impact of the removal of all trade barriers on internal trade, freedom to provide services, economies of scale, effect of competition on corporate behaviour, public procurement and the like. The estimated economic gains were between ECU 175 and 255 billion in 1988 prices. This would increase the EC GNP by 5 per cent of the 1988 level. If economic policies are coordinated, then the increase in the GNP may be between 2.5 and 6.5 per cent in the medium-term. This extra non-inflationary economic growth would create up to 5 million new jobs in the medium-term. Such gains, which may occur under certain conditions, even though they have a once-and-for-all character, are hard to resist.

These results may well be underestimated in that they exclude certain types of continuing and likely dynamic benefits. These indirect effects are difficult to measure. They include: technological

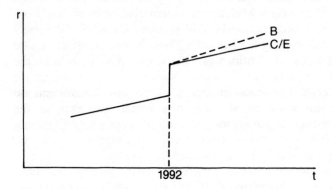

Figure 5.1 Growth effects of the 1992 Programme

innovation, which depends on the existence of competition; the impact of the growth of GNP on long-term savings, investment and rate of growth; dynamic effects of economies of scale and know-how which will be most obvious in the fast-growing, high-technology industries, where the present market segmentation seriously limits the scope for these benefits and jeopardizes performance in the future; and the big EC market will induce the EC companies to change their business strategies in that they will foster the emergence of truly EC companies which are better suited to secure a stronger place in competition both within and without the EC.

The greatest benefits of the 1992 Programme in the EC are not expected from one-step effects, as studies by Cecchini/Emerson suggested, but would come from continuous dynamic effects. Baldwin (1989) argues that Cecchini/Emerson (C/E in Figure 5.1) significantly underestimated the dynamic effects of the 1992 Programme, for they concentrated on the impact of the single market on the level of output. The once-and-for-all efficiency gains from the 1992 Programme will be multiplied into a substantial 'medium-term growth bonus' (B in Figure 5.1). A rise in savings and investment, due to the initial 2.5 to 6.5 per cent growth in the GNP, will increase the EC capital stock. The medium-term growth bonus might evolve into the long-term one, adding permanently between 0.2 and 0.9 per cent to the EC long-term growth rate. The static part of it will be spread over five to seven years, following the completion of the internal market. It may take about 10 years for the realization of half the medium-term growth bonus. Baldwin concludes that the most important impact of the 1992 Programme may be on growth of the EC, not on its effect on resource allocation. If this analysis is correct, then the gains of the 1992 Programme may be between 13 and 33 per cent of the EC GNP. This analysis, along the Romer (1986) lines, may be quite discouraging for all the critics who argued that the Cecchini/Emerson results were high.

The debate about the possible effects of the 1992 Programme on the EC is just beginning. If Baldwin's results are correct, the enthusiasts about integration may be very pleased.

CONCLUSION

The conclusion to this chapter presents the limits of econometric modelling. Econometrics has advanced much since the 1960s, but it is still unable to solve some important issues. It is recognized that it is better to measure somehow than not at all. The problems which appear concern the choice of assumptions: the base year and length of time series before and after integration. The structure of foreign trade changes throughout time, new products appear, old ones disappear while tastes change. The quality of goods changes over time and technology becomes more productive. Capacity utilization within broadly defined sectors escapes scrutiny. All these issues jeopardize generalizations about the long-term structure and pattern of trade. Business cycles make comparisons of prices among countries questionable. A part of trade flows (traditional trade or unique commodities) is independent of international economic integration. Hence, inter-temporal estimates are very complex indeed.

While trade creation indicates new imports of goods from partner countries and a reduction of the same quantity of domestic production, trade diversion indicates reduction of imports from (and production in) off-shore countries, as well as new imports and production in partner countries. Therefore, a comprehensive measurement of the effects of integration requires not only analysis of trade data but also analysis of production data (El-Agraa, 1989, p. 346).

Changes other than international economic integration need to be considered too. They refer to the reduction of tariffs and other barriers to trade under the auspices of the GATT. These changes are not the consequence of the creation of either the EC or the EFTA. Other changes include the introduction of convertibility in the late 1950s and the increase in United States' investment in western Europe. Hence, formal integration is not the only reason for an increase in economic and investment activity.

Assumptions about unchangeable market shares for the purpose of the extrapolation of trends means that technology, competition, costs, tastes, elasticities and economic policy are fixed. Availability and comparability of data may also be criticized, but to a diminishing extent. Actual production and trade does not mean that all potentials are fully utilized. Unfortunately, there does not exist a model which accurately measures unused potential. It is necessary to consider both trade and production data if one wants to obtain a full picture of the effects of international economic integration.

Customs duties are made public, but their implementation is often formidable. Only a part of the reduction in tariffs is passed on to the consumers in the form of lower prices. Prices of imported goods are often formed (by means of various taxes) with reference to competing home goods, if they exist. Technology and inputs for standardized products are available to all producers, but the final goods are often produced at different prices. The answer to this question may be found in X-inefficiency.

Adjustment to integration is not instantaneous. Integration- and growth-induced forces are interlaced. Integration-induced effects may dominate the more sudden the integration. Growth-induced effects may dominate over a longer time. The more gradual the integration and the longer the period of observation, the more the effects will be mixed up (Lipsey, 1976, p. 38). A part of the answer to this problem may be found in models inspired by the work of Romer (1986).

The analysis has revealed that there are serious drawbacks in econometric modelling and the interpretation of results of international economic integration. All models should be viewed with a certain degree of suspicion, for they rely on a number of restrictive assumptions and complexity of effects. One wonders if slightly different assumptions might not have produced a completely different outcome. The final result of all estimations is always a blend of various effects. The whole analysis, therefore, suffers from the identification problem – that is, how to distinguish the effects of integration from the various other effects. This has been hitherto unfortunate for econometrics, not for the effects of international economic integration.

There is, sometimes, a conflicting evidence with respect to the effects of integration – in particular, the EC 1992 Programme. For example, Neven (1990) concluded that the 1992 Programme was relatively unimportant to the northern EC member countries since they have used most of the potential for large-scale production. Alternatively, Smith and Venables (1988) and Cecchini/Emerson believed that the potentials for economies of scale were significant throughout the EC. This puzzle reveals that there does not yet exist a full understanding of the determinants of trade and production patterns in the EC and that the analyses of integration will remain speculative (Norman, 1990, p. 52).

A meaningful comparison of the gap in price for a good in different parts of an integrated area ought to reflect not only the transport costs, as was traditionally the case, but also the consumption pattern in different countries. The problems of measurement become immense because income, tastes, traditions and climate may be very different even within the confines of a single country. The greater the diversity of the integrated countries the harder the test.

A pragmatic way to encounter the effects of international economic integration may be to follow the structure of home consumption (proportions of home made goods, commodities imported from partner countries and goods from third countries). Another way may be to compare the relative prices of equal goods and services on the markets of the integrated countries. In a well integrated area with no differences in tastes, income and climate, these prices may differ only for costs of transport.

The magnitude of the effects of international economic integration will be debated for a long time. It is widely accepted that integration increases the potential for economic gains. The distribution of costs and benefits of these effects matters most. When one participant gains from integration it does not mean that others lose. It is essential that every participant gains more in the long-term than it is able to gain in the situation where it acts alone.

6 Conclusion

Free trade and unimpeded movement of factors is the first-best policy in a world which does not have any distortions. This is only a hypothetical situation. A real situation is full of market imperfections that may be corrected and/or exploited by the employment of economic policy (intervention).

The rationale for international economic integration may be found in the case where there exist market imperfections. When one distortion (a universal tariff of a country) is replaced by another (the common external tariff of a customs union) the net effect may be obscure. International economic integration (introvert economic strategy to a degree) is the analysis of a second-best situation. It is, therefore, not surprising that general principles may not be found. What matters, however, is not solely the prediction of theory, but rather what happens in real life.

When there exist economies of scale, changes in technology, sunk costs, imperfect competition and/or foreign direct investment, it is selected intervention in the form of economic policy (investment/production subsidies, education, protection for a limited period of time) which may successfully correct those market imperfections. The new theory of strategic trade and industrial policy which takes into account market imperfections, supplements the smooth and straightforward conclusions of the neo-classical model. Under certain assumptions, free trade may be an attractive economic policy. Under more realistic conditions, however, smart intervention (of which integration is a part) may fare even better.

In the situation where market imperfections prevail, free trade may exacerbate, rather than iron out various disequilibria. This shortcoming may be successfully overcome by smart cooperation, including international economic integration, among countries.

Integration and cooperation on the global scale as a possible consequence of the play of free market forces, may benefit all partners provided that certain policy requirements are satisfied. Although all countries are not under the same kind of pressure to adjust, a joint action of countries may offer attractive economies of scale in economic policy relative to the situation when each country acts alone.

Countries throughout the world show an interest in economic integration. Their attempts at integration have been achieved with very different degrees of success in relation to their aims and expectations. One of the possible explanations for the slowness in economic integration may be traced to the non-acceptance of supranationality. Small countries, in particular, have to learn that it is much less a matter of sovereignty and integration and much more a choice between one or another form of interdependence.

International economic integration is not an enterprise without risks of adjustment. On these grounds some countries may accept protectionism as an attractive alternative. In the short run, national protectionism may offer some advantages over an outward-oriented economic policy that includes integration. This choice is defensive in its nature. International markets and technology continuously increase their speed of change. To petrify the status quo by endless protection is the surest way to economic disaster, since every country will face the need to adjust in the long run. If economic policy provides the environment for continuous adjustment, then the costs of relatively smooth shifts may be smaller than the big-bang adjustment which may occur after a long period of protection.

International economic integration limits, to an extent, the possibility for unnecessary public intervention in the economy because of the fact that it extends the scope of economic policy on at least two countries. The result is increased competition which creates more efficient industry and service sectors. However, integration is not a cure for all economic illnesses. It creates opportunities for increased competition on an enlarged market, but it is up to smart economic policies in education, R&D and investment to take advantage of the newly created environment.

A free competition within the group is unlikely to destroy all business in some of the participating countries. Two instruments would prevent such a disastrous scenario. First, the adjustment period to new circumstances would enable firms to reallocate resources. A country with serious adjustment problems may ask for free access to the markets of partner countries some time before it offers the same concession to the partners. Exchange rate is the second safety valve which would prevent such a disastrous scenario. The experience of the EC and EFTA shows that economic adjustment to the new circumstances took place smoothly, and that trade, production, growth and employment will have an increasing trend in the long term. If structural problems did occur, then they were due to increases in prices for oil and competition from the newly industrializing countries, not to integration.

One of the difficulties of international economic integration is that its gains accrue in the long run to everybody, but in relatively small instalments. The costs of integration may be more easily identified. They affect certain segments of business and population, but their effects may be short-term in nature. The coordination of economic policies which may be brought about by integration has the potential to exercise its full beneficial effect only in the long run. These joint policies should not be abandoned even if they do not bring the desired results in the short run. Enhanced competition and economies of scale exert a downward pressure on costs and prices. This enables an increase in non-inflationary growth. However, it is unclear how this will happen in practice. It may occur through increased output with unchanged inflation or less price inflation or, and most likely, a mixture of both. A real problem is that the gains of international economic integration may not be easily comprehended by non-economists.

Off-shore countries may feel the unfavourable effects of integration. Trade diversion is an example. However, if integrated countries grow at a faster rate than in the case without integration, their income may increase and, by this acceleration, the integrated countries may expand their economic relations with outside countries. Such a result may be uncertain. Third countries will have to count on some degree of discrimination (or reduced preference) from the integrated countries. Technology will force on small countries some kind of economic integration which may reduce costs of structural adjustment, which will inevitably be significantly higher in the future than is currently the case.

A relatively big and integrated market is not a guarantee in itself that international economic integration will bring both satisfactory and desired economic outcomes. Evidence for this may be found in the case of China and India. A contrasting evidence may be traced in the impressive experience in individualistic development of South Korea, Taiwan, Singapore and Hong Kong. The success of these countries may be exceptional, but it does not undermine the case for regional integration as a strategy for a large number of LDCs (Robson, 1987, p. 197). Relatively larger markets may have potentials for a greater capacity for coping with various distortions than smaller markets, because they may more easily offset the impact of both favourable and unfavourable effects.

The theory of international economic integration is basically Euro-centric, for this is the area where integration may have had its most significant impact. Its application to the case of LDCs may be enhanced by cost–benefit analysis. The classical theory of customs unions may find that a customs union among LDCs may be trade-diverting in most cases. This is due to the fact that for many goods and services LDCs are higher-cost suppliers than industrialized and newly industrialized countries. The existing structure of production and trade does not provide a rationale for economic integration among many developing countries. It is the potential for change in this structure which provides the rationale for integration among LDCs. Integration and adequate intervention (economic policy) may offer attractive gains.

The theory of international economic integration as a part of international economics may also be a part of the theory of economic development. LDCs may enhance their development in one of the combinations of reallocation of home resources, mineral discovery, integration, foreign loans and external aid.

The developing countries correctly find dynamic effects as their grounds for integration. An exclusive removal of tariffs and quotas may not bring a significant increase in trade among LDCs because they may not offer product diversity. Their cooperation in other fields – such as a common policy of industrial development, regional and social policy – may be indispensable for the survival and success of the scheme because of polarization effects that bring market imperfections.

The main conclusion is that international economic integration is a desirable economic strategy for small and medium-sized countries in a world with continuous technological and market change. Integration can increase and secure markets for a variety of a country's goods in the future and, hence, mitigate the inevitable costs of adjustment to change. The gains of integration include improvement in the efficient use of resources – due to increased competition, specialization, returns to scale, increase in investment, trade creation and diversion, as well as monetary stability. The opponents of integration for small countries would have to answer the question: how much is it worth to lose the market and potentials for gain in order to keep the right to carry on with a home economic policy which is insulated from international influences?

In the situation with imperfect competition, a score of various economic outcomes can happen. This is different from the case with perfect competition where a narrow range of outcomes is clear. The aim of this book is not to give *carte blanche* to intervention, it is much more modest. This book argues that in the situation with market imperfections, intervention (integration is a part of it), under certain conditions, may have a more favourable welfare outcome than the free play of market forces. Any theoretically respectable case for intervention may often find support for the wrong reasons (Krugman, 1990, p. 253). Intervention is capable of provoking a chain of retaliations which may impoverish everybody.

Dr Samuel Johnson's (1709–84) remark 'Like a dog walking on his hind legs. It is not well done, but you are surprised to find it done at all' aptly describes integration arrangements among countries. International economic integration increases the potential for significant world-wide improvements in economic welfare. But countries have to organize themselves both individually and collectively to reap these gains. Economic policies concerning investment, industrial change, R&D, and education 'on the efficiency side of the economy' and regional and social matters 'on the equity side of it' are absolutely crucial for the success and survival of economic integration. The equity side of economic life is provoked by the polarization effect due to market imperfections, and it is requested by the desire of the losers to share the benefits of integration. In a constantly changing situation in the market and technology, countries which do not adapt to change face troubles and fall behind their competitors, who have different attitudes.

It is hard to forecast with a high degree of accuracy when and how the effects of integration will happen. In the short-term 'just after the lifting of barriers to trade', production, GNP and trade may increase while some prices fall. Also, some increase in unemployment may occur in the short run because of increased competition and an unfinished adjustment process. In the medium- and long-term, structural adjustment takes place and economies of scale occur, retraining and mobility of labour reduces unemployment because new jobs are being created. Market rigidities are being reduced, for agents change their behaviour due to increased opportunities and competition. It is in this context where the dynamic effects of integration are materialized. International economic integration is not an economic policy choice which would frighten small and medium-sized countries. The only thing which these countries would lose while integrating is the illusion that international economic integration is a bad policy choice.

Bibliography

Adams, G. (1983) 'Criteria for US industrial policy strategies', in *Industrial Policies for Growth and Competitiveness* (eds G. Adams and L. Klein), Lexington, MA: Lexington Books, pp. 393–418.

—— and Bolino, A. (1983) 'Meaning of industrial policy', in *Industrial Policies for Growth and Competitiveness* (eds G. Adams and L. Klein), Lexington, MA: Lexington Books, pp. 13–20.

—— and Klein, L. (1983) 'Economic evolution of industrial policies for growth and competitiveness: overview', in *Industrial Policies for Growth and Competitiveness* (eds G. Adams and L. Klein), Lexington, MA: Lexington Books, pp. 3–11.

Allen, P. (1983) 'Policies to correct cyclical imbalance within a monetary union'. *Journal of Common Market Studies*, pp. 313–27.

—— and Kenen, P. (1980) *Asset Markets, Exchange Rates and Economic Integration*. Cambridge: Cambridge University Press.

Ardy, B. (1988) 'The national incidence of the EC budget', *Journal of Common Market Studies*, pp. 401–29.

Armington, P. (1969) 'A theory of demand for products distinguished by place of production', *IMF Staff Papers*, pp. 159–78.

Armstrong, H. (1985) 'The reform of European Community regional policy', *Journal of Common Market Studies*, pp. 319–43.

Ashcroft, B. (1980) *The Evaluation of Regional Policy in Europe: A Survey and Critique*, Glasgow: University of Strathclyde.

Balassa, B. (1967) 'Trade creation and trade diversion in the European Common market', *Economic Journal*, pp. 1–17.

—— (1973) *The Theory of Economic Integration*, London: George Allen & Unwin.

—— (1986a) 'Intra-industry specialisation', *European Economic Review*, pp. 27–42.

—— (1986b) 'The determinants of intra-industry specialization in the United States trade', *Oxford Economic Papers*, pp. 220–33.

—— and Bauwens, L. (1988) 'The determinants of intra-European trade in manufactured goods', *European Economic Review*, pp. 1421–37.

Baldwin, R. (1989) 'The growth effects of 1992', *Economic Policy*, pp. 248–70.

Bayliss, B. (1985) 'Competition and industrial policy', in *The Economics of the European Community* (ed. A. El-Agraa), Oxford: Philip Allan, pp. 209–27.

Beije, P., Groenewegen, J., van Paridon, K. and Paelinck, J. (eds) (1985) *A Competitive Future for Europe?* Rotterdam: Erasmus University.

Berglas, E. (1979) 'Preferential trading theory: the n commodity case'. *Journal of Political Economy*, pp. 315–31.

Bhagwati, J. (1971) 'Trade diverting customs unions and welfare improvement: a clarification', *Economic Journal*, pp. 580–87.

—— (1973) 'A reply to Professor Kirman', *Economic Journal*, pp. 895–97.

Bhatia, R. (1985) *The West African Monetary Union*, Washington: IMF.

Bird, R. (1972) 'The need for regional policy in a common market', in *International Economic Integration* (ed. P. Robson), Harmondsworth: Penguin Books, pp. 257–77.

—— (1975) 'International aspects of integration', *National Tax Journal*, pp. 302–14.

—— and Brean, D. (1985) 'Canada/US tax relations: issues and perspectives', in *Canada/United States Trade and Investment Issues* (eds D. Fretz, R. Stern and J. Whalley), Toronto: Ontario Economic Council, pp. 391–425.

Blais, A. (1986) 'Industrial policy in advanced capitalist democracies', in *Industrial Policy* (ed. A. Blais), Toronto: University of Toronto Press, pp. 1–53.

Bos, M. and Nelson, H. (1988) 'Indirect taxation and the completion of the internal market of the EC', *Journal of Common Market Studies*, pp. 27–44.

Brander, J. (1987) 'Shaping comparative advantage: trade policy, industrial policy, and economic performance', in *Shaping Comparative Advantage* (eds R.G. Lipsey and W. Dobson), Toronto: C.D. Howe Institute, pp. 1–55.

—— and Spencer, B. (1985) 'Export subsidies and international market share rivalry', *Journal of International Economics*, pp. 83–100.

Buckley, P. and Artisien, P. (1987) 'Policy issues of intra-EC direct investment', *Journal of Common Market Studies*, pp. 207–30.

Bunce, V. (1985) 'The empire strides back: the evolution of the eastern bloc from a Soviet asset to a Soviet liability', *International Organization*, pp. 1–46.

Cantwell, J. (1987) 'The reorganization of European industries after integration: selected evidence on the role of multinational enterprise activities', *Journal of Common Market Studies*, pp. 127–51.

Canzoneri, M. and Rogers, C. (1990) 'Is the European Community an optimal currency area? Optimal taxation versus the cost of multiple currencies', *American Economic Review*, pp. 419–33.

Carliner, G. (1988) 'Industrial policies for emerging industries', in *Strategic Trade Policy and the New International Economics* (ed. P. Krugman), Cambridge, MA: The MIT Press, pp. 147–68.

Caves, R. (1985) *Multinational Enterprise and Economic Analysis*. Cambridge: Cambridge University Press.

—— and Jones, R. (1985) *World Trade and Payments*, Boston: Little, Brown and Company.

Cecchini, P. (1988) *The European Challenge 1992*, Aldershot: Wildwood House.

Choi, J. and Yu, E. (1984) 'Customs unions under increasing returns to scale', *Economica*, pp. 195–203.

Cnossen, S. (1986) 'Tax harmonization in the European Community', *Bulletin for International Fiscal Documentation*, pp. 545–63.

Cobham, D. (1989) 'Strategies for monetary integration revisited', *Journal of Common Market Studies*, pp. 203–18.

Coffey, P. (ed.) (1988) *Main Economic Policy Areas of the EEC Towards 1992*, Dordrecht: Kluwer.

Collier, P. (1979) 'The welfare effects of customs unions: an anatomy', *Economic Journal*, pp. 84–95

Collins, C. (1985) 'Social policy', in *The Economics of the European Economic Community* (ed. A. El-Agraa), Oxford: Philip Allan, pp. 262–87.

Commission of the EC (1990) 'One market, one money', *European Economy*, October.

Conklin, D. and Courchene, T. (eds) (1985) *Canadian Trade at Crossroads: Options for New International Agreements*, Toronto: Ontario Economic Council.

Cooper, C. and Massel, B. (1965a) 'A new look at customs union theory'. *Economic Journal*, pp. 742–47.

―― (1965b) 'Toward a general theory of customs unions for developing countries', *Journal of Political Economy*, pp. 461–76.

Corado, C. and de Melo, J. (1986) 'An ex-ante model for estimating the impact on trade flows of a country's joining a customs union', *Journal of Development Economics*, pp. 153–66.

Corden, W. (1972a) 'Economies of scale and customs union theory', *Journal of Political Economy*, pp. 465–75.

―― (1972b) *Monetary Integration*, Princeton: Essays in International Finance, Princeton University.

―― (1976) 'Customs union theory and the nonuniformity of tariffs', *Journal of International Economics*, pp. 99–106.

―― (1979) 'Intra-industry trade and factors proportion theory', in *On the Economics of Intra-Industry Trade* (ed. H. Giersch), Tubingen: J.C.B. Mohr, pp. 3–12.

―― (1984) 'The normative theory of international trade', in *Handbook of International Economics* (eds R. Jones and P. Kenen), Amsterdam: North Holland, pp. 63–130.

Courchene, T. (1987) *Social Policy in the 1990s, Agenda for Reform*, Toronto: C.D. Howe Institute.

Croxford, G., Wise, M. and Chalkley, B. (1987) 'The reform of the European Development Fund', *Journal of Common Market Studies*, pp. 25–38.

Curzon, V. (1974) *The Essentials of Economic Integration*, London: Macmillan.

Curzon Price, V. (1981) *Industrial Policies in the European Community*, London: Macmillan.

―― (1987) *Free Trade Areas, the European Experience*, Toronto: C.D. Howe Institute.

—— (1988a) 'The European Free Trade Association', in *International Economic Integration* (ed. A. El-Agraa), London: Macmillan, pp. 96–127.

—— (1988b) *1992: Europe's Last Chance? From Common Market to Single Market*, London: Institute of Economic Affairs.

d'Arge, R. (1969) 'Note on customs unions and direct foreign investment', *Economic Journal*, pp. 324–33.

—— (1971a) 'Customs unions and direct foreign investment', *Economic Journal*, pp. 352–5.

—— (1971b) 'A reply', *Economic Journal*, pp. 357–59.

de Bandt, J. (1985) 'French industrial policies', in *A Competitive Future for Europe?* (eds P. Beije, J. Groenewegen, K. van Paridon and J. Paelinck), Rotterdam: Erasmus University, pp. 65–79.

Defraigne, P. (1984) 'Towards concerted industrial policies in the EC', in *European Industry: Public Policy and Corporate Strategy* (ed. A. Jacquemin), Oxford: Clarendon Press, pp. 368–77.

de Ghellinck, E. (1988) 'European industrial policy against the background of the single European Act', in *Main Economic Policy Areas of the EEC – Towards 1992* (ed. P. Coffey), Dordrecht: Kluwer, pp. 133–56.

de Grauwe, P. (1975a) 'Conditions for monetary integration – a geometric interpretation', *Weltwirschaftliches Archiv*, pp. 634–46.

—— (1975b) 'The interaction of monetary policies in a group of European countries', *Journal of International Economics*, pp. 207–28.

—— (1987) 'International trade and economic growth in the European monetary system', *European Economic Review*, pp. 389–98.

—— (1989) 'Economic policy and political democracy', *European Affairs*, no. 1, pp. 66–72.

Dell'Aringa, C. and Neri, F. (1989) 'Illegal immigrants and the informal economy in Italy', in *European Factor Mobility* (eds I. Gordon and A. Thirlwall), New York: St. Martin's Press, pp. 133–47.

Delors, J. (1989) *Report on Economic and Monetary Union in the European Community*, Brussels: EC.

Dennis, G. (1981) 'United Kingdom's monetary independence and membership of the European monetary system', in *European Monetary System and International Monetary Reform* (eds J. Abraham and M. Vanden Abeele), Bruxelles: Éditions de l'Université de Bruxelles, pp. 139–55.

Dertouzos, M., Lester, R. and Solow, R. (1990) *Made in America*, New York: Harper Perennial.

Devarajan, S. and de Melo, J. (1987) 'Evaluating participation in African monetary unions: a statistical analysis of the CFA zones', *World Development*, pp. 483–96.

Dietz, R. (1986) 'Soviet forgone gains in trade with the CMEA six: a reapprisal', *Comparative Economic Studies*, pp. 69–94.

Dore, R. (1986) *Structural Adjustment in Japan, 1970–82*, Geneva: ILO.

Drabek, Z. and Greenaway, D. (1984) 'Economic integration and intra-industry trade: the EEC and CMEA compared', *Kyklos*, pp. 444–69.

Dunning, J. (1969) 'Foreign capital and economic growth in Europe', in *Economic Integration in Europe* (ed. G. Denton), London: Weidenfeld & Nicolson, pp. 246–85.

—— (1988) *Explaining International Production*, London: Unwin Hyman.
—— and Robson, P. (1987) 'Multinational corporate integration and regional economic integration', *Journal of Common Market Studies*, pp. 103–24.
EFTA Secretariat (1969) 'The effects of EFTA on the economies of member states', *EFTA Bulletin* (January).
El-Agraa, A. (1985a) 'General introduction', in *The Economics of the European Community* (ed. A. El-Agraa), Oxford: Philip Allan, pp. 1–8.
—— (1985b) 'European monetary integration', in *The Economics of the European Economic Community* (ed. A. El-Agraa), Oxford: Philip Allan, pp. 93–111.
—— (ed.) (1988) *International Economic Integration*, London: Macmillan.
—— (1989) *The Theory and Measurement of International Economic Integration*, New York: St. Martin's Press.
Emerson, M., Aujean, M., Catinat, M., Goybet, P. and Jacquemin, A. (1988) 'The economics of 1992', *European Economy*, March.
Ethier, W. and Svensson, L. (1986) 'The theorems of international trade with factor mobility', *Journal of International Economics*, pp. 21–42.
Flam, H. and Helpman, E. (1987) 'Industrial policy under monopolistic competition', *Journal of International Economics*, pp. 79–102.
Fleming, M. (1971) 'On exchange rate unification', *Economic Journal*, pp. 467–86.
Folkerts-Landau, D. and Mathieson, D. (1989) *The European Monetary System in the Context of the Integration of European Financial Markets*, Washington: IMF.
Franko, L. (1977) 'European multinational enterprises in the integration process', in *The Multinational Enterprise in a Hostile World* (eds G. Curzon and V. Curzon), London: Macmillan, pp. 58–67.
Fretz, D., Stern, R. and Whalley, J. (eds) (1985) *Canada/United States Trade and Investment Issues*, Toronto: Ontario Economic Council.
Geroski, P. (1987) 'Brander's "Shaping Comparative Advantage": some comments', in *Shaping Comparative Advantage* (eds R.G. Lipsey and W. Dobson), Toronto: C.D. Howe Institute, pp. 57–64.
—— (1989) 'European industrial policy and industrial policy in Europe', *Oxford Review of Economic Policy*, pp. 20–36.
Gleiser, H., Jacquemin, A. and Petit, J. (1980) 'Exports in an imperfect competition framework: an analysis of 1,446 exporters', *Quarterly Journal of Economics*, pp. 507–24.
Gray, P., Pugel, T. and Walter, I. (1986) *International Trade, Employment and Structural Adjustment: The United States*, Geneva: ILO.
Greenaway, D. (1987) 'Intra-industry trade, intra-firm trade and European integration', *Journal of Common Market Studies*, pp. 153–72.
—— and Milner, C. (1987) 'Intra-industry trade: current perspectives and unresolved issues', *Weltwirschaftliches Archiv*, pp. 39–57.
—— and Tharakan, P. (eds) (1986) *Imperfect Competition and International Trade*, Brighton: Wheatsheaf Books.
Gremmen, H. (1985) 'Testing the factor price equalization theorem in the EC: an alternative approach', *Journal of Common Market Studies*, pp. 277–86.

Gros, D. (1989) 'Paradigms for the monetary union of Europe', *Journal of Common Market Studies*, pp. 219–30.

Grubel, H. (1967) 'Intra-industry specialization and the pattern of trade', *Canadian Journal of Economics and Political Science*, pp. 374–88.

—— (1970) 'The theory of optimum currency areas', *Canadian Journal of Economics*, pp. 318–24.

—— (1984) *The International Monetary System*, Harmondsworth: Penguin Books.

Guillaumont, P. and Guillaumont, S. (1989) 'The implications of European monetary union for African countries', *Journal of Common Market Studies*, pp. 139–53.

Hall, G. (ed.) (1986) *European Industrial Policy*. London: Croom Helm.

Hamilton, B. and Whalley, J. (1986) 'Border tax adjustment and US trade', *Journal of International Economics*. pp. 377–83.

Harris, R. (1984) *Trade, Industrial Policy and Canadian Manufacturing*, Toronto: Ontario Economic Council.

—— (1985a) *Trade, Industrial Policy and International Competition*, Toronto: University of Toronto Press.

—— (1985b) 'Summary of a project on the general equilibrium evaluation of Canadian trade policy', in *Canada–US Free Trade* (ed. J. Whalley), Toronto: University of Toronto Press, pp. 157–77.

Helpman, E. (1984) 'Increasing returns, imperfect markets and trade theory', in *Handbook of International economics* (eds. R. Jones and P. Kenen), Amsterdam: North Holland, pp. 325–66.

—— and Krugman, P. (1986) *Market Structure and Foreign Trade*, Cambridge, MA: The MIT Press.

Hill, T. (1977) 'On goods and services', *Review of Income and Wealth*, pp. 315–38.

Holzman, F. (1976) *International Trade under Communism*, New York: Basic Books.

Ishiyama, Y. (1975) 'The theory of optimum currency areas: a survey', *IMF Staff Papers*, pp. 344–78.

Jacquemin, A. (1979) 'European industrial policies and competition', in *Economic Policies of the Common Market* (ed. P. Coffey), London: Macmillan, pp. 22–51.

—— (1983) 'Industrial policies and the Community', in *Main Economic Policy Areas of the EEC* (ed. P. Coffey), The Hague: Martinus Nijhoff, pp. 27–58.

—— (ed.) (1984) *European Industry: Public Policy and Corporate Strategy*, Oxford: Clarendon Press.

—— and Sapir, A. (eds) (1989) *The European Internal Market*, Oxford: Oxford University Press.

Johnson, H. (1962) *Money, Trade and Economic Growth*, London: George Allen & Unwin.

—— (1973) 'An economic theory of protectionism, tariff bargaining and the formation of customs unions', in *The Economics of Integration* (ed. M. Krauss), London: George Allen & Unwin, pp. 64–103.

—— (1974) 'Trade-diverting customs unions: a comment', *Economic Journal*, pp. 618–21.

—— and Krauss, M. (1973) 'Border taxes, border tax adjustment, comparative advantage and the balance of payments', in *Economics of Integration* (ed. M. Krauss), London: George Allen & Unwin, pp. 239–53.

Jones, A. (1985) 'The theory of economic integration', in *The Economics of European Community* (ed. A. El-Agraa), Oxford: Philip Allan, pp. 71–92.

Jones, R. and Neary, J. (1984) 'The positive theory of international trade', in *Handbook of International Economics* (eds. R. Jones and P. Kenen), Amsterdam: North Holland, pp. 1–62.

Jovanović, M. (1984) 'Pet godina Evropskog monetarnog sistema', *Jugoslovensko bankarstvo*, March, pp. 42–7.

—— (1984) 'Ekonomska teorija o medjunarodnoj monetarnoj integraciji', *Jugoslovensko bankarstvo*, December, pp. 41–6.

—— (1985) *Ekonomika Evropske ekonomske zajednice*, Belgrade: Savremena administracija.

—— (1989) 'Industrial policy and international trade (shaping comparative advantage)', *Economic Analysis*, pp. 55–77.

Kaldor, N. (1971) 'The dynamic effects of the common market', in *Destiny or Delusion: Britain and the Common Market* (ed. D. Evans), London: Victor Gollancz, pp. 59–83.

Kay, J. (1990) 'Tax policy: a survey', *Economic Journal*, pp. 18–75.

Kemp, M. and Wan, H. (1976) 'An elementary proposal concerning the formation of customs unions', *Journal of International Economics*, pp. 95–7.

Kenen, P. (1969) 'The theory of optimum currency areas: an eclectic view', in *Monetary Problems of the International Economy* (eds. R. Mundell and A. Swoboda), Chicago: University of Chicago Press, pp. 41–60.

Kindleberger, C. and Audretsch, D. (eds) (1984) *The Multinational Corporation in the 1980s*. Cambridge, MA: The MIT Press.

Kirman, A. (1973) 'Trade diverting customs unions and welfare improvement: a comment', *Economic Journal*, pp. 890–93.

Krauss, M. (1972) 'Recent developments in customs unions theory: an interpretative survey', *Journal of Economic Literature*, pp. 413–36.

—— (ed.) (1973) *The Economics of Integration*, London: George Allen & Unwin.

—— and Bird, R. (1973) 'The value added tax: critique of a review', in *Economics of Integration* (ed. M. Krauss), London: George Allen & Unwin, pp. 254–64.

Kreinin, M. (1964) 'On the dynamic effects of a customs union', *Journal of Political Economy*, pp. 193–5.

—— (1969) 'Trade creation and trade diversion by the EEC and EFTA', *Economia Internazionale*, pp. 273–80.

Krugman, P. (1981) 'Intraindustry specialization and the gains from trade', *Journal of Political Economy*, pp. 959–73.

—— (ed.) (1988) *Strategic Trade Policy and the New International Economics*, Cambridge, MA: The MIT Press.

—— (1990) *Rethinking International Trade*. Cambridge, MA: The MIT Press.

Kumar, M. (1985) 'International trade and industrial concentration', *Oxford Economic Papers*, pp. 125–33.

Lancaster, K. (1980) 'Intra-industry trade under perfect monopolistic competition', *Journal of International Economics*, pp. 151–75.

Leamer, E. (1984) *Sources of International Comparative Advantage*, Cambridge, MA: The MIT Press.

Linder, S. (1961) *An Essay on Trade and Transformation*, New York: John Wiley.

Lipsey, R.G. (1957) 'The theory of customs unions: trade diversion and welfare', *Economica*, pp. 40–6.

—— (1960) 'The theory of customs unions: a general survey', *Economic Journal*, pp. 496–513.

—— (1970) *The Theory of Customs Unions: A general Equilibrium Analysis*, London: Weidenfeld and Nicolson.

—— (1976) 'Comments', in *Economic Integration Worldwide, Regional, Sectoral* (ed. F. Machlup), London: Macmillan, pp. 37–40.

—— (1984) 'Can the market economy survive?' in *Probing Leviathan: An Investigation of Government in the Economy* (ed. G. Lermer), Vancouver: The Frazer Institute, pp. 3–37.

—— (1985) 'Canada and the United States: the economic dimension', in *Canada and the United States: Enduring Friendship, Persistent Stress* (eds. C. Doran and J. Stigler), New York: Prentice Hall, pp. 69–108.

—— (1987a) 'Report on the workshop', in *Shaping Comparative Advantage* (eds. R.G. Lipsey and W. Dobson), Toronto: C.D. Howe Institute, pp. 109–53.

—— (1987b) 'Models matter when discussing competitiveness: a technical note', in *Shaping Comparative Advantage* (eds. R.G. Lipsey and W. Dobson), Toronto: C.D. Howe Institute, pp. 155–66.

—— (1989) 'Unsettled issues in the great free trade debate', *Canadian Journal of Economics*, pp. 1–21.

—— and Dobson, W. (eds) (1987) *Shaping Comparative Advantage*, Toronto: C.D. Howe Institute.

—— and Lancaster, K. (1956–7) 'The general theory of the second best', *Review of Economic Studies*, pp. 11–32.

—— and Smith, M. (1986) *Taking the Initiative: Canada's Trade Options in a Turbulent World*, Toronto: C.D. Howe Institute.

—— and York, R. (1988) *Evaluating the Free Trade Deal: A Guided Tour through the Canada-US Agreement*, Toronto: C.D. Howe Institute.

Lloyd, P. (1982) '3 × 3 theory of customs unions', *Journal of International Economics*, pp. 41–63.

Lundgren, N. (1969) 'Customs unions of industrialized West European countries', in *Economic Integration in Europe* (ed. G. Denton), London: Weidenfeld & Nicolson, pp. 25–54.

Lunn, J. (1980) 'Determinants of US direct investment in the EEC', *European Economic Review*, pp. 93–101.

—— (1983) 'Determinants of US direct investment in the EEC', *European Economic Review*, pp. 391–3.

MacDougall, G. (1977) *Report of the Study Group on the Role of Public Finance in European Integration*, Brussels: EC.

McFetridge, D. (1985) 'The economics of industrial policy', in *Canadian Industrial Policy in Action* (ed. D. McFetridge), Toronto: University of Toronto Press, pp. 1–49.

—— (ed.) (1986) *Economics of Industrial Policy and Strategy*, Toronto: University of Toronto Press.
McKay, D. and Grant, W. (1983) 'Industrial policies in OECD countries: an overview', *Journal of Public Policy*, pp. 1–12.
McKinnon, R. (1963) 'Optimum currency area', *American Economic Review*, pp. 717–25.
Machlup, F. (ed.) (1976) *Economic Integration Worldwide, Regional, Sectoral*, London: Macmillan.
—— (1979) *A History of Thought on Economic Integration*, London: Macmillan.
Maksimova, M. (1976) 'Comments on paper types of economic integration by B. Balassa', in *Economic Integration Worldwide, Regional, Sectoral* (ed. F. Machlup), London: Macmillan, pp. 32–6.
Markusen, J. (1983) 'Factor movements and commodity trade as complements', *Journal of International Economics*, pp. 341–56.
—— and Melvin, J. (1984) *The Theory of International Trade and Its Canadian Applications*, Toronto: Butterworths.
Marer, P. and Montias, J. (1988) 'The Council for Mutual Economic Assistance', in *International Economic Integration* (ed. A. El-Agraa), London: Macmillan, pp. 128–65.
Marrese, M. (1986) 'CMEA: effective but cumbersome political economy', *International Organization*, pp. 287–327.
—— and Vanous, J. (1983) *Soviet Subsidization of Trade with Eastern Europe: A Soviet Perspective*, Berkeley: Institute of International Studies, University of California.
Mayes, D. (1978) 'The effects of economic integration on trade', *Journal of Common Market Studies*, pp. 1–23.
—— (1985) 'Factor mobility', in *The Economics of the European Community* (ed. A.El-Agraa), Oxford: Philip Allan, pp. 124–50.
—— (1988) 'The problems of quantitative estimation of integration effects', in *International Economic Integration* (ed. A. El-Agraa), London: Macmillan, pp. 42–58.
Mayes, G. (1987) 'European industrial policy', in *European Integration and Industry* (eds. M. Macmillen, D. Mayes and P. van Veen), Tilburg: Tilburg University Press, pp. 247–65.
Meade, J. (1968) *The Pure Theory of Customs Unions*, Amsterdam: North Holland.
—— (1973) 'The balance of payments problems of a European free-trade area', in *The Economics of Integration* (ed. M. Krauss), London: George Allen and Unwin, pp. 155–76.
Melvin, J. (1985) 'The regional impact of tariffs', in *Canada-United States Free Trade* (ed. J. Whalley), Toronto: University of Toronto Press, pp. 313–24.
Melvin, M. (1985) 'Currency substitution and western European monetary unification', *Economica*, pp. 79–91.
Mendershausen, H. (1959) 'Terms of trade between the Soviet Union and smaller communist countries 1955–57', *Review of Economics and Statistics*, pp. 106–18.
—— (1960) 'Terms of Soviet-satellite trade: a broadened analysis', *Review of Economics and Statistics*, pp. 152–63.
Mendes, A. Marques (1986) 'The contribution of the European Community to economic growth', *Journal of Common Market Studies*, pp. 260–77.

—— (1987) *Economic Integration and Growth in Europe*, London: Croom Helm.

Mennis, B. and Sauvant, K. (1976) *Emerging Forms of Transnational Community*, Lexington: Lexington Books.

Merrit, G. (1988) 'Social policy rethink', *European Affairs*, no. 1, pp. 88–94.

Michaely, M. (1976) 'The assumptions of Jacob Viner's theory of customs unions', *Journal of International Economics*, pp. 75–93.

—— (1977) *Theory of Commercial Policy*, Oxford: Philip Allan.

Mishan, E. (1976) 'The welfare gains of a trade diverting customs union reinterpreted', *Economic Journal*, pp. 669–72.

Molle, W. (1988) ' Regional policy', in *Main Economic Policy Areas of the EEC Towards 1992* (ed. P. Coffey), Dordrecht: Kluwer, pp. 67–97.

—— and van Mourik, A. (1988) 'International movements of labour under conditions of economic integration: the case of western Europe', *Journal of Common Market Studies*, pp. 317–42.

Mundell, R. (1957) 'International trade and factor mobility', *American Economic Review*, pp. 321–35.

—— (1961) 'A theory of optimum currency areas', *American Economic Review*, pp. 657–65.

Mytelka, L. and Delapierre, M. (1987) 'The alliance strategies of European firms in the information technology industry and the role of ESPRIT', *Journal of Common Market Studies*, pp. 231–53.

Nayyar, D. (1988) 'The political economy of international trade in services', *Cambridge Journal of Economics*, pp. 279–98.

Neven, D. (1990) 'EEC integration towards 1992: some distributional aspects', *Economic Policy*, 14–46.

Nevin, E. (1985) 'Regional policy', in *The Economics of the European Community* (ed. A. El-Agraa), Oxford: Philip Allan, pp. 338–61.

Norman, V. (1990) 'Discussion of D. Neven's paper', *Economic Policy*, pp. 49–52.

Owen, N. (1976) 'Scale economies in the EEC', *European Economic Review*, pp. 143–63.

Panić, M. (1988) *National Management of the International Economy*, London: Macmillan.

—— (1991) 'The impact of multinationals on national economic policies', in *Multinationals and Europe 1992* (eds. B. Burgenmeier and J. Mucchelli), London: Routledge, pp. 204–22.

—— and Schioppa, C. (1989) 'Europe's long-term capital flows since 1971', in *European Factor Mobility* (eds. I. Gordon and A. Thirlwall), New York: St. Martin's Press, pp. 166–94.

Pelkmans, J. (1980) 'Economic theories of integration revisited', *Journal of Common Market Studies*, pp. 333–53.

—— (1984) *Market Integration in the European Community*, The Hague: Martinus Nijhoff.

—— and Winters, A. (1988) *Europe's Domestic Market*, London, Routledge.

Petith, H. (1977) 'European integration and the terms of trade', *Economic Journal*, pp. 262–72.

Pinder, J. (1969) 'Problems of European integration', in *Economic*

Integration in Europe (ed. G. Denton), London: Weidenfeld and Nicolson, pp. 143–70.

—— Hosomi, T. and Diebold, W. (1979) *Industrial Policy and International Economy*, New York: The Trilateral Commission.

Pomfret, R. (1986) 'The trade-diverting bias of preferential trading arrangements', *Journal of Common Market Studies*, pp. 109–17.

President's Commission on Industrial Competitiveness (1985) *Global Competition: The New Reality* (volumes 1 and 2), Washington: US Government Printing Office.

Prest, A. (1979) 'Fiscal policy', in *Economic Policies of the Common Market* (ed. P. Coffey), London: Macmillan, pp. 69–97.

—— (1983) 'Fiscal policy', in *Main Economic Policy Areas of the EEC* (ed. P. Coffey), The Hague: Martinus Nijhoff, pp. 58–90.

Purvis. D. (1972) 'Technology, trade and factor mobility', *Economic Journal*, pp. 991–9.

Reich, S. (1989) 'Roads to follow: regulating direct foreign investment', *International Organization*, pp. 543–84.

Renshaw, G. (1986) *Adjustment and Economic Performance in Industrialised Countries: A Synthesis*, Geneva: ILO.

Riezman, R. (1979) 'A 3 × 3 model of customs unions', *Journal of International Economics*, pp. 341–54.

Robson, P. (1968) *Economic Integration in Africa*, London: George Allen & Unwin.

—— (ed.) (1972) *International Economic Integration*, Harmondsworth: Penguin Books.

—— (1983) *Integration, Development and Equity*, London: George Allen & Unwin.

—— (1984) *The Economics of International Integration*, London: Allen & Unwin.

—— (1987) *The Economics of International Integration*, London: George Allen and Unwin.

Romer, P. (1986) 'Increasing returns and long-run growth', *Journal of Political Economy*, pp. 1002–37.

Rubin, S. (1970) 'The international firm and the national jurisdiction', in *The International Corporation* (ed. C. Kindleberger), Cambridge, MA: The MIT Press, pp. 179–204.

Rugman, A. (1985) 'The behaviour of US subsidiaries in Canada: implications for trade and investment', in *Canada/United States Trade and Investments Issues* (eds. D. Fretz, R. Stern and J. Whalley), Toronto: Ontario Economic Council, pp. 460–73.

Scaperlanda, A. (1967) 'The EEC and US foreign investment: some empirical evidence', *Economic Journal*, pp. 22–6.

—— and Balough, R. (1983) 'Determinants of US direct investment in Europe', *European Economic Journal*, pp. 381–90.

—— and Reiling, E. (1971) 'A comment on a note on customs unions and direct foreign investment', *Economic Journal*, pp. 355–7.

Schatz, K. and Wolter, F. (1987) *Structural Adjustment in the Federal Republic of Germany*, Geneva: ILO.

Schmalensee, R. (1988) 'Industrial economics: an overview', *Economic Journal*, pp. 643–81.

Schott, J. and Smith, M. (1988) 'Services and investment', in *The Canada-US Free Trade Agreement* (eds. J. Schott and M. Smith), Washington: Institute for International Economics, pp. 137–58.

Scitowsky, T. (1967) *Economic Theory and Western European Integration*, London: George Allen & Unwin.

Scott, A. (1986) 'Britain and the EMS: an appraisal of the report of the Treasury and Civil Service Committee', *Journal of Common Market Studies*, pp. 187–201.

Sellekaerts, W. (1973) 'How meaningful are empirical studies on trade creation and diversion?' *Weltwirschaftliches Archiv*, pp. 519–53.

Sharp, M. and Shepherd, G. (1987) *Managing Change in British Industry*, Geneva: ILO.

Shoup, C. (1972) 'Taxation aspects of international economic integration', in *International Economic Integration* (ed. P. Robson), Harmondsworth: Penguin Books, pp. 197–218.

Sleuwaegen, L. (1987) 'Multinationals, the European Community and Belgium', *Journal of Common Market Studies*, pp. 255–72.

Smith, A. and Venables, A. (1988) 'Completing the internal market in the European Community', *European Economic Review*, pp. 1501–25.

Snape, R. (1990) 'Principles in trade in services', in *The Uruguay Round: Services in the World Economy* (eds. P. Messerlin and K. Sauvant), New York: United Nations Centre on Transnational Corporations, pp. 5–11.

Sobell, V. (1984) *The Red Market-Industrial Co-operation and Specialisation in Comecon*, Aldershot: Gower.

Spinelli, A. (1973) *Action Programme in the Field of Technological and Industrial Policy*, Brussels: EC.

Straubhaar, T. (1988) 'International labour migration within a common market: some aspects of EC experience', *Journal of Common Market Studies*, pp. 45–62.

Swann, D. (1978) *The Economics of the Common Market*, Harmondsworth: Penguin Books.

Thirsk, W. (1985) 'Should taxes be included in trade agreements?' in *Canadian Trade at Crossroads: Options for New International Agreements* (eds. D. Conklin and T. Courchene), Toronto: Ontario Economic Council, pp. 138–52.

Thygesen, N. (1987) 'Is the EEC an optimal currency area?' in *The ECU Market* (eds. R. Levics and A. Sommariva), Toronto: D. C. Heath, Lexington Books.

Tinbergen, J. (1954) *International Economic Integration*, Amsterdam: Elsevier.

Tironi, E. (1982) 'Customs union theory in the presence of foreign firms', *Oxford Economic Papers*, pp. 150–71.

Tovias, A. (1982) 'Testing factor price equalization in the EEC', *Journal of Common Market Studies*, pp. 375–88.

Trebilcock, M. (1986) *The Political Economy of Economic Adjustment*, Toronto: University of Toronto Press.

Tyson, L. (1987) 'Comments on Brander's "Shaping Comparative Advantage": creating advantage, an industrial policy perspective', in *Shaping*

Comparative Advantage (eds. R.G. Lipsey and W. Dobson), Toronto: C.D. Howe Institute, pp. 65–82.

—— and Zysman, J. (1987a) 'American industry in international competition', in *American Industry in International Competition* (eds. J. Zysman and L. Tyson), Ithaca: Cornell University Press, pp. 15–59.

—— (1987b) 'Conclusion: what to do now?' in *American Industry in International Competition* (eds. J. Zysman and L. Tyson), Ithaca: Cornell University Press, pp. 422–7.

UNCTC (1988) *Transnational Corporations in World Development*, New York: United Nations.

—— (1989) *Transnational Corporations and International Economic Relations: Recent Developments and Selected Issues*, New York: United Nations.

—— (1990) *Regional Economic Integration and Transnational Corporations in the 1990s: Europe 1992, North America and Developing Countries*, New York: United Nations.

Ungerer, H., Evans, O., Mayer, T. and Young, P. (1986) *The European Monetary System: Recent Development*, Washington: IMF.

Utton, M. (1986) 'Developments in British industrial and competition policies', in *European Industrial Policy* (ed. G. Hall), London: Croom Helm, pp. 59–83.

van Brabant, J. (1980) *Socialist Economic Integration*, Cambridge: Cambridge University Press.

—— (1988) 'Product specialisation in the CMEA – concepts and empirical evidence', *Journal of Common Market Studies*, pp. 287–315.

Vanek, J. (1962) *International Trade*, Homewood: Richard D. Irwin.

—— (1965) *General Equilibrium of International Discrimination*, Cambridge, MA: Harvard University Press.

van Meerhaeghe, M. (1985) *International Economic Institutions*, Dordrecht: Martinus Nijhoff.

van Mourik, A. (1987) 'Testing the factor price equalisation theorem in the EC: an alternative approach', *Journal of Common Market Studies*, pp. 79–86.

Varian, H. (1984) *Microeconomic Analysis*, New York: Norton.

Vaubel, P. (1978) 'Real exchange rate changes in the European Community', *Journal of International Economics*, pp. 319–39.

—— (1990) 'Currency competition and European monetary integration', *Economic Journal*, pp. 936–46.

Verdoorn, P. and van Bochove, C. (1972) 'Measuring integration effects: a survey', *European Economic Review*, pp. 337–49.

Viner, J. (1950) *The Customs Union Issue*, London: Stevens & Sons Limited for the Carnegie Endowment for International Peace.

—— (1976) 'A letter to W.M. Corden', *Journal of International Economics*, pp. 107–8.

Vosgerau, H. (1989) 'International capital movements and trade in an intertemporal setting', in *European Factor Mobility* (eds. I. Gordon and A. Thirlwall), New York: St. Martin's Press, pp. 215–32.

Wallis, K. (1968) 'The EEC and United States foreign investment: some empirical evidence re-examined', *Economic Journal*, pp. 717–19.

Werner, P. (1970) *Report to the Council and the Commission on the*

Realization by Stages of Economic and Monetary Union in the Community, Luxembourg: European Communities.

Wescott, R. (1983) 'US approaches to industrial policy', in *Industrial Policies for Growth and Competitiveness* (eds. G. Adams and L. Klein), Lexington, MA: Lexington Books, pp. 87–151.

Whalley, J. (ed.) (1985) *Canada-United States Free Trade*, Toronto: University of Toronto Press.

—— (1987) 'Brander's "Shaping Comparative Advantage"': remarks', in *Shaping Comparative Advantage* (eds. R.G. Lipsey and W. Dobson), Toronto: C.D. Howe Institute, pp. 83–9.

White Paper (Completing the Internal Market) (1985) Luxembourg: EC.

Whitman, M. (1967) *International and Interregional Payments Adjustment: A Synthetic View*, Princeton: Essays in International Finance, Princeton University.

Wilkinson, B. (1985) 'Canada/US free trade and Canadian economic, cultural and political sovereignty', in *Canadian Trade at Crossroads: Options for New International Agreements* (eds. D. Conklin and T. Chourchene), Toronto: Ontario Economic Council, pp. 291–307.

Wilkinson, C. (1984) 'Trends in industrial policy in the EC: theory and practice', in *European Industry: Public Policy and Corporate Strategy* (ed. A. Jacquemin), Oxford: Clarendon Press, pp. 39–78.

Williamson, J. and Bottrill, A. (1973) 'The impact of customs unions on trade in manufactures', in *The Economics of Integration* (ed. M. Krauss), London: George Allen & Unwin, pp. 118–51.

Winters, A. (1987) 'Negotiating the abolition of non-tariff barriers', *Oxford Economic Papers*, pp. 465–80.

Wong, J. (1988) 'The Association of Southeast Asian Nations', in *International Economic Integration* (ed. A. El-Agraa), London: Macmillan, pp. 314–28.

Wonnacott, P. (1987) *The United States and Canada: The Quest For Free Trade*, Washington: Institute for International Economics.

—— and Wonnacott, R. (1981) 'Is unilateral tariff reduction preferable to a customs union? The customs union of the missing foreign tariffs', *American Economic Review*, pp. 703–13.

Yannopoulos, G. (1988) *Customs Unions and Trade Conflicts*, London: Routledge.

—— (1990) 'Foreign direct investment and European integration: the evidence from the formative years of the European community', *Journal of Common Market Studies*, pp. 235–59.

Zysman, J. (1983) *Governments, Markets and Growth*, Ithaca: Cornell University Press.

Index